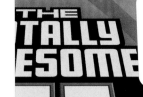

THE TOTALLY AWESOME HULK

MY BEST FRIENDS ARE MONSTERS

TOTALLY AWESOME HULK #19

GREG PAK
WRITER

ROBERT GILL
ARTIST

NOLAN WOODARD
COLOR ARTIST

VC's CORY PETIT
LETTERER

STONEHOUSE
COVER ART

MOON GIRL AND DEVIL DINOSAUR #4

BRANDON MONTCLARE & AMY REEDER
WRITERS

NATACHA BUSTOS
ARTIST

TAMRA BONVILLAIN
COLOR ARTIST

VC's TRAVIS LANHAM
LETTERER

AMY REEDER
COVER ART

TOTALLY AWESOME HULK #1.MU
"FLAWLESS VICTORY"

BRYAN EDWARD HILL
WRITER

TY TEMPLETON
ARTIST

MAT LOPES
COLOR ARTIST

VC's CORY PETIT
LETTERER

"MATH IS MAGIC"

LEAH WILLIAMS
WRITER

JAHNOY LINDSAY
ARTIST

ESTHER SANZ
COLOR ARTIST

VC's CORY PETIT
LETTERER

RAHZZAH
COVER ART

GENERATIONS: BANNER HULK & THE TOTALLY AWESOME HULK #1

GREG PAK
WRITER

MATTEO BUFFAGNI
ARTIST

DONO SÁNCHEZ-ALMARA
COLOR ARTIST

VC's CORY PETIT
LETTERER

JORGE MOLINA
COVER ART

TOTALLY AWESOME HULK #23

GREG PAK
WRITER

IBRAIM ROBERSON
ARTIST

NOLAN WOODARD
COLOR ARTIST

VC'S CORY PETIT
LETTERER

JORGE MOLINA
COVER ART

MARK PANICCIA, CHRIS ROBINSON & EMILY SHAW
EDITORS

HULK CREATED BY
STAN LEE & JACK KIRBY

PREVIOUSLY IN

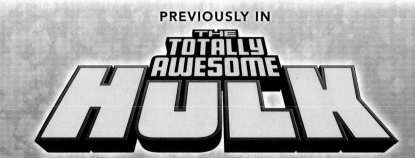

THE TOTALLY AWESOME HULK

SUPER-GENIUS TEENAGER AMADEUS CHO CURED BRUCE BANNER AND TOOK ON THE POWERS AND MANTLE OF THE HULK!

BEING THE HULK HAS HAD ITS UPS AND DOWNS: WHILE SAVING LIVES AND MAKING FRIENDS WITH OTHER HEROES HAS BEEN GREAT, AMADEUS HAS STRUGGLED TO KEEP HIS EMOTIONS IN CHECK, WHICH HAS CAUSED A SPLIT WITH HIS SISTER MADDY.

MEANWHILE, THE EVIL MINDS BEHIND THE WEAPON X PROGRAM HOPE TO CAPITALIZE ON THE GENETIC GIFTS OF MUTANTS TO WIPE OUT ALL OF MUTANT-KIND! USING ADAMANTIUM CYBORGS IMBUED WITH THE ABILITIES OF OLD MAN LOGAN, SABRETOOTH, WARPATH, AND LADY DEATHSTRIKE, THE WEAPON X PROGRAM HUNTS THEIR NEXT TARGET...

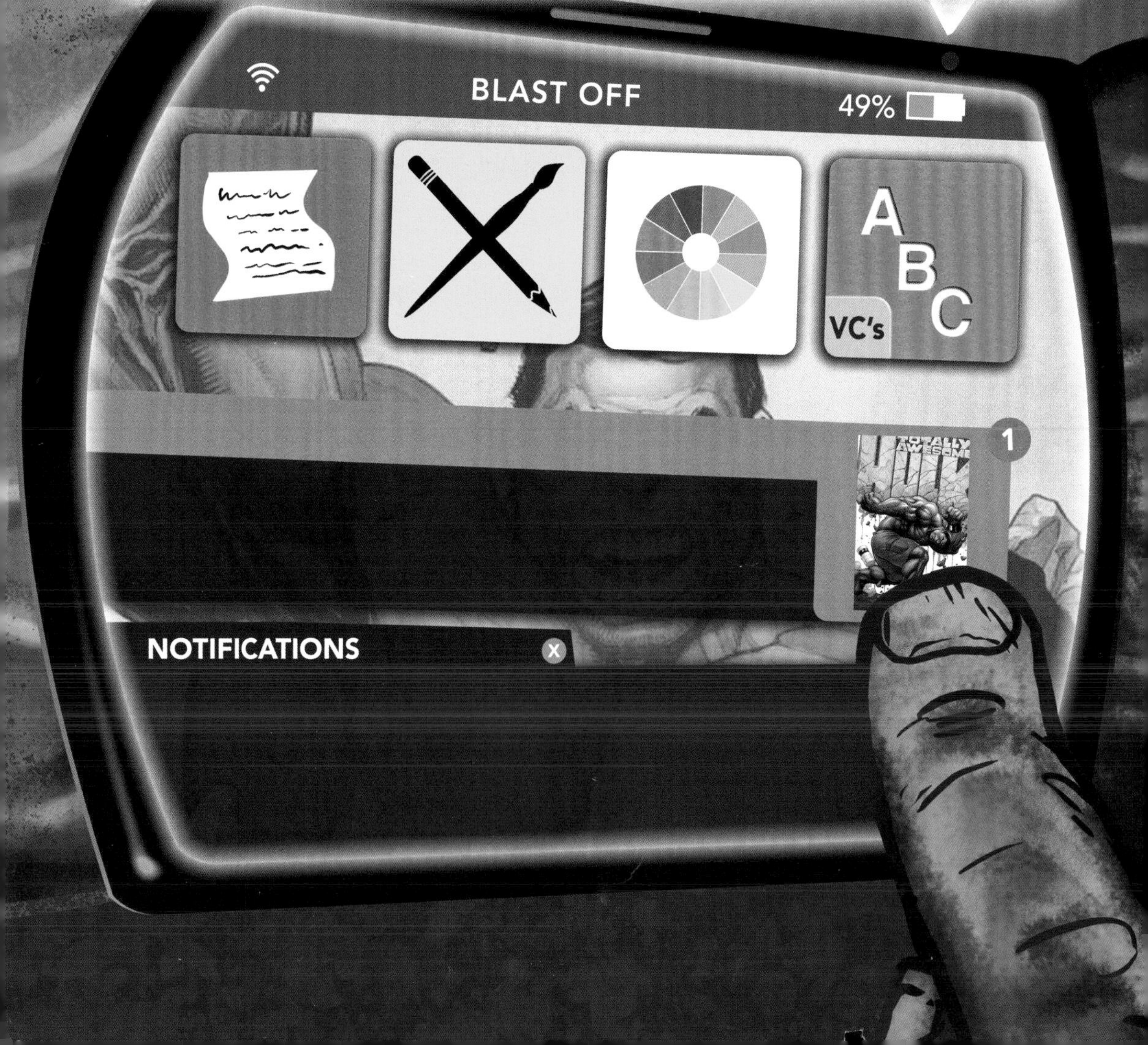

BLAST OFF
49%
A
B
C
VC's
TOTALLY AWESOME
1
NOTIFICATIONS
x

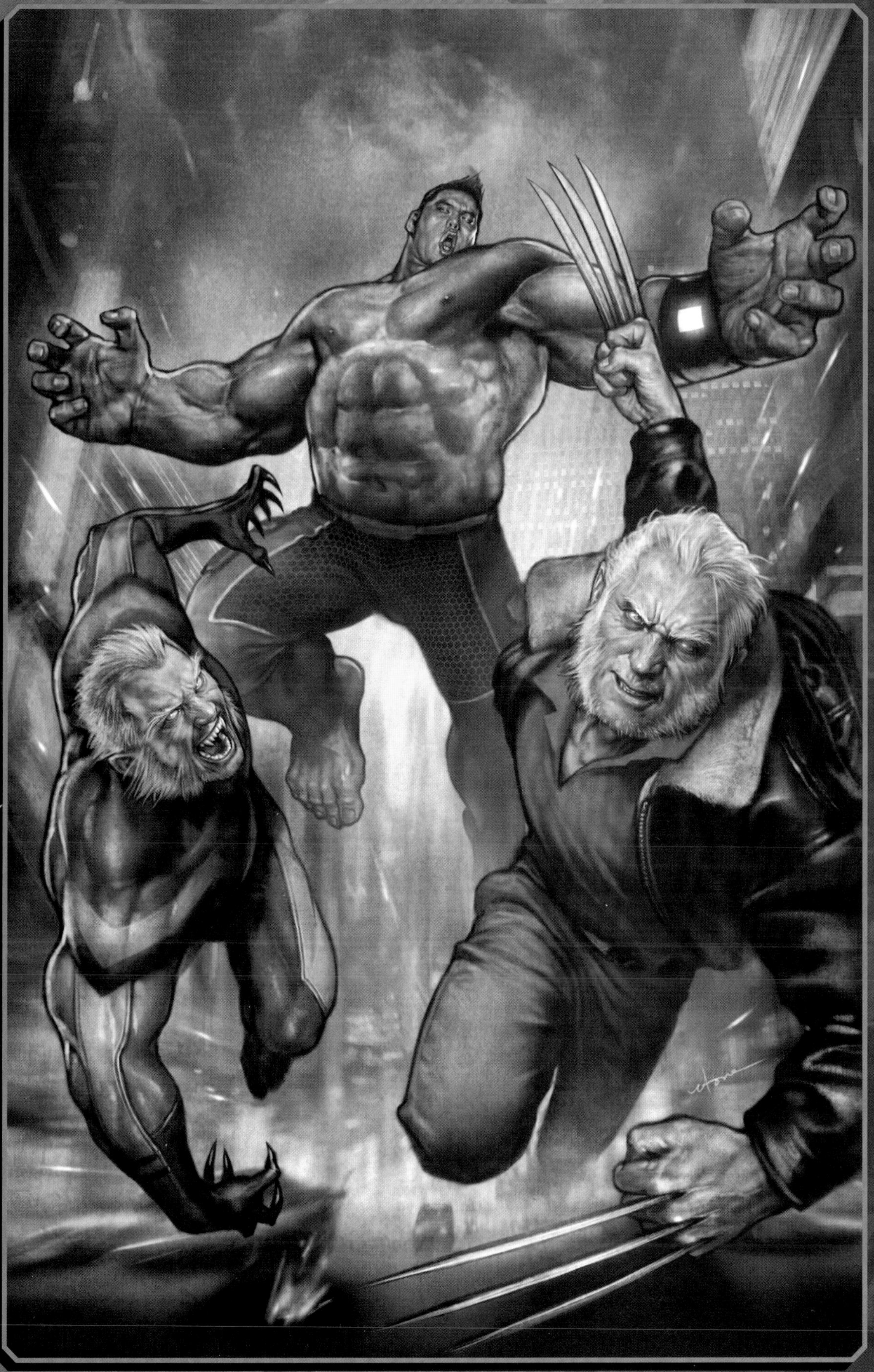

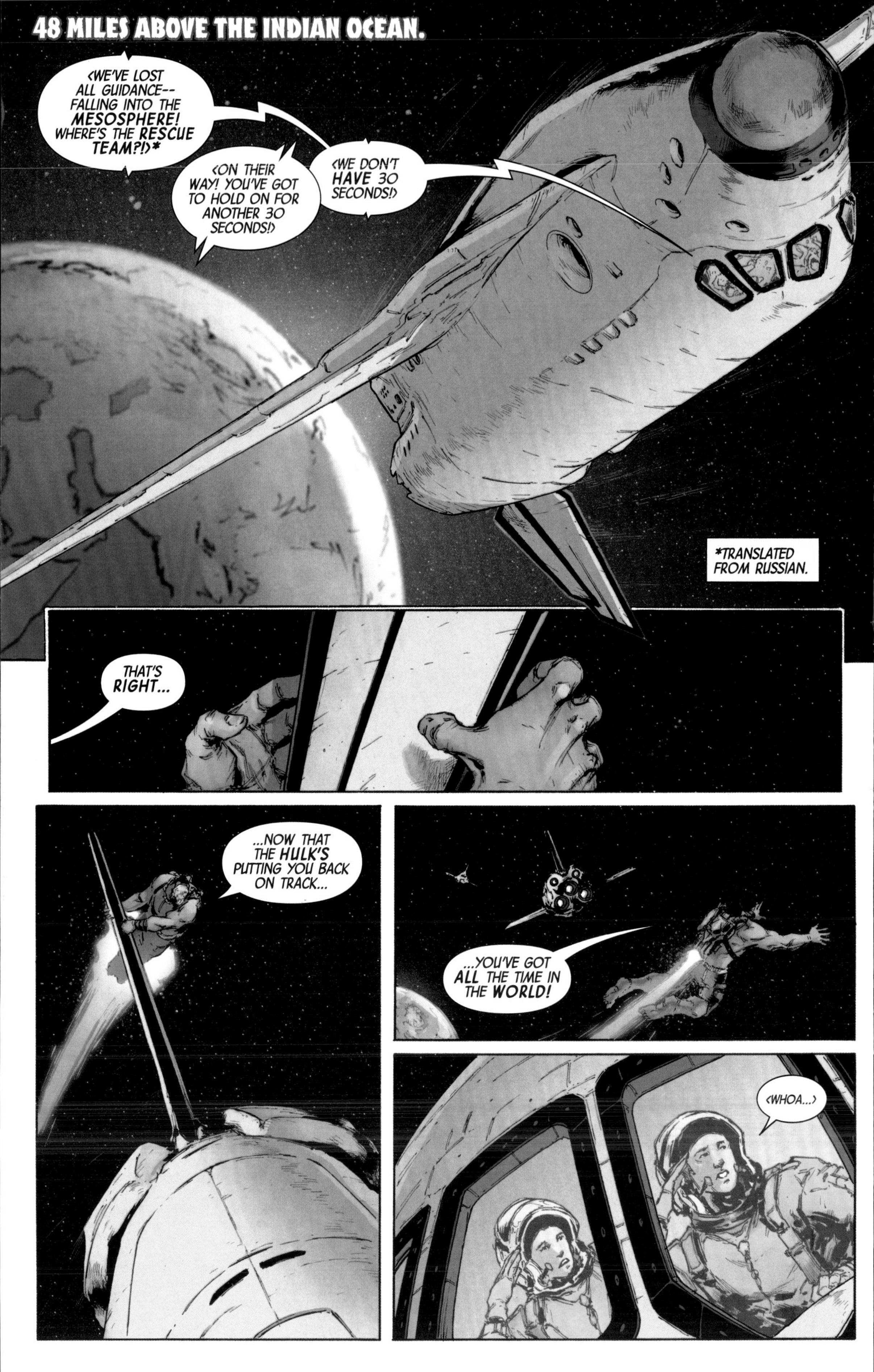
48 MILES ABOVE THE INDIAN OCEAN.
‹WE'VE LOST ALL GUIDANCE--FALLING INTO THE MESOSPHERE! WHERE'S THE RESCUE TEAM?!›*
‹ON THEIR WAY! YOU'VE GOT TO HOLD ON FOR ANOTHER 30 SECONDS!›
‹WE DON'T HAVE 30 SECONDS!›
*TRANSLATED FROM RUSSIAN.
THAT'S RIGHT...
...NOW THAT THE HULK'S PUTTING YOU BACK ON TRACK...
...YOU'VE GOT ALL THE TIME IN THE WORLD!
‹WHOA...›

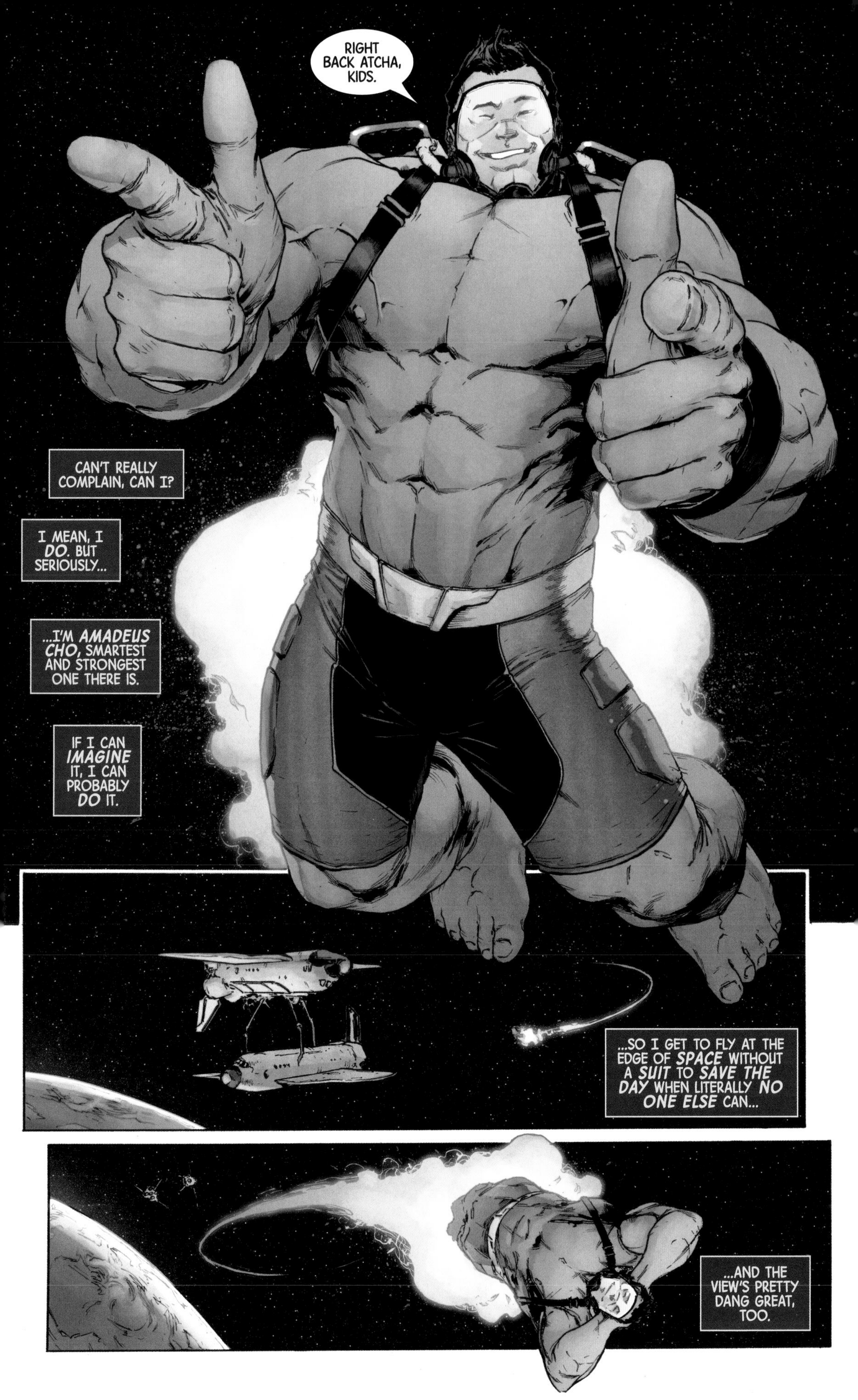
RIGHT BACK ATCHA, KIDS.
CAN'T REALLY COMPLAIN, CAN I?
I MEAN, I DO. BUT SERIOUSLY...
...I'M AMADEUS CHO, SMARTEST AND STRONGEST ONE THERE IS.
IF I CAN IMAGINE IT, I CAN PROBABLY DO IT.
...SO I GET TO FLY AT THE EDGE OF SPACE WITHOUT A SUIT TO SAVE THE DAY WHEN LITERALLY NO ONE ELSE CAN...
...AND THE VIEW'S PRETTY DANG GREAT, TOO.

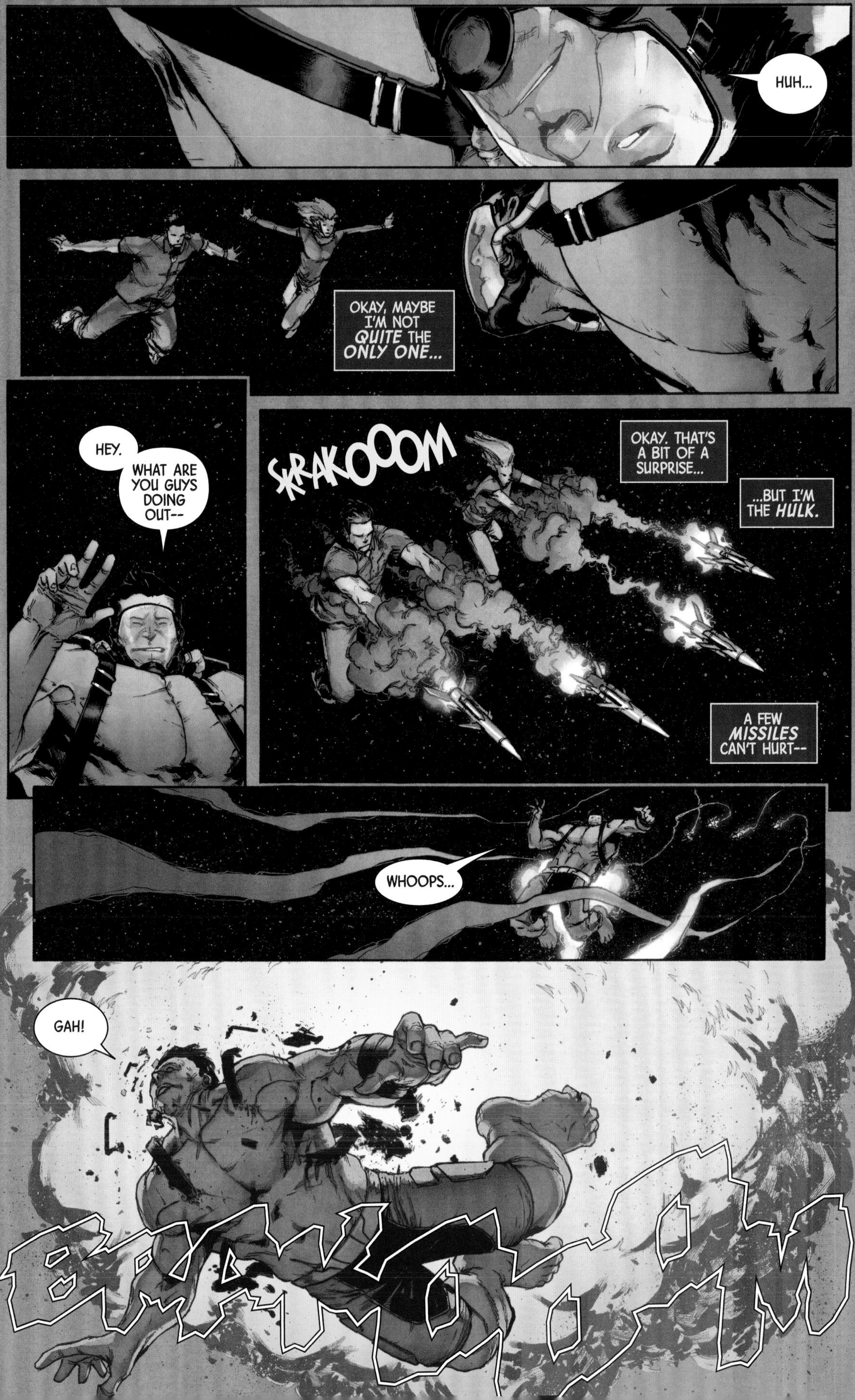
HUH...
OKAY, MAYBE I'M NOT QUITE THE ONLY ONE...
HEY.
WHAT ARE YOU GUYS DOING OUT--
SKRAKOOOM
OKAY. THAT'S A BIT OF A SURPRISE...
...BUT I'M THE HULK.
A FEW MISSILES CAN'T HURT--
WHOOPS...
GAH!

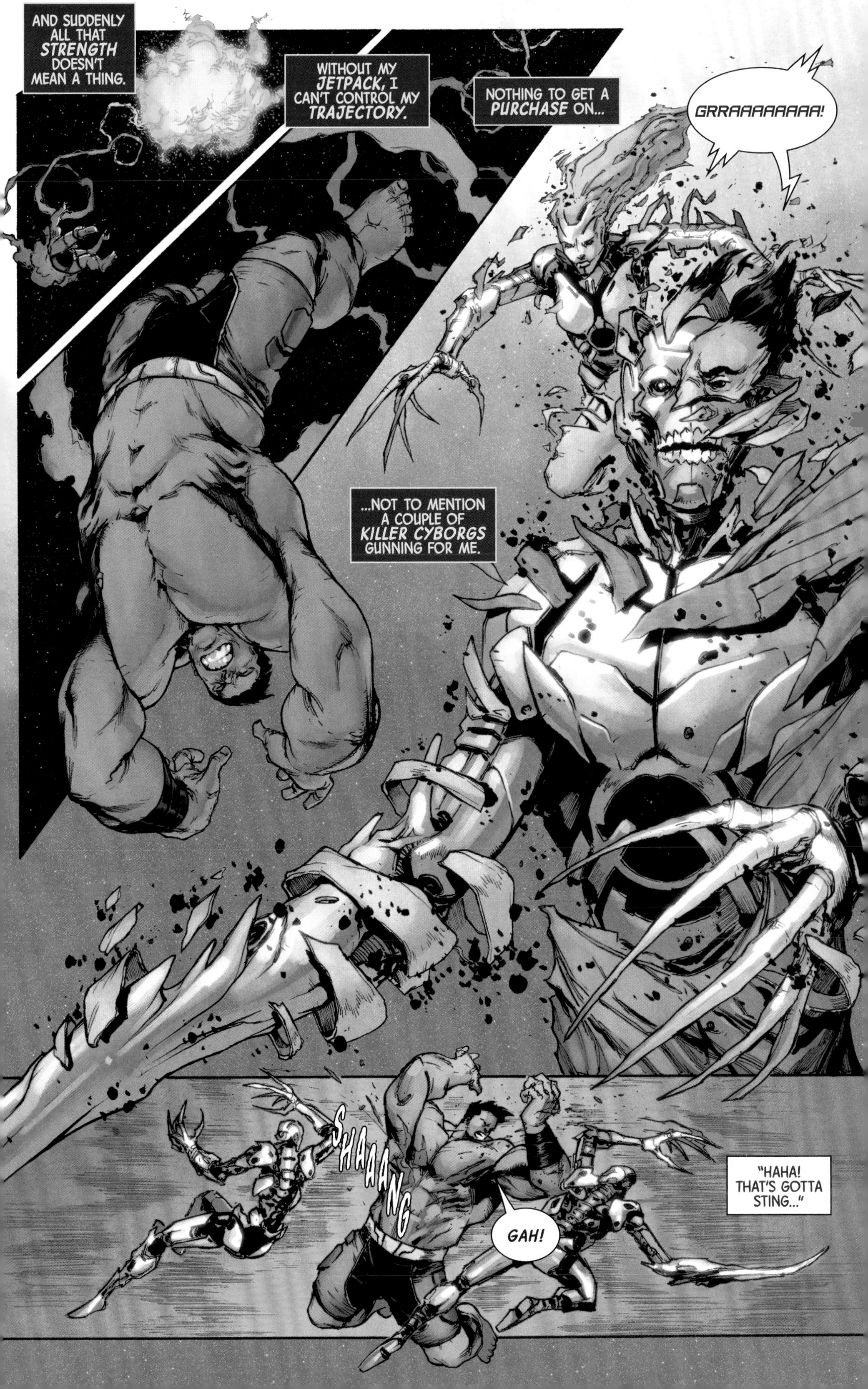
AND SUDDENLY ALL THAT STRENGTH DOESN'T MEAN A THING.
WITHOUT MY JETPACK, I CAN'T CONTROL MY TRAJECTORY.
NOTHING TO GET A PURCHASE ON...
GRRAAAAAAAA!
...NOT TO MENTION A COUPLE OF KILLER CYBORGS GUNNING FOR ME.
SHAAANG
GAH!
"HAHA! THAT'S GOTTA STING..."

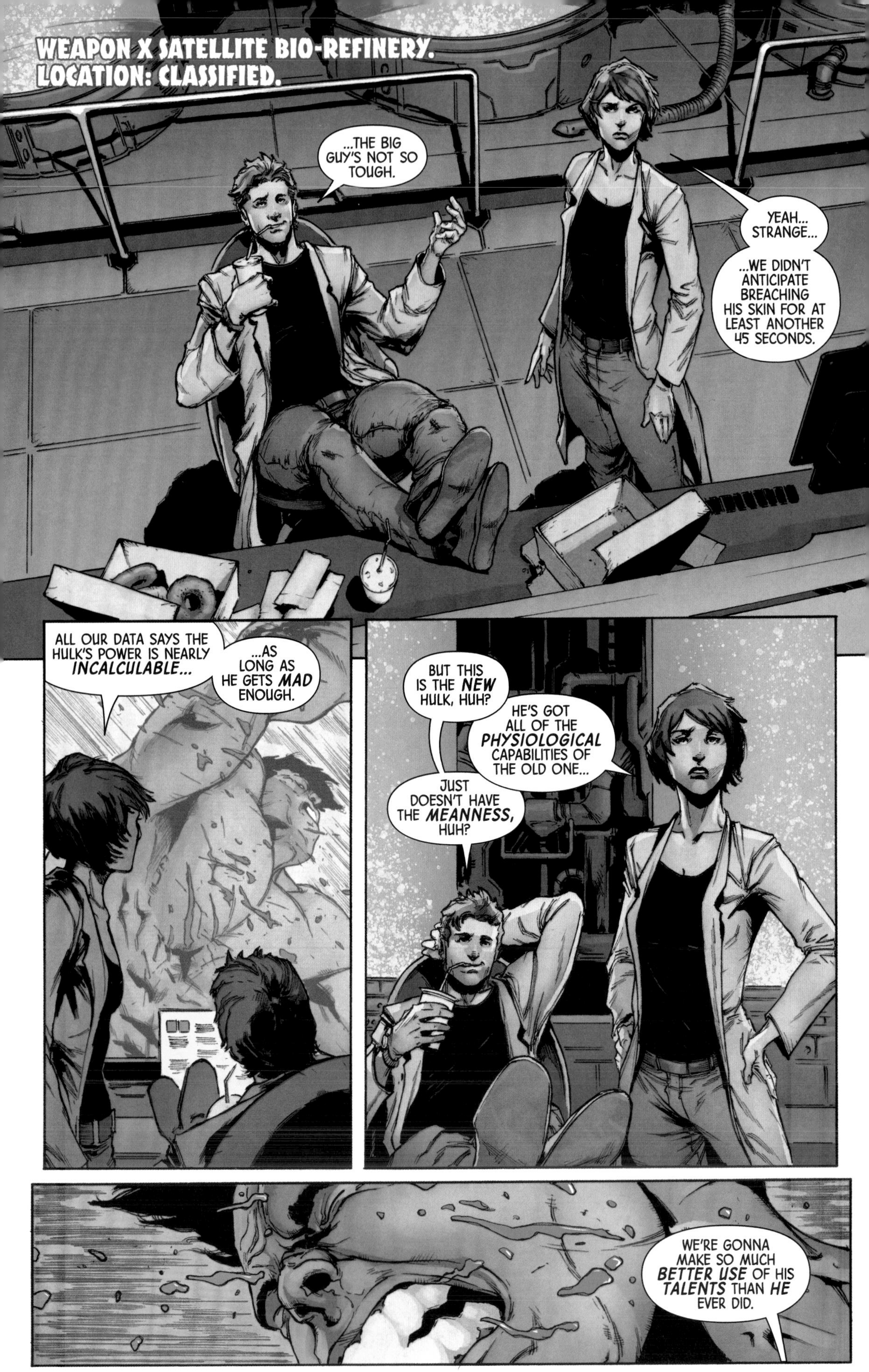
WEAPON X SATELLITE BIO-REFINERY.
LOCATION: CLASSIFIED.
...THE BIG GUY'S NOT SO TOUGH.
YEAH... STRANGE...
...WE DIDN'T ANTICIPATE BREACHING HIS SKIN FOR AT LEAST ANOTHER 45 SECONDS.
ALL OUR DATA SAYS THE HULK'S POWER IS NEARLY *INCALCULABLE...*
...AS LONG AS HE GETS *MAD* ENOUGH.
BUT THIS IS THE *NEW* HULK, HUH?
HE'S GOT ALL OF THE *PHYSIOLOGICAL* CAPABILITIES OF THE OLD ONE...
JUST DOESN'T HAVE THE *MEANNESS,* HUH?
WE'RE GONNA MAKE SO MUCH *BETTER USE* OF HIS *TALENTS* THAN *HE* EVER DID.

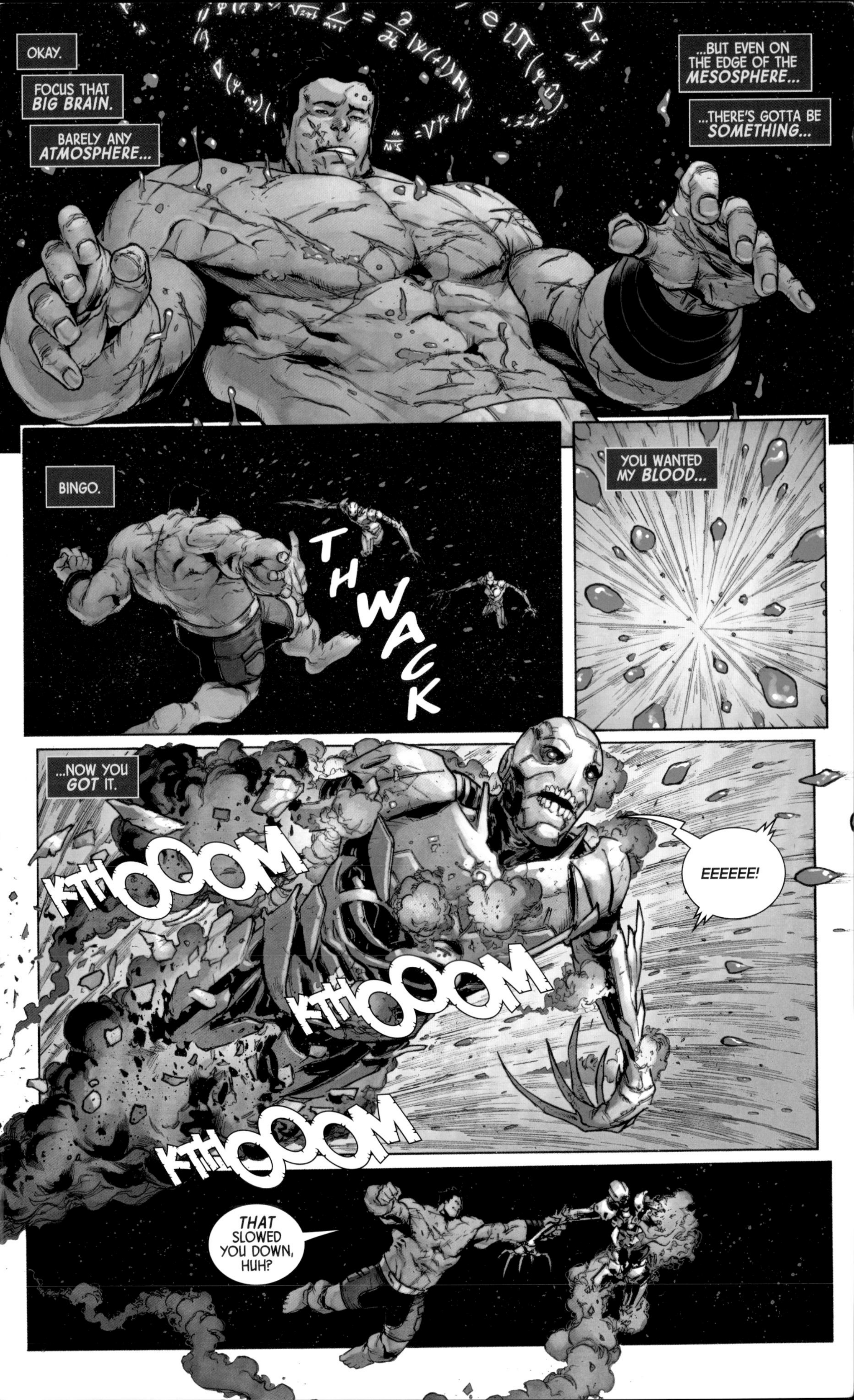
OKAY.
FOCUS THAT BIG BRAIN.
BARELY ANY ATMOSPHERE...
...BUT EVEN ON THE EDGE OF THE MESOSPHERE...
...THERE'S GOTTA BE SOMETHING...
BINGO.
THWACK
YOU WANTED MY BLOOD...
...NOW YOU GOT IT.
KTHOOOM
EEEEEE!
KTHOOOM
KTHOOOM
THAT SLOWED YOU DOWN, HUH?

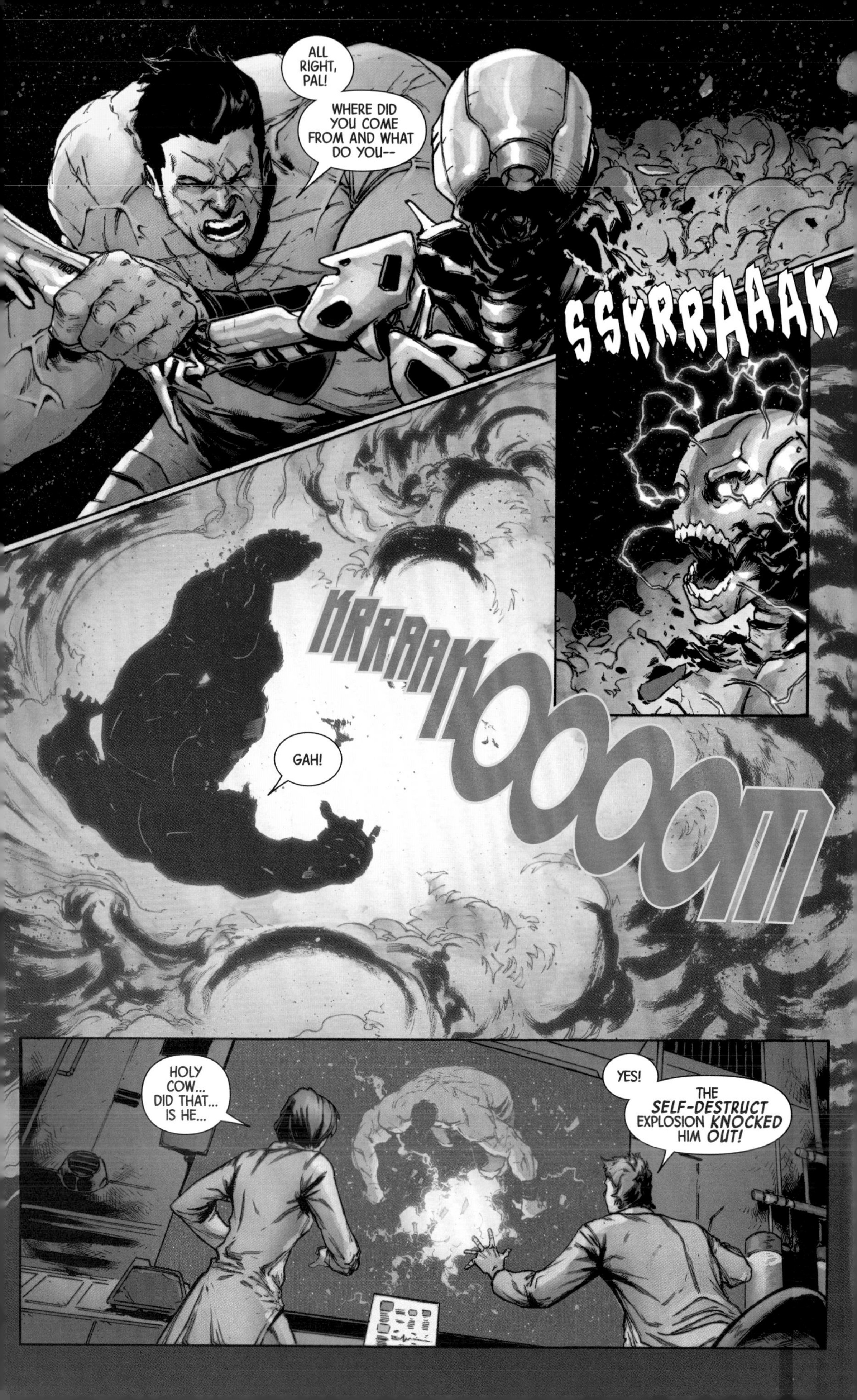
ALL RIGHT, PAL!
WHERE DID YOU COME FROM AND WHAT DO YOU--
SSKRRAAAK
KRRAAKOOOOOM
GAH!
HOLY COW... DID THAT... IS HE...
YES!
THE SELF-DESTRUCT EXPLOSION KNOCKED HIM OUT!

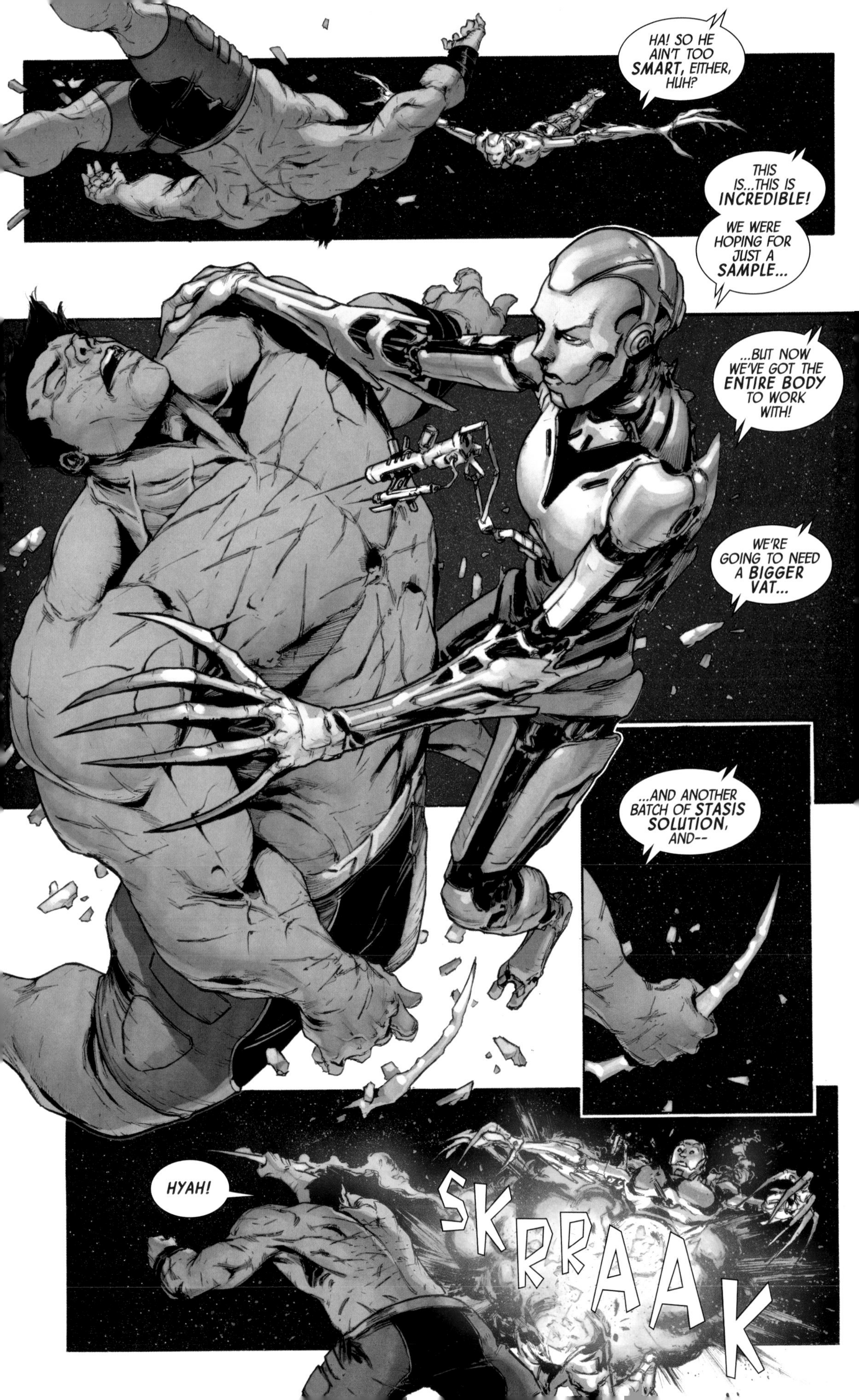
HA! SO HE AIN'T TOO SMART, EITHER, HUH?
THIS IS...THIS IS INCREDIBLE!
WE WERE HOPING FOR JUST A SAMPLE...
...BUT NOW WE'VE GOT THE ENTIRE BODY TO WORK WITH!
WE'RE GOING TO NEED A BIGGER VAT...
...AND ANOTHER BATCH OF STASIS SOLUTION, AND--
HYAH!
SKRRAAK

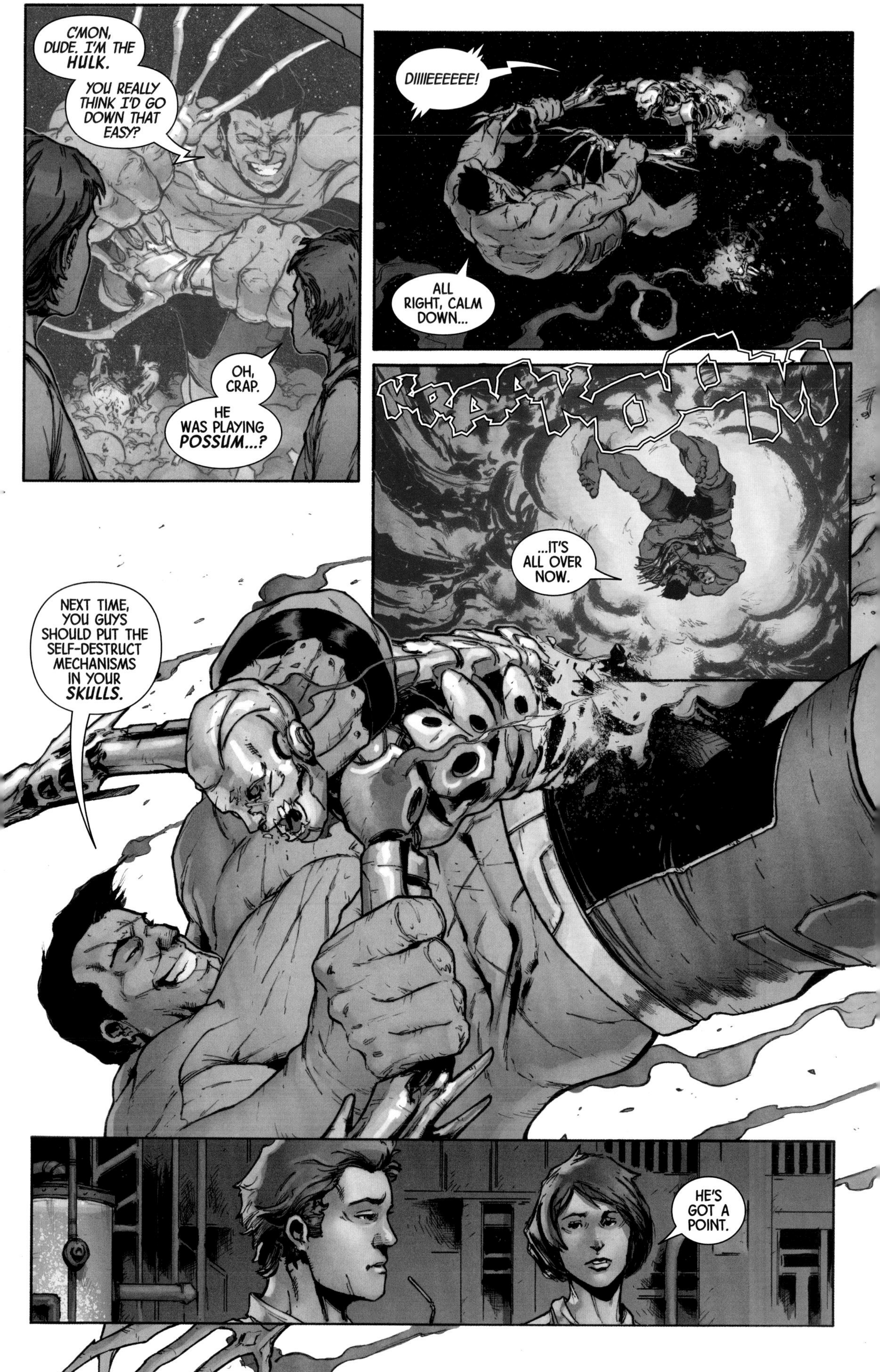
C'MON, DUDE. I'M THE HULK.
YOU REALLY THINK I'D GO DOWN THAT EASY?
OH, CRAP.
HE WAS PLAYING POSSUM...?
DIIIIEEEEEE!
ALL RIGHT, CALM DOWN...
KRAAKOOOM
...IT'S ALL OVER NOW.
NEXT TIME, YOU GUYS SHOULD PUT THE SELF-DESTRUCT MECHANISMS IN YOUR SKULLS.
HE'S GOT A POINT.

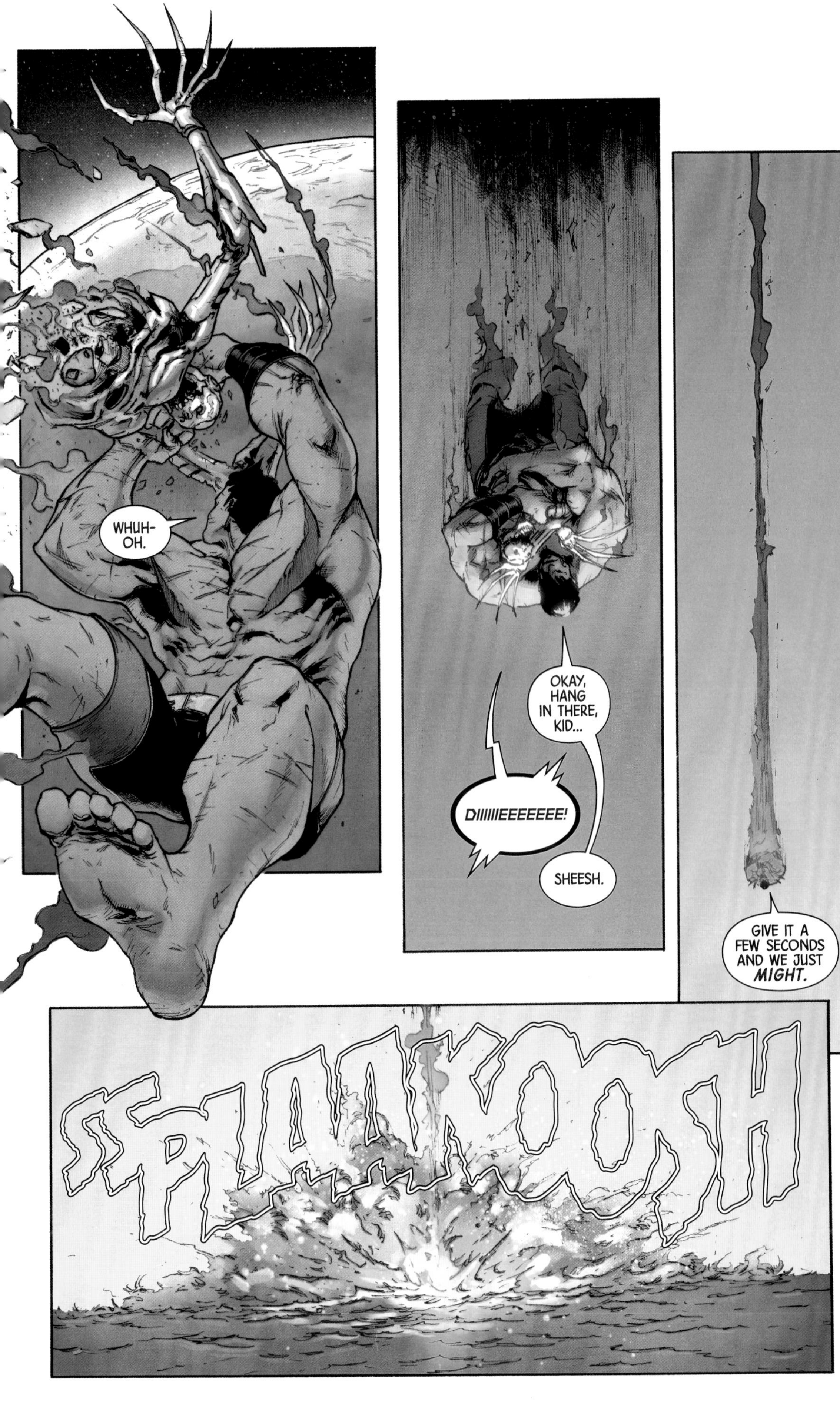
WHUH-
OH.
OKAY,
HANG
IN THERE,
KID...
DIIIIIEEEEEEE!
SHEESH.
GIVE IT A
FEW SECONDS
AND WE JUST
MIGHT.
SPLAAKOOSH

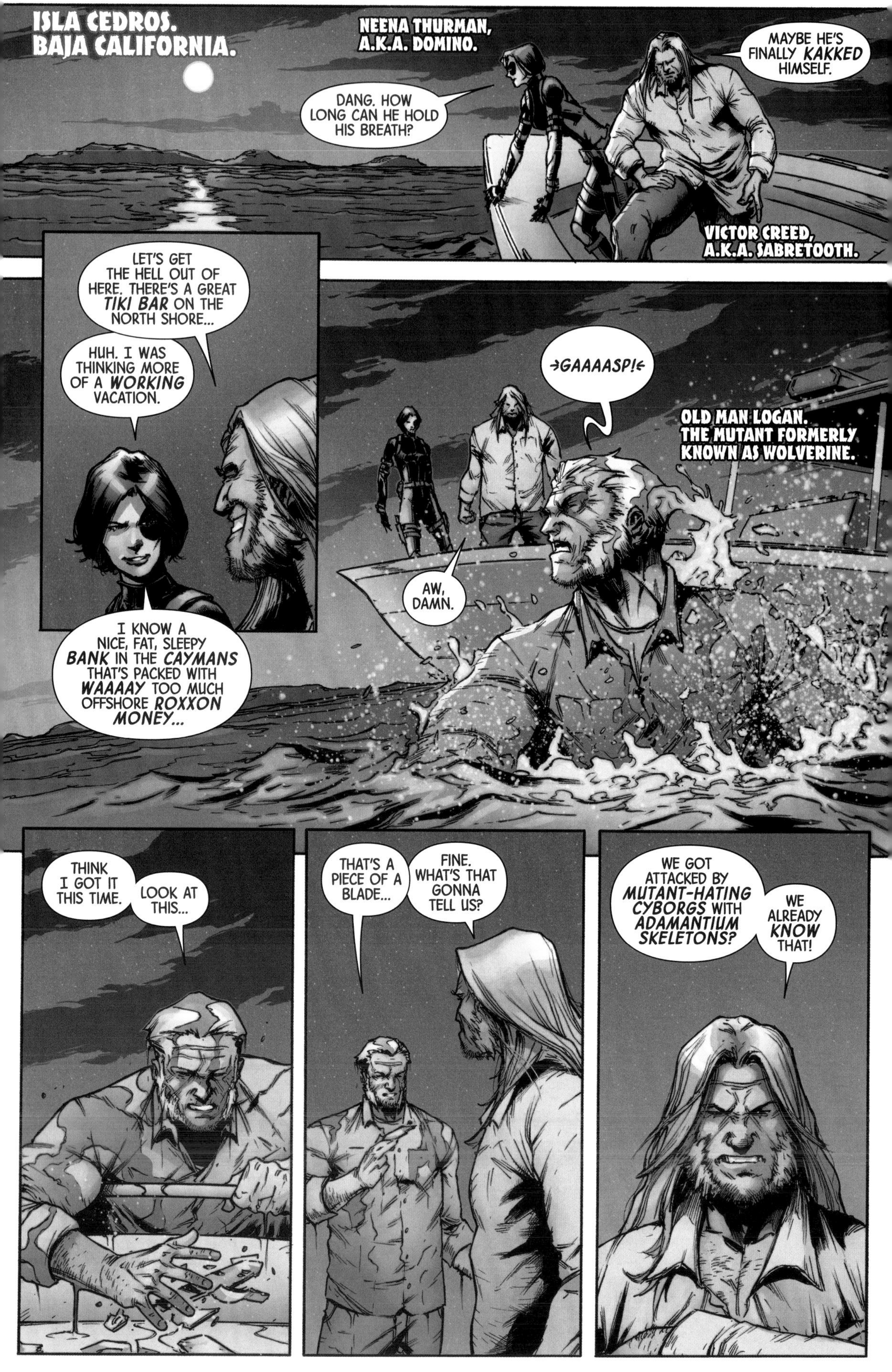
ISLA CEDROS. BAJA CALIFORNIA.
NEENA THURMAN, A.K.A. DOMINO.
DANG. HOW LONG CAN HE HOLD HIS BREATH?
MAYBE HE'S FINALLY KAKKED HIMSELF.
VICTOR CREED, A.K.A. SABRETOOTH.
LET'S GET THE HELL OUT OF HERE. THERE'S A GREAT TIKI BAR ON THE NORTH SHORE...
HUH. I WAS THINKING MORE OF A WORKING VACATION.
I KNOW A NICE, FAT, SLEEPY BANK IN THE CAYMANS THAT'S PACKED WITH WAAAAY TOO MUCH OFFSHORE ROXXON MONEY...
→GAAAASP!←
OLD MAN LOGAN. THE MUTANT FORMERLY KNOWN AS WOLVERINE.
AW, DAMN.
THINK I GOT IT THIS TIME.
LOOK AT THIS...
THAT'S A PIECE OF A BLADE...
FINE. WHAT'S THAT GONNA TELL US?
WE GOT ATTACKED BY MUTANT-HATING CYBORGS WITH ADAMANTIUM SKELETONS?
WE ALREADY KNOW THAT!

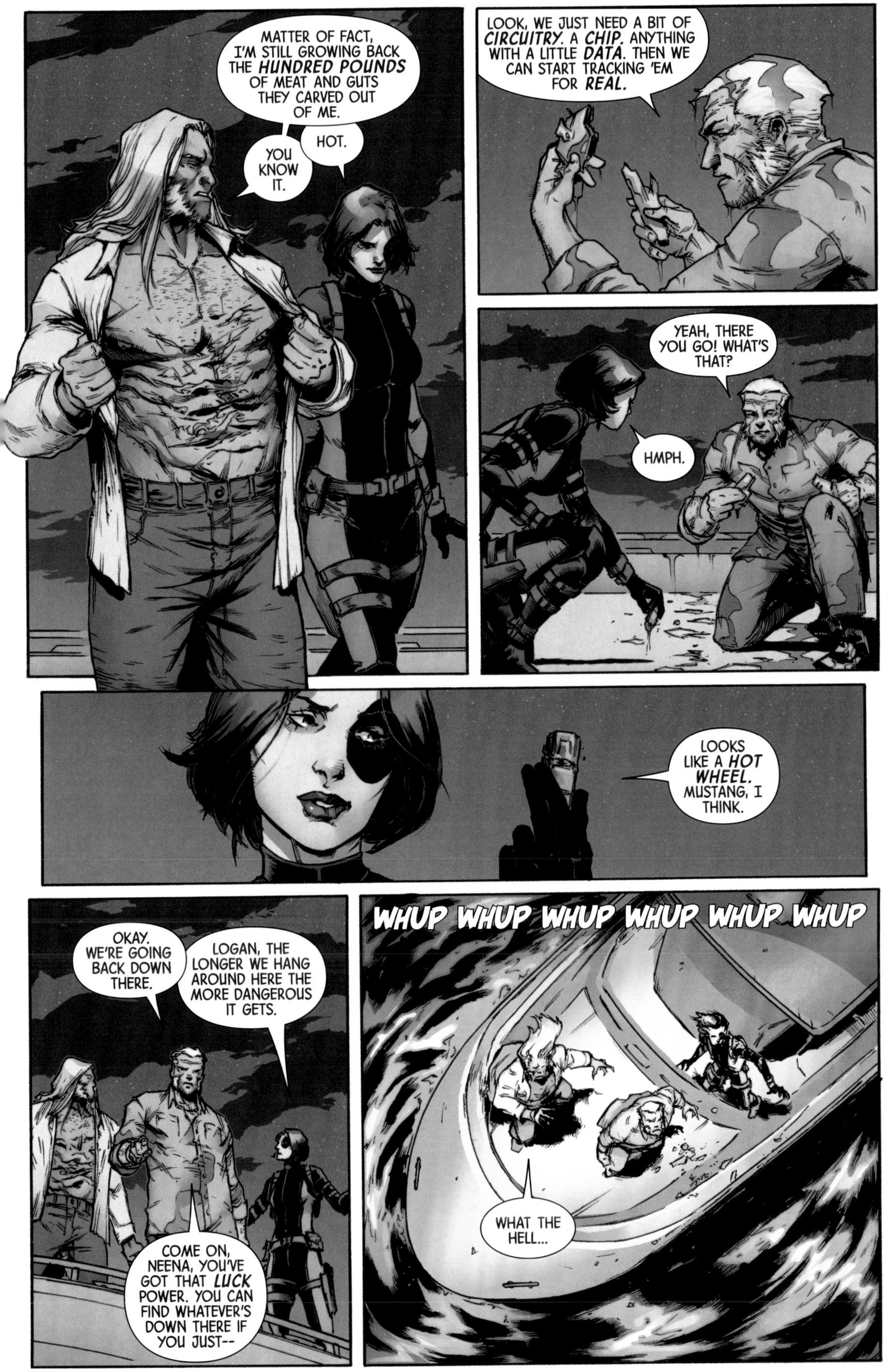
MATTER OF FACT, I'M STILL GROWING BACK THE HUNDRED POUNDS OF MEAT AND GUTS THEY CARVED OUT OF ME.
HOT.
YOU KNOW IT.
LOOK, WE JUST NEED A BIT OF CIRCUITRY. A CHIP. ANYTHING WITH A LITTLE DATA. THEN WE CAN START TRACKING 'EM FOR REAL.
YEAH, THERE YOU GO! WHAT'S THAT?
HMPH.
LOOKS LIKE A HOT WHEEL. MUSTANG, I THINK.
OKAY. WE'RE GOING BACK DOWN THERE.
LOGAN, THE LONGER WE HANG AROUND HERE THE MORE DANGEROUS IT GETS.
COME ON, NEENA, YOU'VE GOT THAT LUCK POWER. YOU CAN FIND WHATEVER'S DOWN THERE IF YOU JUST--
WHUP WHUP WHUP WHUP WHUP WHUP
WHAT THE HELL...

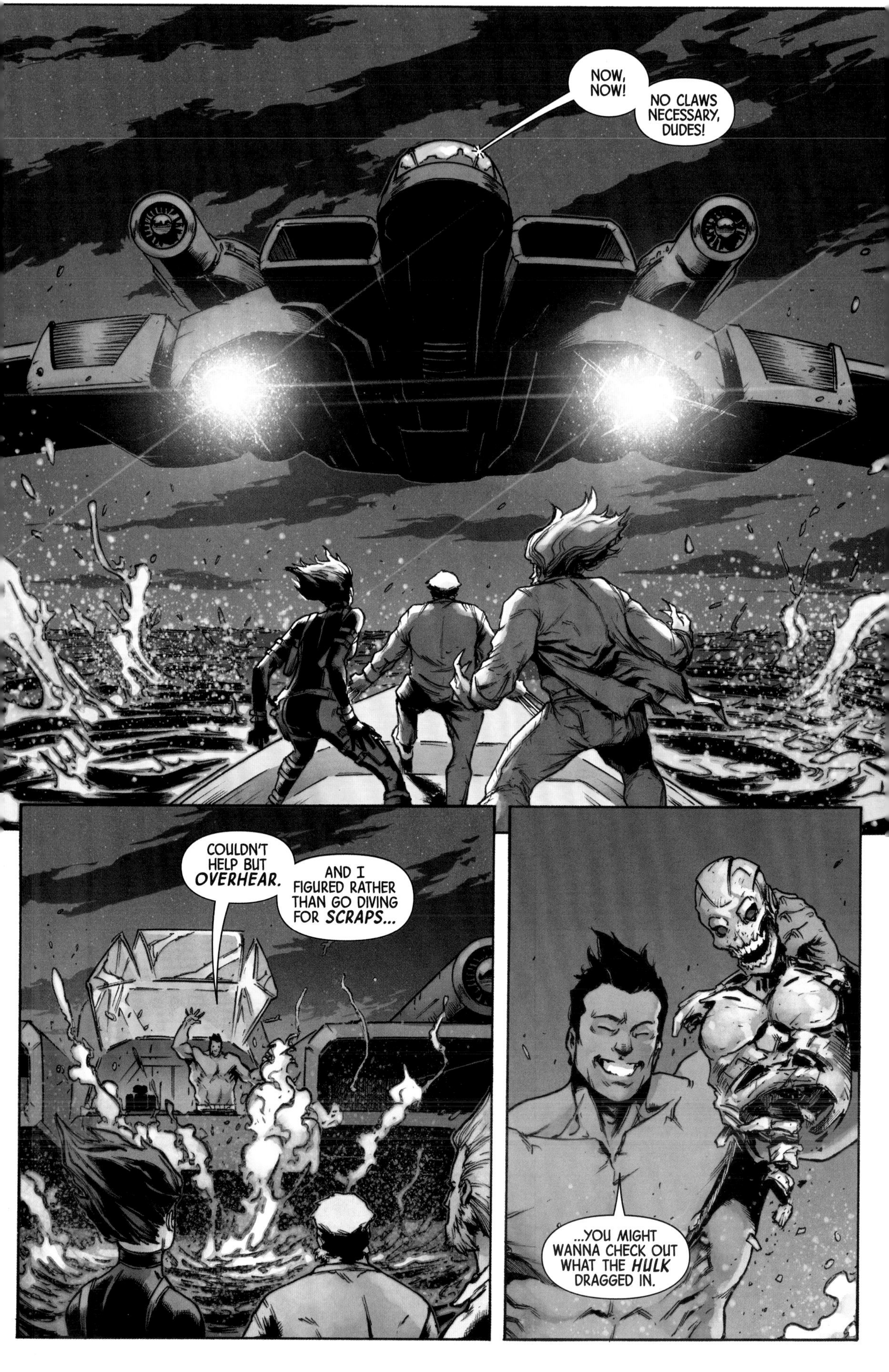
NOW, NOW!
NO CLAWS NECESSARY, DUDES!
COULDN'T HELP BUT OVERHEAR.
AND I FIGURED RATHER THAN GO DIVING FOR SCRAPS...
...YOU MIGHT WANNA CHECK OUT WHAT THE HULK DRAGGED IN.

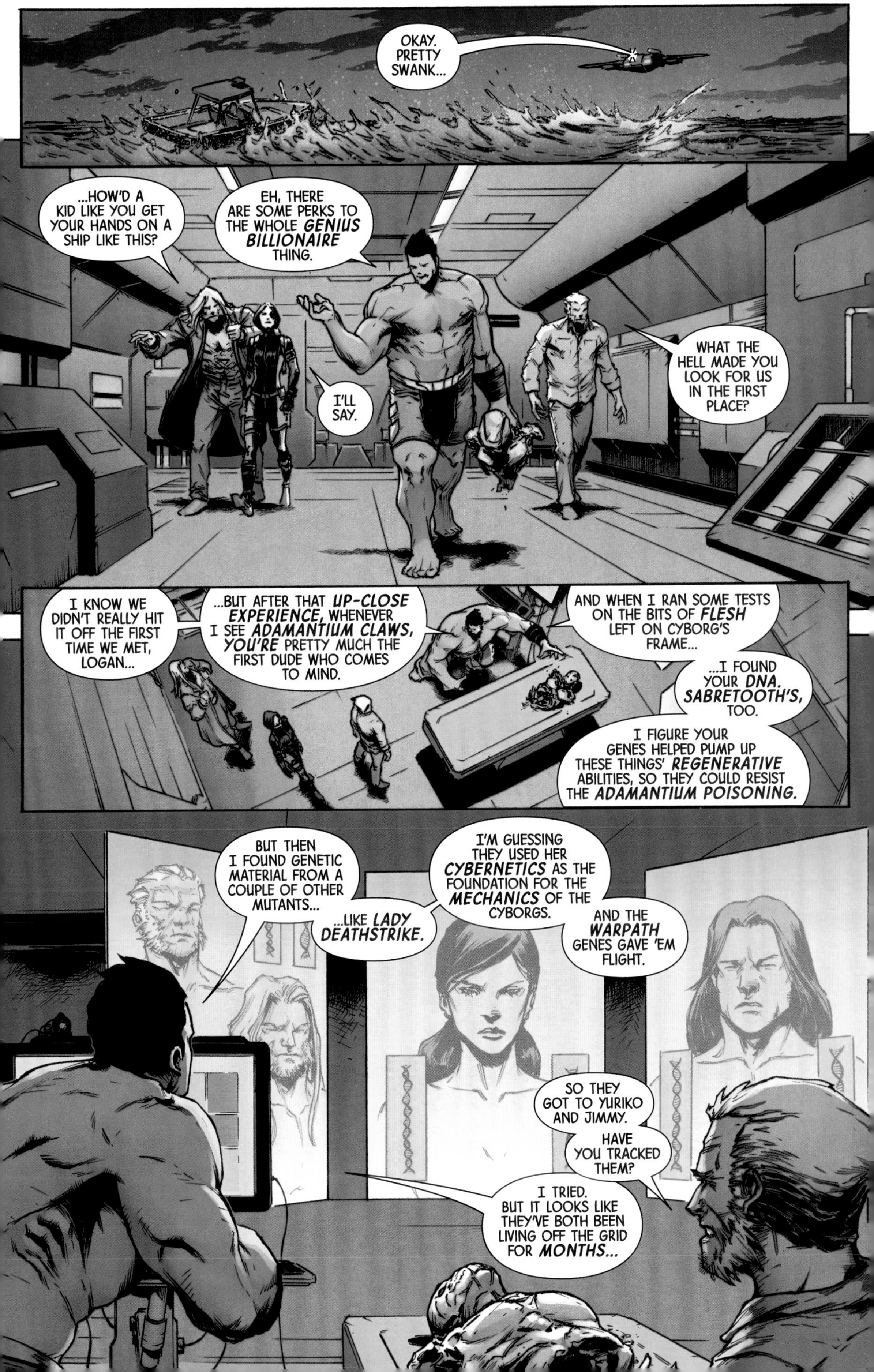

OKAY. PRETTY SWANK...
...HOW'D A KID LIKE YOU GET YOUR HANDS ON A SHIP LIKE THIS?
EH, THERE ARE SOME PERKS TO THE WHOLE GENIUS BILLIONAIRE THING.
I'LL SAY.
WHAT THE HELL MADE YOU LOOK FOR US IN THE FIRST PLACE?
I KNOW WE DIDN'T REALLY HIT IT OFF THE FIRST TIME WE MET, LOGAN...
...BUT AFTER THAT UP-CLOSE EXPERIENCE, WHENEVER I SEE ADAMANTIUM CLAWS, YOU'RE PRETTY MUCH THE FIRST DUDE WHO COMES TO MIND.
AND WHEN I RAN SOME TESTS ON THE BITS OF FLESH LEFT ON CYBORG'S FRAME...
...I FOUND YOUR DNA. SABRETOOTH'S, TOO.
I FIGURE YOUR GENES HELPED PUMP UP THESE THINGS' REGENERATIVE ABILITIES, SO THEY COULD RESIST THE ADAMANTIUM POISONING.
BUT THEN I FOUND GENETIC MATERIAL FROM A COUPLE OF OTHER MUTANTS...
...LIKE LADY DEATHSTRIKE.
I'M GUESSING THEY USED HER CYBERNETICS AS THE FOUNDATION FOR THE MECHANICS OF THE CYBORGS.
AND THE WARPATH GENES GAVE 'EM FLIGHT.
SO THEY GOT TO YURIKO AND JIMMY.
HAVE YOU TRACKED THEM?
I TRIED. BUT IT LOOKS LIKE THEY'VE BOTH BEEN LIVING OFF THE GRID FOR MONTHS...

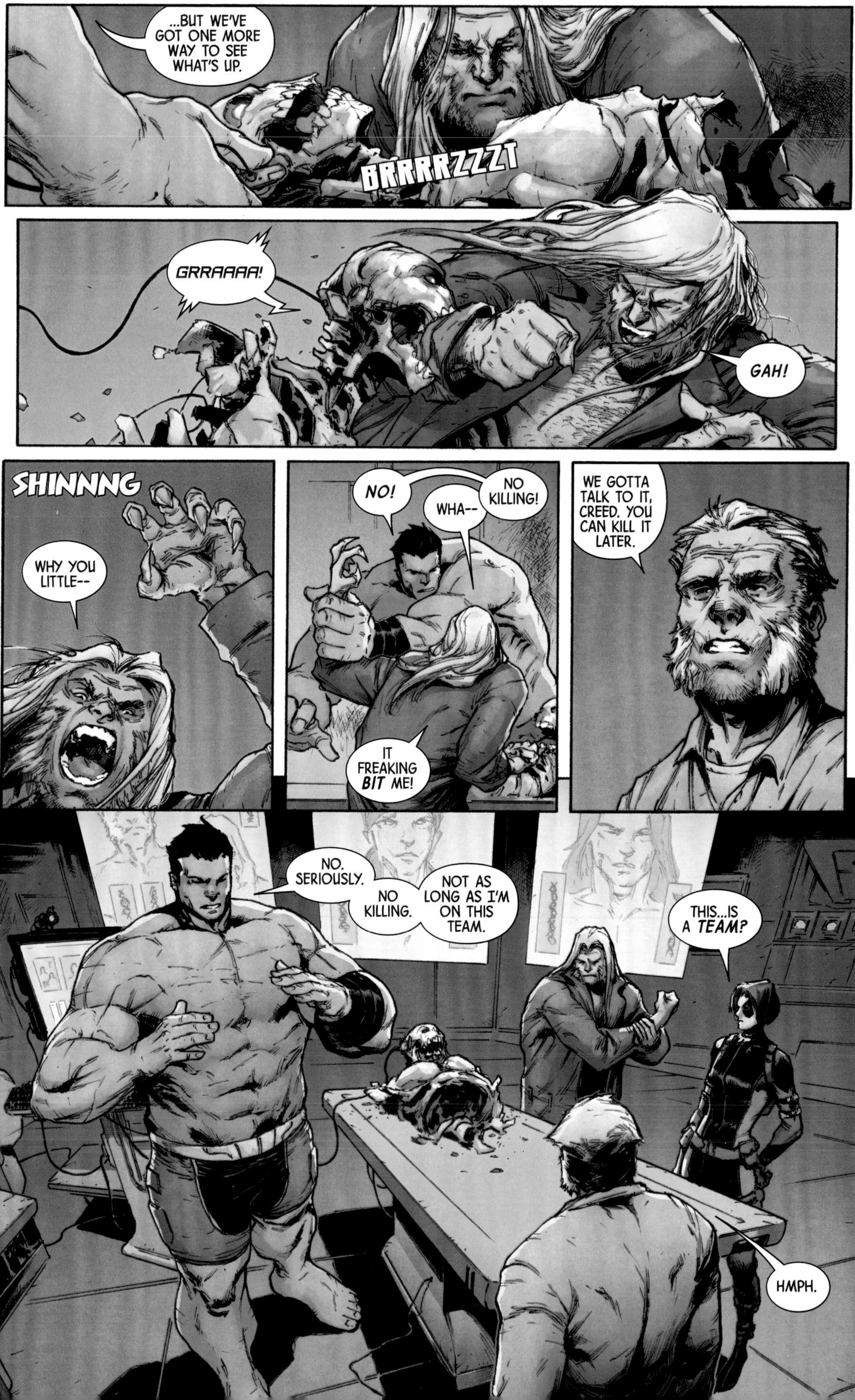
...BUT WE'VE GOT ONE MORE WAY TO SEE WHAT'S UP.
BRRRRZZZT
GRRAAAA!
GAH!
SHINNNG
WHY YOU LITTLE--
NO!
WHA--
NO KILLING!
IT FREAKING BIT ME!
WE GOTTA TALK TO IT, CREED. YOU CAN KILL IT LATER.
NO. SERIOUSLY.
NO KILLING.
NOT AS LONG AS I'M ON THIS TEAM.
THIS...IS A TEAM?
HMPH.

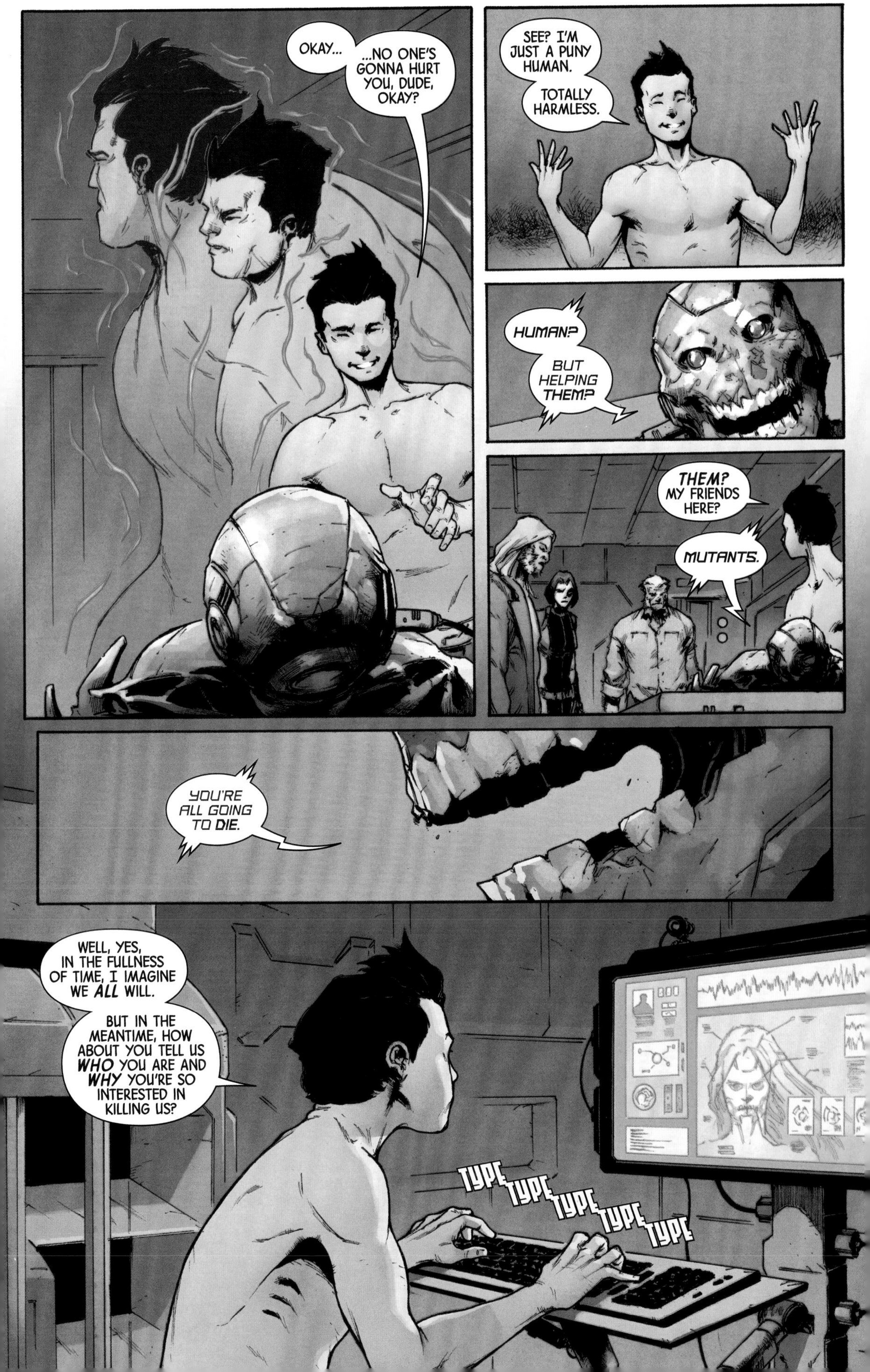
OKAY...
...NO ONE'S GONNA HURT YOU, DUDE, OKAY?
SEE? I'M JUST A PUNY HUMAN.
TOTALLY HARMLESS.
HUMAN?
BUT HELPING THEM?
THEM? MY FRIENDS HERE?
MUTANTS.
YOU'RE ALL GOING TO DIE.
WELL, YES, IN THE FULLNESS OF TIME, I IMAGINE WE ALL WILL.
BUT IN THE MEANTIME, HOW ABOUT YOU TELL US WHO YOU ARE AND WHY YOU'RE SO INTERESTED IN KILLING US?
TYPE TYPE TYPE TYPE TYPE

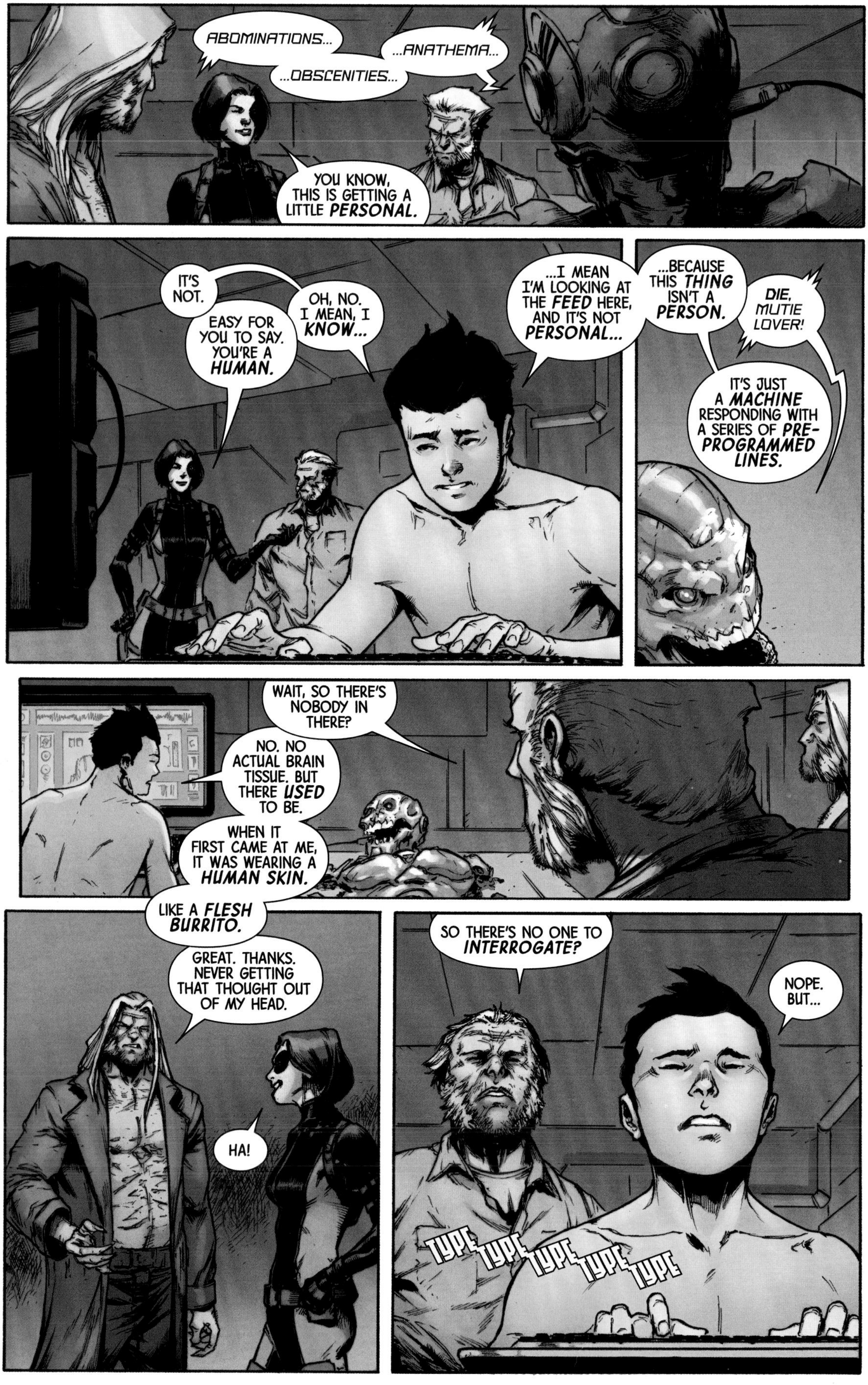
ABOMINATIONS...
...OBSCENITIES...
...ANATHEMA...
YOU KNOW, THIS IS GETTING A LITTLE PERSONAL.
IT'S NOT.
EASY FOR YOU TO SAY. YOU'RE A HUMAN.
OH, NO. I MEAN, I KNOW...
...I MEAN I'M LOOKING AT THE FEED HERE, AND IT'S NOT PERSONAL...
...BECAUSE THIS THING ISN'T A PERSON.
DIE, MUTIE LOVER!
IT'S JUST A MACHINE RESPONDING WITH A SERIES OF PRE-PROGRAMMED LINES.
WAIT, SO THERE'S NOBODY IN THERE?
NO. NO ACTUAL BRAIN TISSUE. BUT THERE USED TO BE.
WHEN IT FIRST CAME AT ME, IT WAS WEARING A HUMAN SKIN.
LIKE A FLESH BURRITO.
GREAT. THANKS. NEVER GETTING THAT THOUGHT OUT OF MY HEAD.
HA!
SO THERE'S NO ONE TO INTERROGATE?
NOPE. BUT...
TYPE TYPE TYPE TYPE TYPE

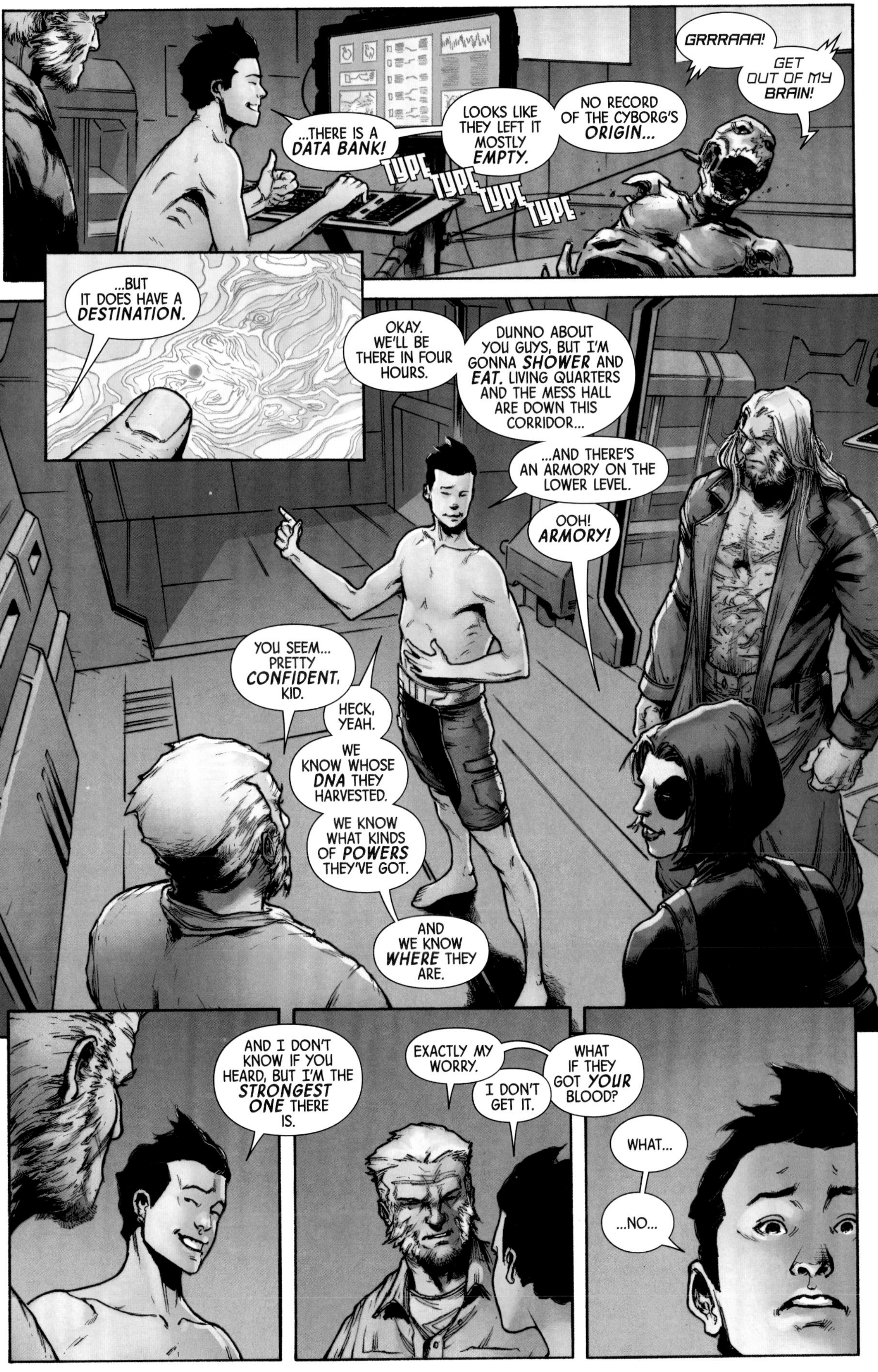

...THERE IS A DATA BANK!
LOOKS LIKE THEY LEFT IT MOSTLY EMPTY.
NO RECORD OF THE CYBORG'S ORIGIN...
TYPE TYPE TYPE TYPE
GRRRAAA!
GET OUT OF MY BRAIN!
...BUT IT DOES HAVE A DESTINATION.
OKAY. WE'LL BE THERE IN FOUR HOURS.
DUNNO ABOUT YOU GUYS, BUT I'M GONNA SHOWER AND EAT. LIVING QUARTERS AND THE MESS HALL ARE DOWN THIS CORRIDOR...
...AND THERE'S AN ARMORY ON THE LOWER LEVEL.
OOH! ARMORY!
YOU SEEM... PRETTY CONFIDENT, KID.
HECK, YEAH.
WE KNOW WHOSE DNA THEY HARVESTED.
WE KNOW WHAT KINDS OF POWERS THEY'VE GOT.
AND WE KNOW WHERE THEY ARE.
AND I DON'T KNOW IF YOU HEARD, BUT I'M THE STRONGEST ONE THERE IS.
EXACTLY MY WORRY.
I DON'T GET IT.
WHAT IF THEY GOT YOUR BLOOD?
WHAT...
...NO...

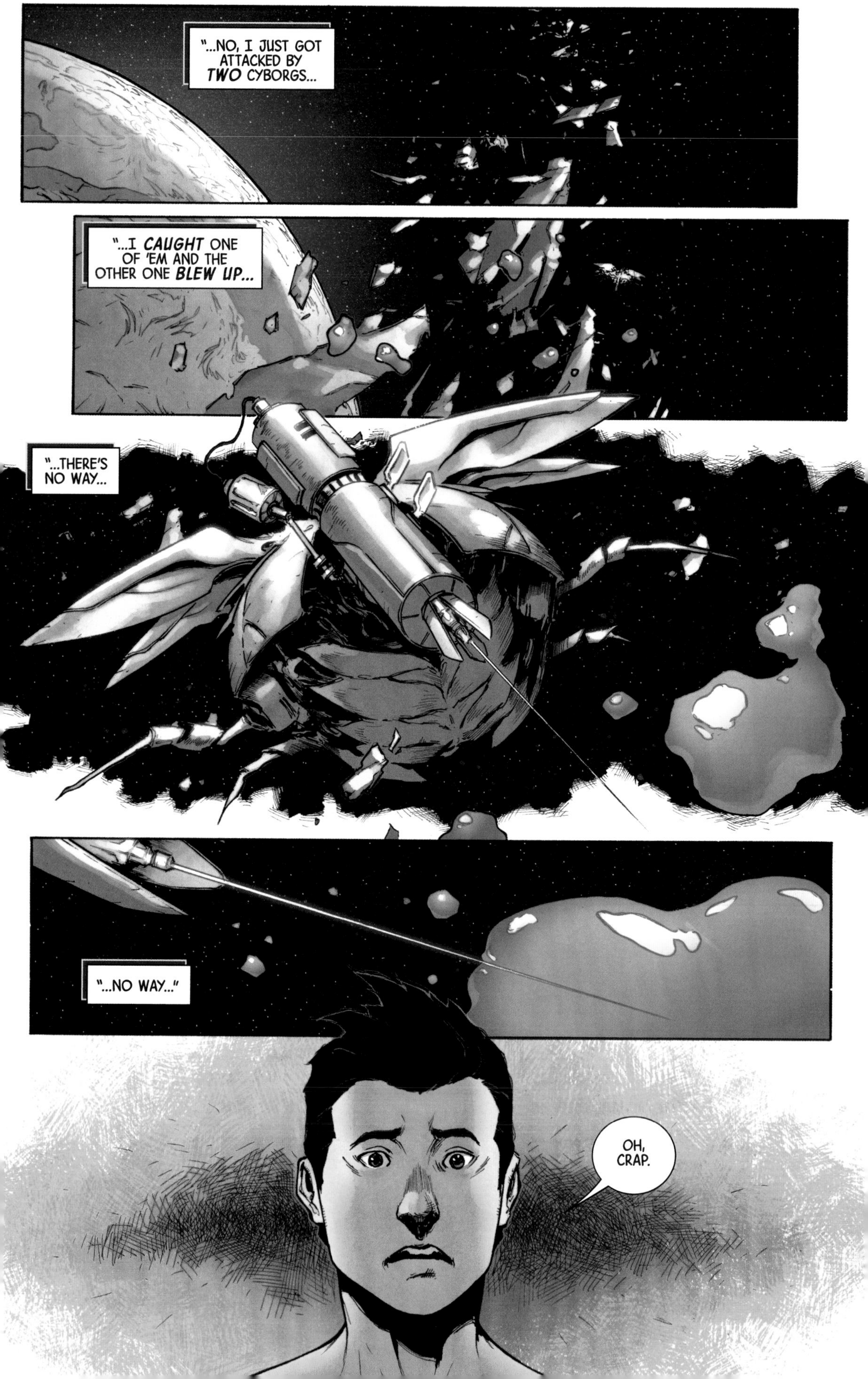
"...NO, I JUST GOT ATTACKED BY TWO CYBORGS...
"...I CAUGHT ONE OF 'EM AND THE OTHER ONE BLEW UP...
"...THERE'S NO WAY...
"...NO WAY..."
OH, CRAP.

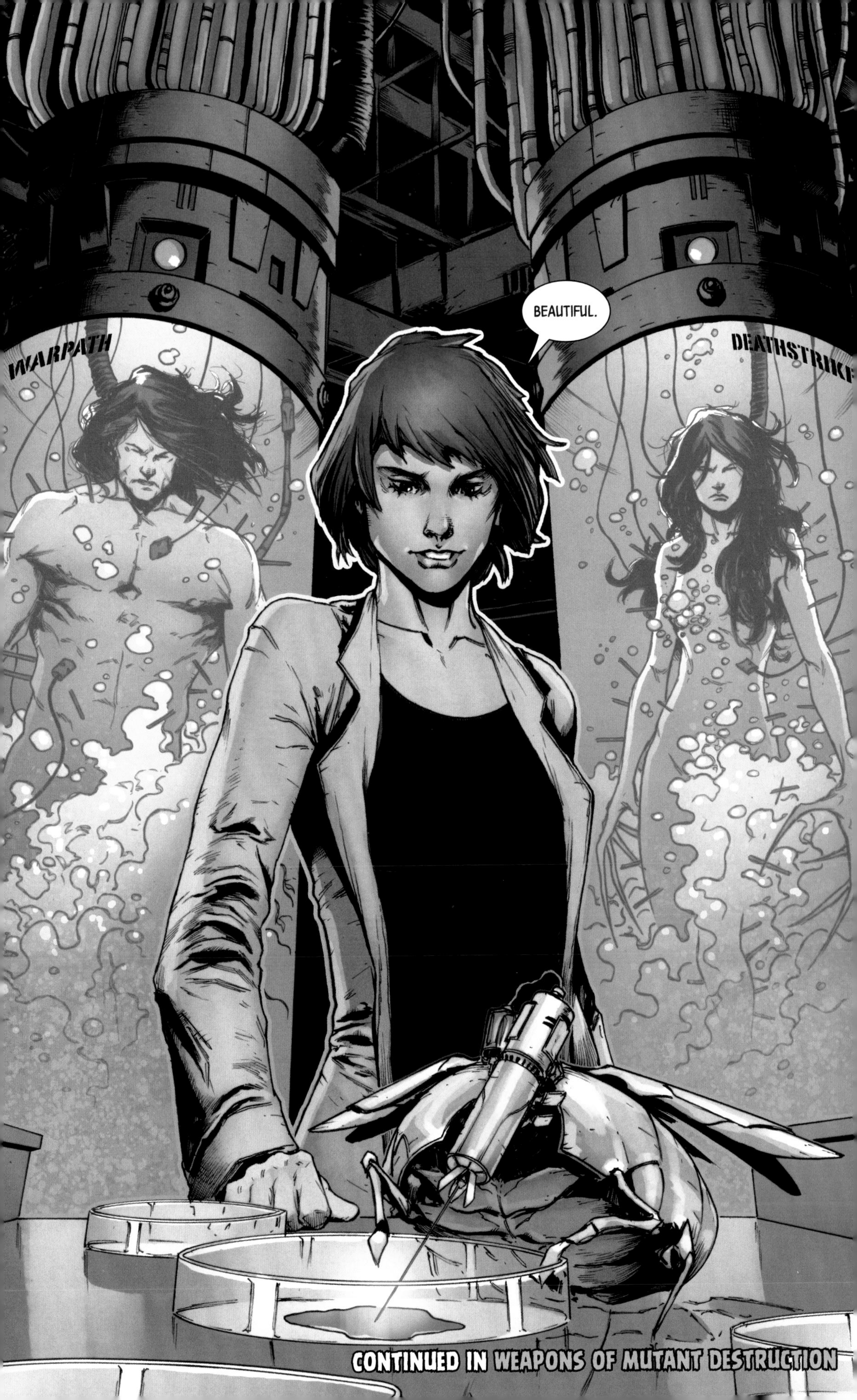
WARPATH
BEAUTIFUL.
DEATHSTRIKE
CONTINUED IN WEAPONS OF MUTANT DESTRUCTION

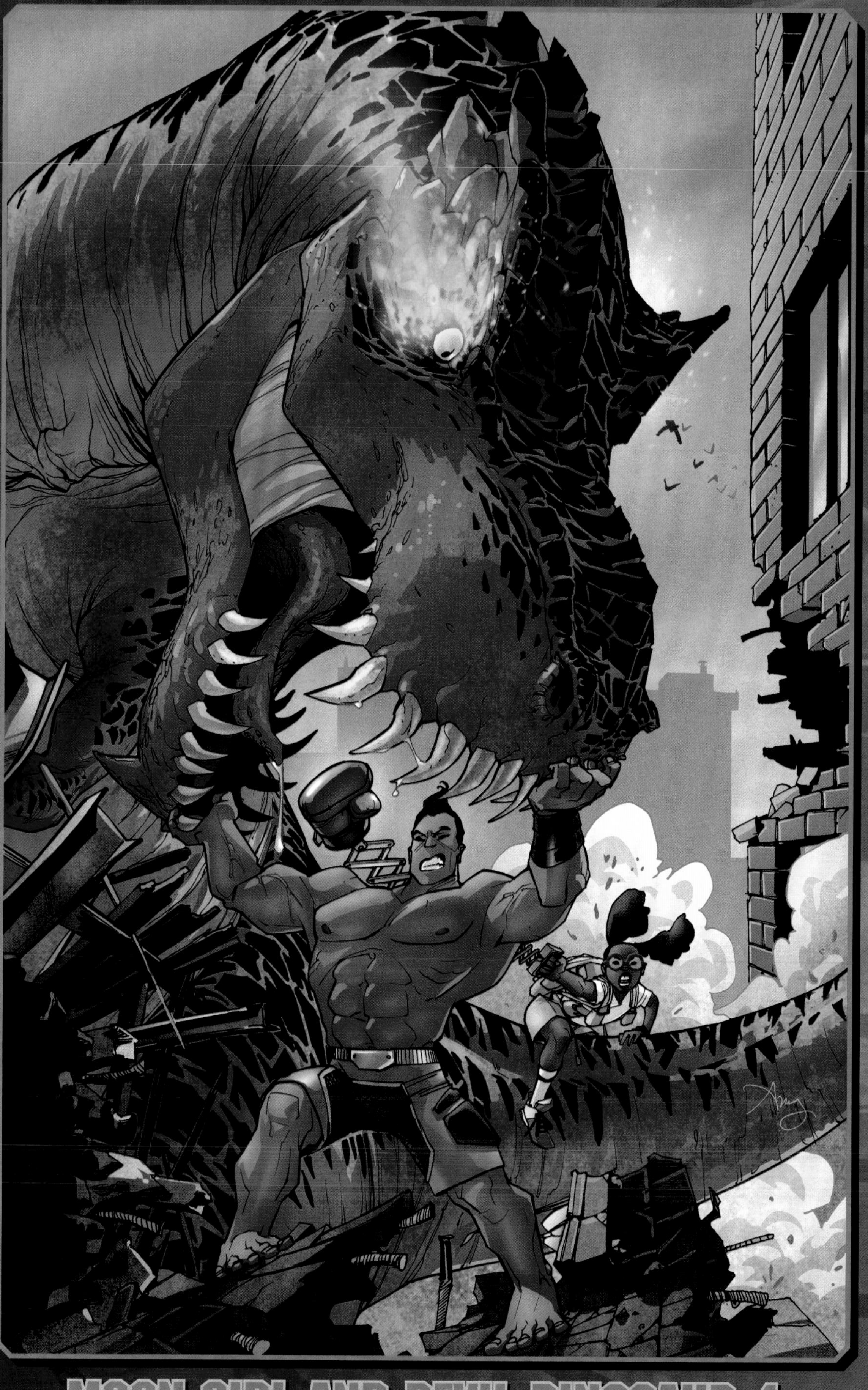

MOON GIRL AND DEVIL DINOSAUR 4

MOON GIRL AND DEVIL DINOSAUR

LUNELLA LAFAYETTE is teased by other kids, who call her MOON GIRL and laugh at her inventions. Who needs friends when you have gizmos and books? She's just biding her time until she can get into a REAL school for genius kids like her.

There's only one problem: Lunella has the INHUMAN gene, which means she could transform into a freak with powers at any moment! She found a device that could help stop it – the OMNI-WAVE PROJECTOR.

When activated, it created a TIME PORTAL that brought forth angry cavemen called KILLER FOLK and a BIG, RED DINOSAUR! The Killer Folk stole the projector and fled, leaving Lunella eager to retrieve it!

While hiding the dinosaur in her secret lab at school, a fire broke out. Devil Dinosaur and Lunella helped rescue everyone inside, but another hero has finally found them: THE HULK. Despite their heroism, he has demanded Devil Dinosaur leave with him...

DEVIL DINOSAUR
CREATED BY JACK KIRBY

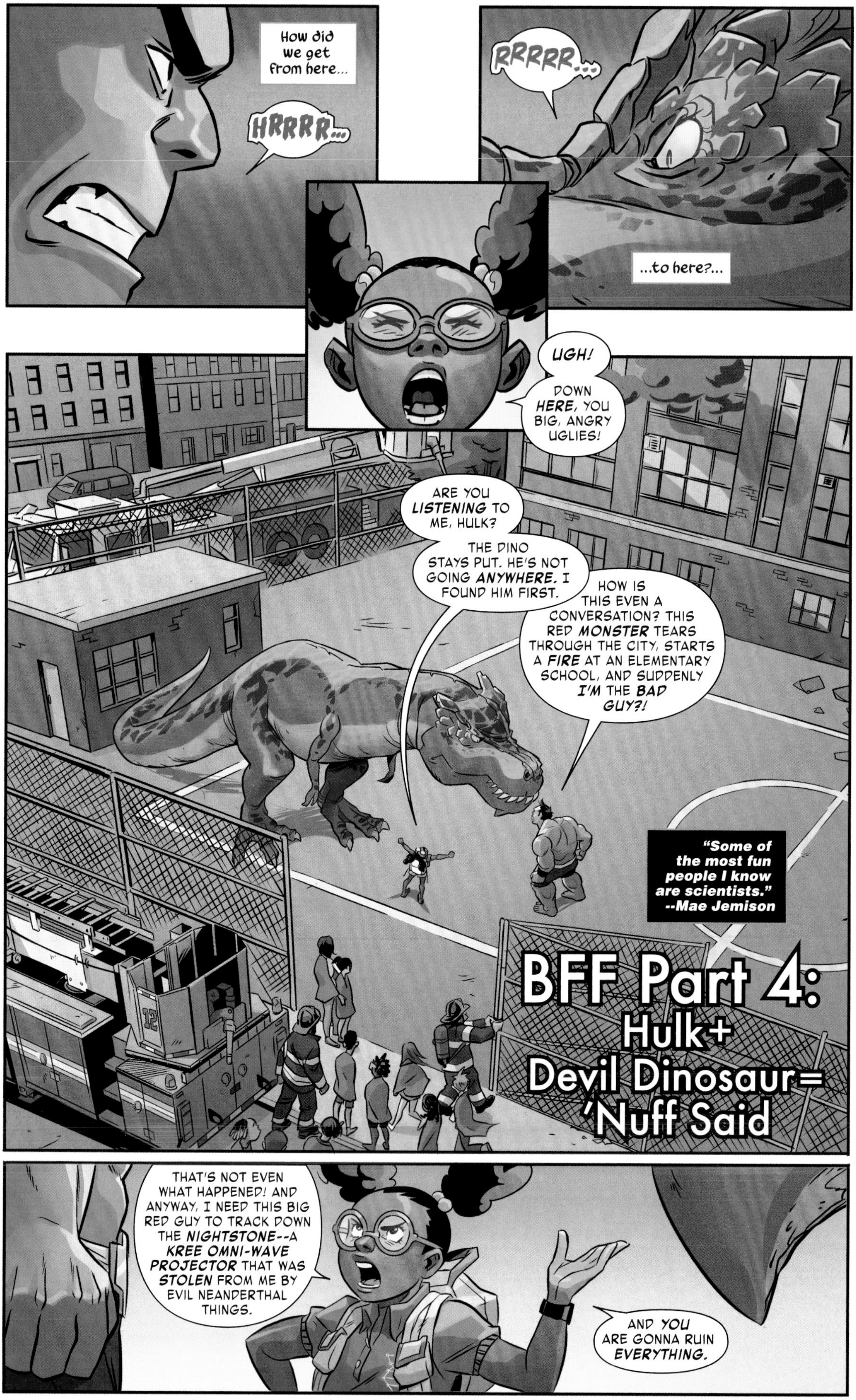
How did we get from here...
HRRRR...
RRRRR...
...to here?...
UGH!
DOWN HERE, YOU BIG, ANGRY UGLIES!
ARE YOU LISTENING TO ME, HULK?
THE DINO STAYS PUT. HE'S NOT GOING ANYWHERE. I FOUND HIM FIRST.
HOW IS THIS EVEN A CONVERSATION? THIS RED MONSTER TEARS THROUGH THE CITY, STARTS A FIRE AT AN ELEMENTARY SCHOOL, AND SUDDENLY I'M THE BAD GUY?!
"Some of the most fun people I know are scientists." --Mae Jemison
BFF Part 4:
Hulk+ Devil Dinosaur= 'Nuff Said
THAT'S NOT EVEN WHAT HAPPENED! AND ANYWAY, I NEED THIS BIG RED GUY TO TRACK DOWN THE NIGHTSTONE--A KREE OMNI-WAVE PROJECTOR THAT WAS STOLEN FROM ME BY EVIL NEANDERTHAL THINGS.
AND YOU ARE GONNA RUIN EVERYTHING.

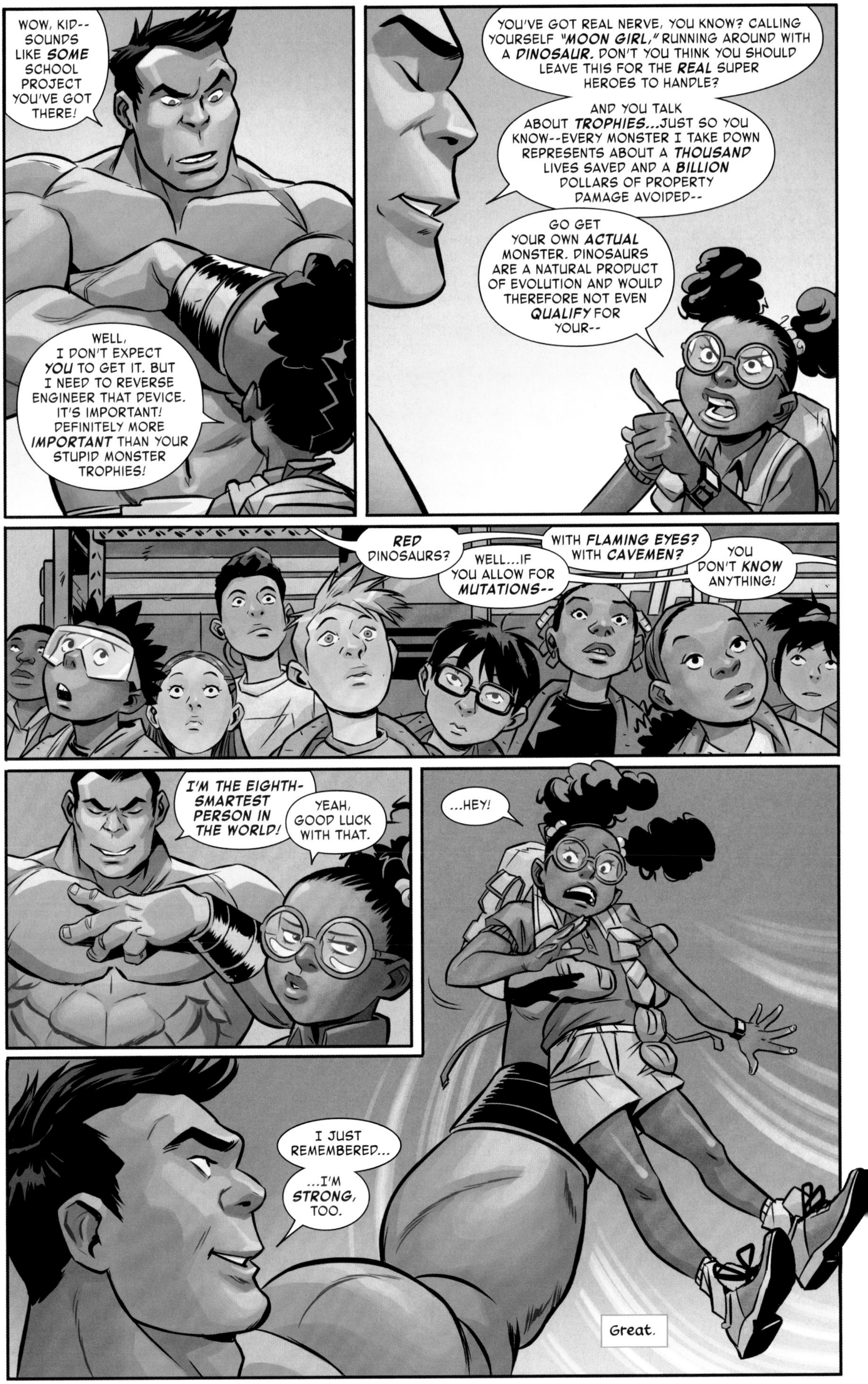

WOW, KID-- SOUNDS LIKE SOME SCHOOL PROJECT YOU'VE GOT THERE!
WELL, I DON'T EXPECT YOU TO GET IT. BUT I NEED TO REVERSE ENGINEER THAT DEVICE. IT'S IMPORTANT! DEFINITELY MORE IMPORTANT THAN YOUR STUPID MONSTER TROPHIES!
YOU'VE GOT REAL NERVE, YOU KNOW? CALLING YOURSELF "MOON GIRL," RUNNING AROUND WITH A DINOSAUR. DON'T YOU THINK YOU SHOULD LEAVE THIS FOR THE REAL SUPER HEROES TO HANDLE?
AND YOU TALK ABOUT TROPHIES...JUST SO YOU KNOW--EVERY MONSTER I TAKE DOWN REPRESENTS ABOUT A THOUSAND LIVES SAVED AND A BILLION DOLLARS OF PROPERTY DAMAGE AVOIDED--
GO GET YOUR OWN ACTUAL MONSTER. DINOSAURS ARE A NATURAL PRODUCT OF EVOLUTION AND WOULD THEREFORE NOT EVEN QUALIFY FOR YOUR--
RED DINOSAURS?
WELL...IF YOU ALLOW FOR MUTATIONS--
WITH FLAMING EYES? WITH CAVEMEN?
YOU DON'T KNOW ANYTHING!
I'M THE EIGHTH-SMARTEST PERSON IN THE WORLD!
YEAH, GOOD LUCK WITH THAT.
...HEY!
I JUST REMEMBERED...
...I'M STRONG, TOO.
Great.

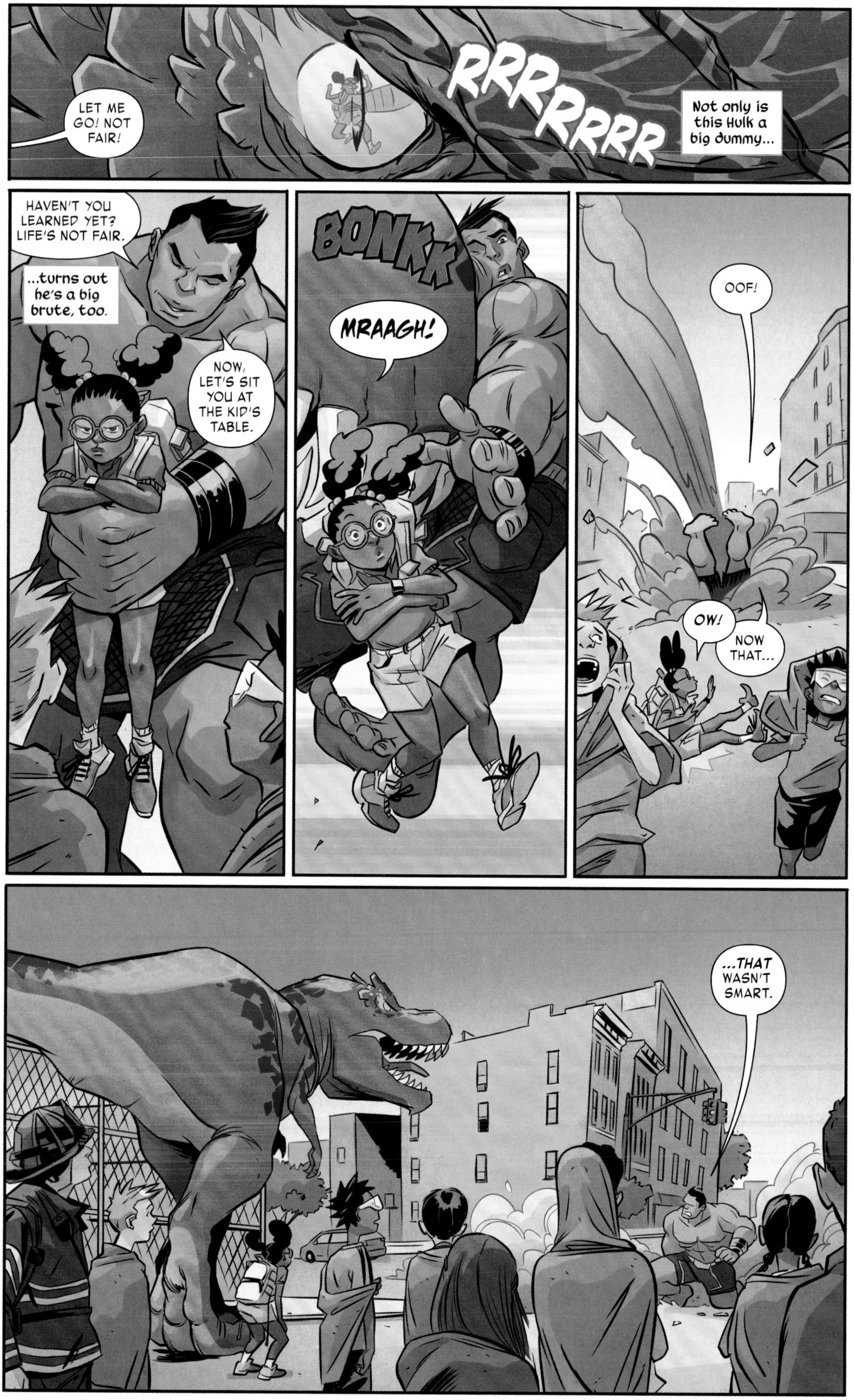
LET ME GO! NOT FAIR!
RRRRRRR
Not only is this Hulk a big dummy...
HAVEN'T YOU LEARNED YET? LIFE'S NOT FAIR.
...turns out he's a big brute, too.
NOW, LET'S SIT YOU AT THE KID'S TABLE.
BONKK
MRAAGH!
OOF!
OW!
NOW THAT...
...THAT WASN'T SMART.

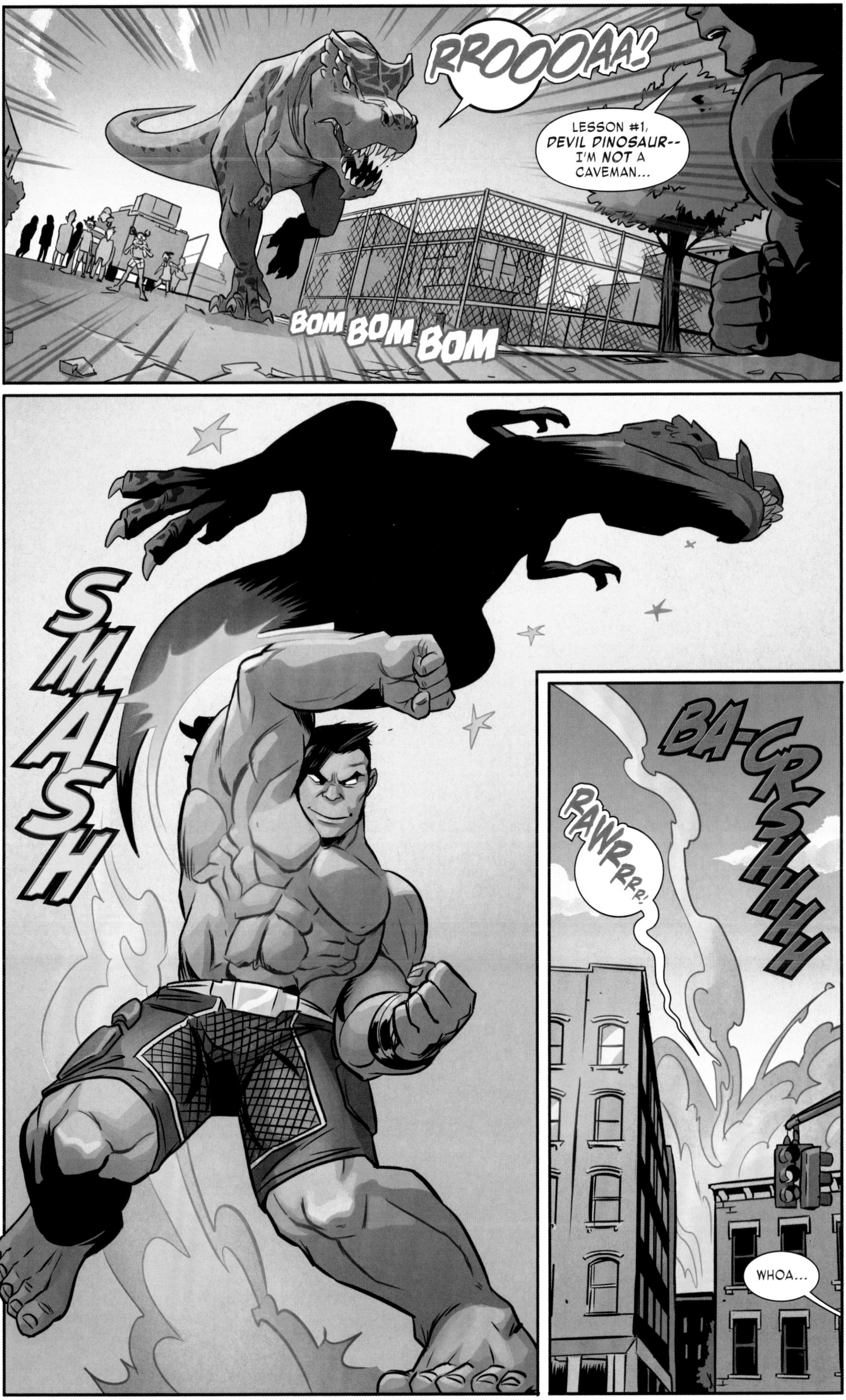
RROOOAA!
LESSON #1, DEVIL DINOSAUR-- I'M NOT A CAVEMAN...
BOM BOM BOM
SMASH
BA-CRSHHHH
RAWRRRR!
WHOA...

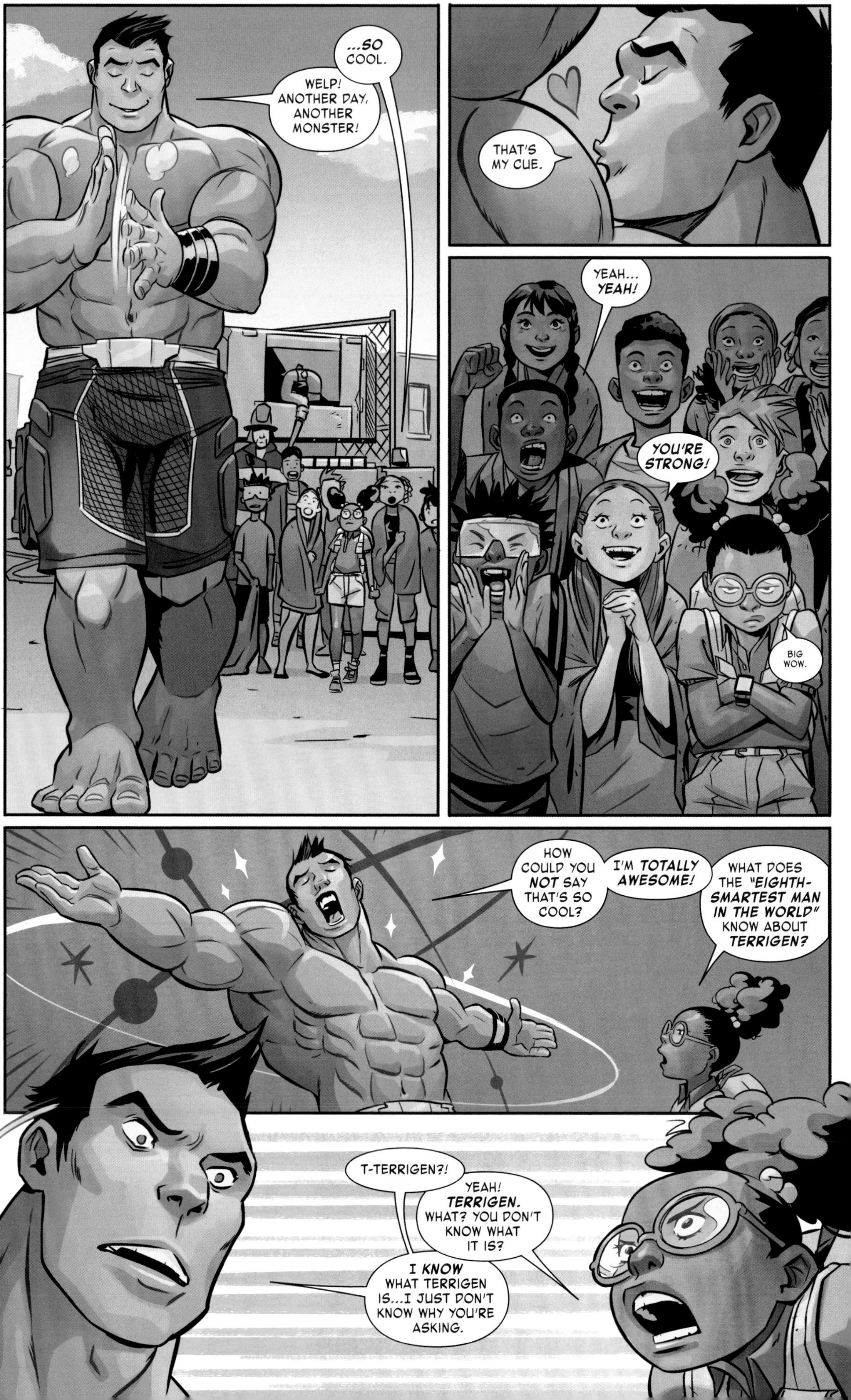

WELP! ANOTHER DAY, ANOTHER MONSTER!
...SO COOL.
THAT'S MY CUE.
YEAH... YEAH!
YOU'RE STRONG!
BIG WOW.
HOW COULD YOU NOT SAY THAT'S SO COOL?
I'M TOTALLY AWESOME!
WHAT DOES THE "EIGHTH-SMARTEST MAN IN THE WORLD" KNOW ABOUT TERRIGEN?
T-TERRIGEN?!
YEAH! TERRIGEN. WHAT? YOU DON'T KNOW WHAT IT IS?
I KNOW WHAT TERRIGEN IS...I JUST DON'T KNOW WHY YOU'RE ASKING.

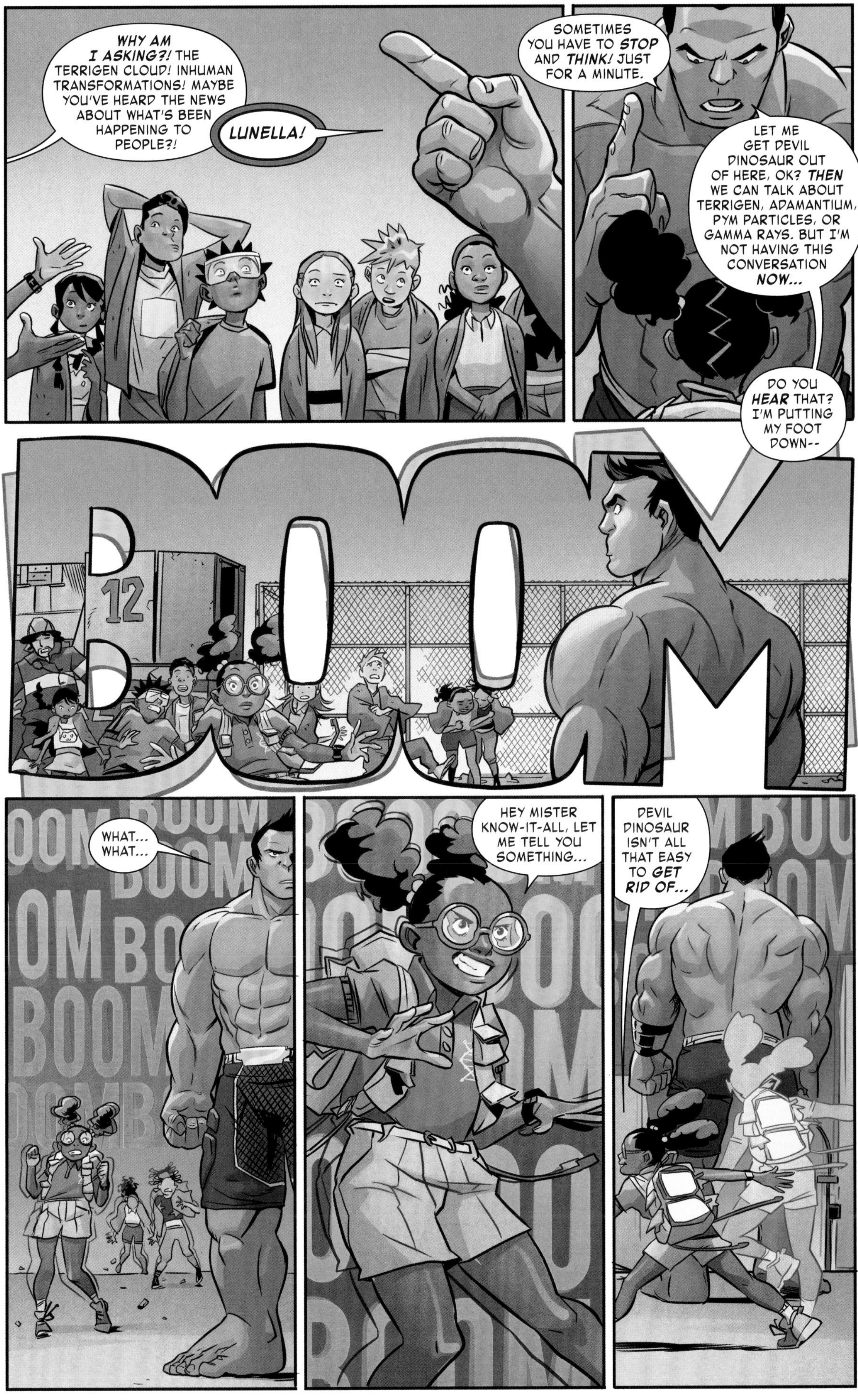
WHY AM I ASKING?! THE TERRIGEN CLOUD! INHUMAN TRANSFORMATIONS! MAYBE YOU'VE HEARD THE NEWS ABOUT WHAT'S BEEN HAPPENING TO PEOPLE?!
LUNELLA!
SOMETIMES YOU HAVE TO STOP AND THINK! JUST FOR A MINUTE.
LET ME GET DEVIL DINOSAUR OUT OF HERE, OK? THEN WE CAN TALK ABOUT TERRIGEN, ADAMANTIUM, PYM PARTICLES, OR GAMMA RAYS. BUT I'M NOT HAVING THIS CONVERSATION NOW...
DO YOU HEAR THAT? I'M PUTTING MY FOOT DOWN--
BOOM
12
WHAT... WHAT...
HEY MISTER KNOW-IT-ALL, LET ME TELL YOU SOMETHING...
DEVIL DINOSAUR ISN'T ALL THAT EASY TO GET RID OF...

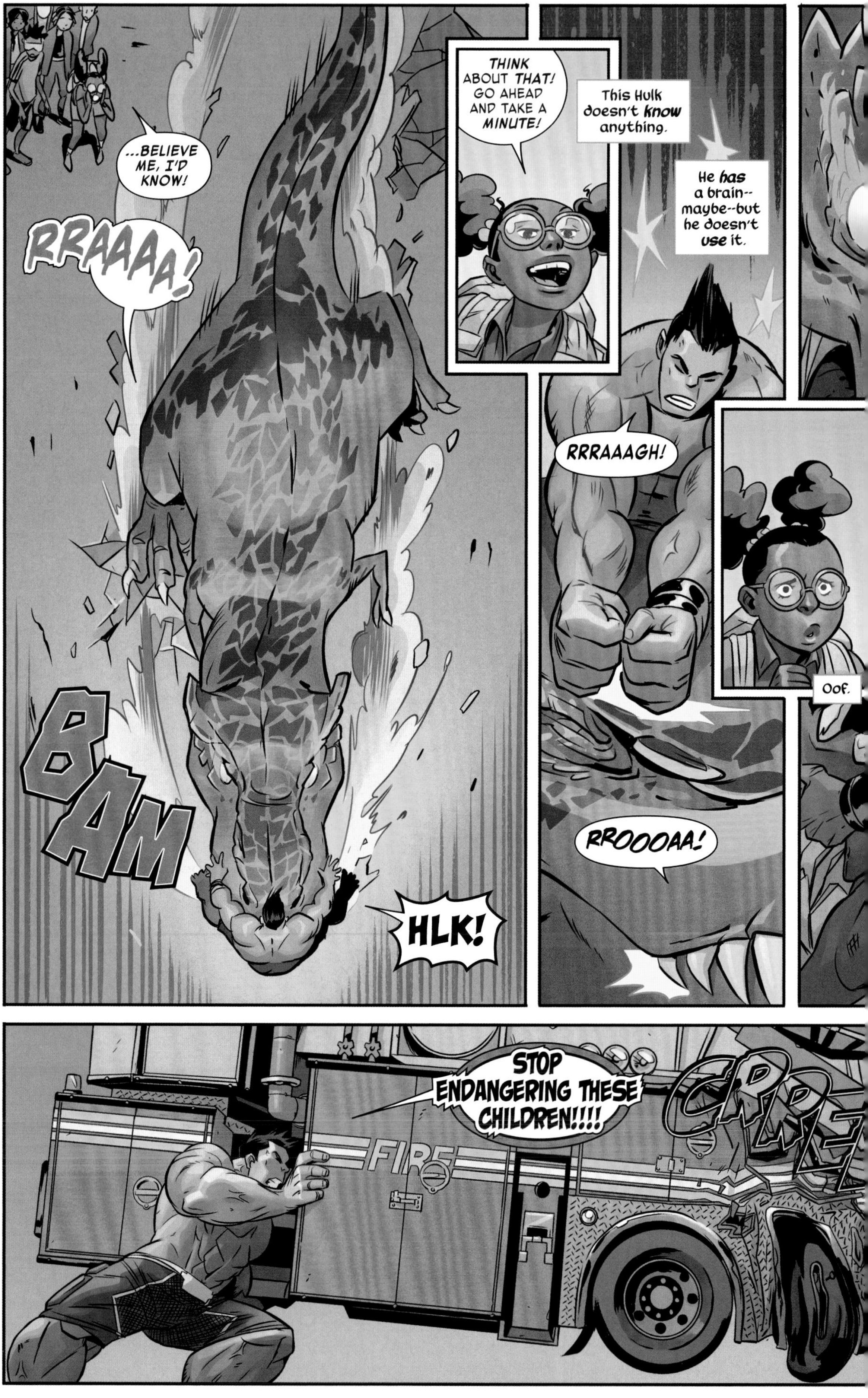
...BELIEVE ME, I'D KNOW!
RRAAAAA!
BAM
HLK!
THINK ABOUT THAT! GO AHEAD AND TAKE A MINUTE!
This Hulk doesn't know anything.
He has a brain--maybe--but he doesn't use it.
RRRAAAGH!
RROOOAA!
Oof.
STOP ENDANGERING THESE CHILDREN!!!!
FIRE

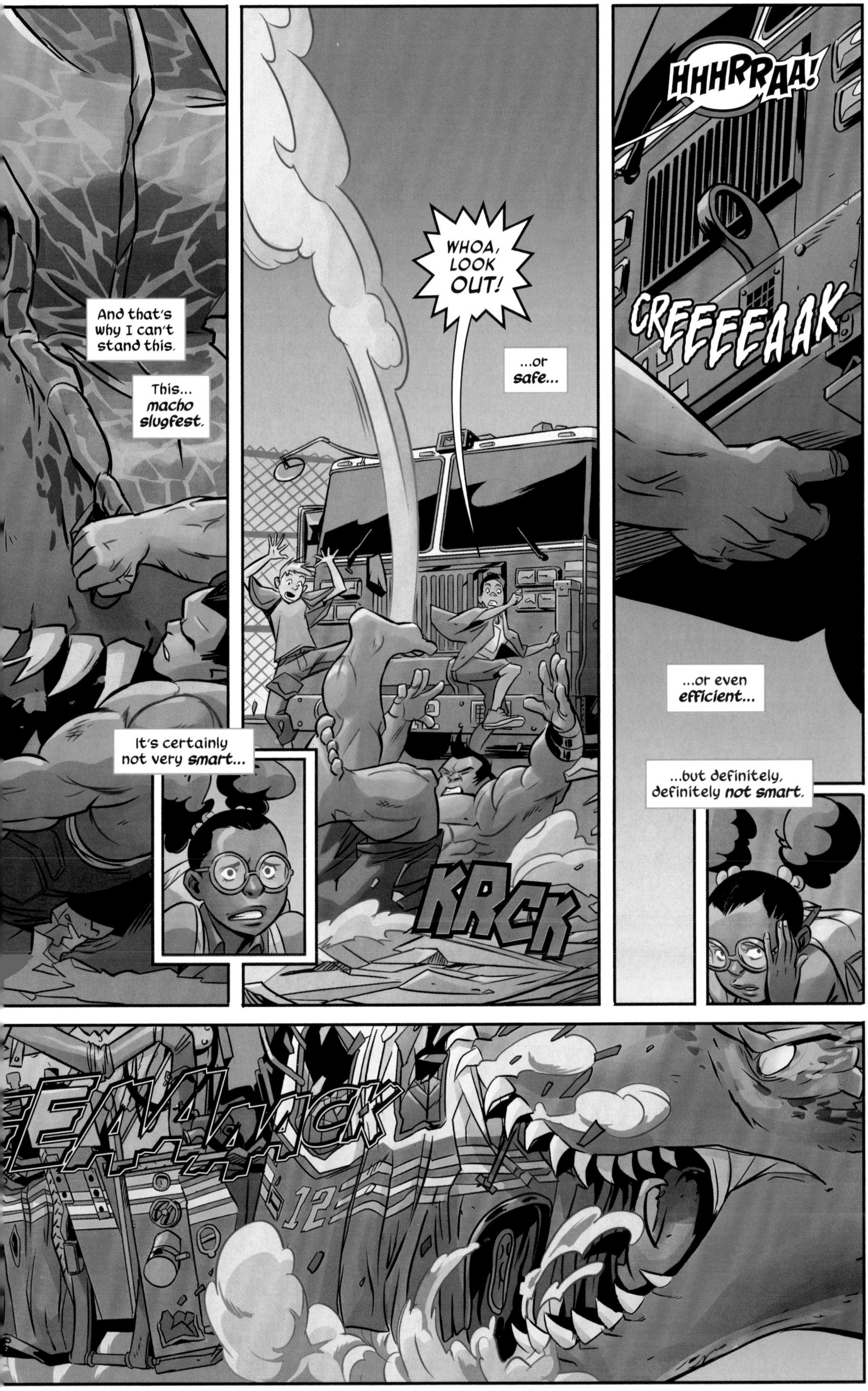
And that's why I can't stand this.
This... macho slugfest.
It's certainly not very smart...
WHOA, LOOK OUT!
...or safe...
KRCK
HHHRRAA!
CREEEEAAK
...or even efficient...
...but definitely, definitely not smart.
KRAAAACK
12

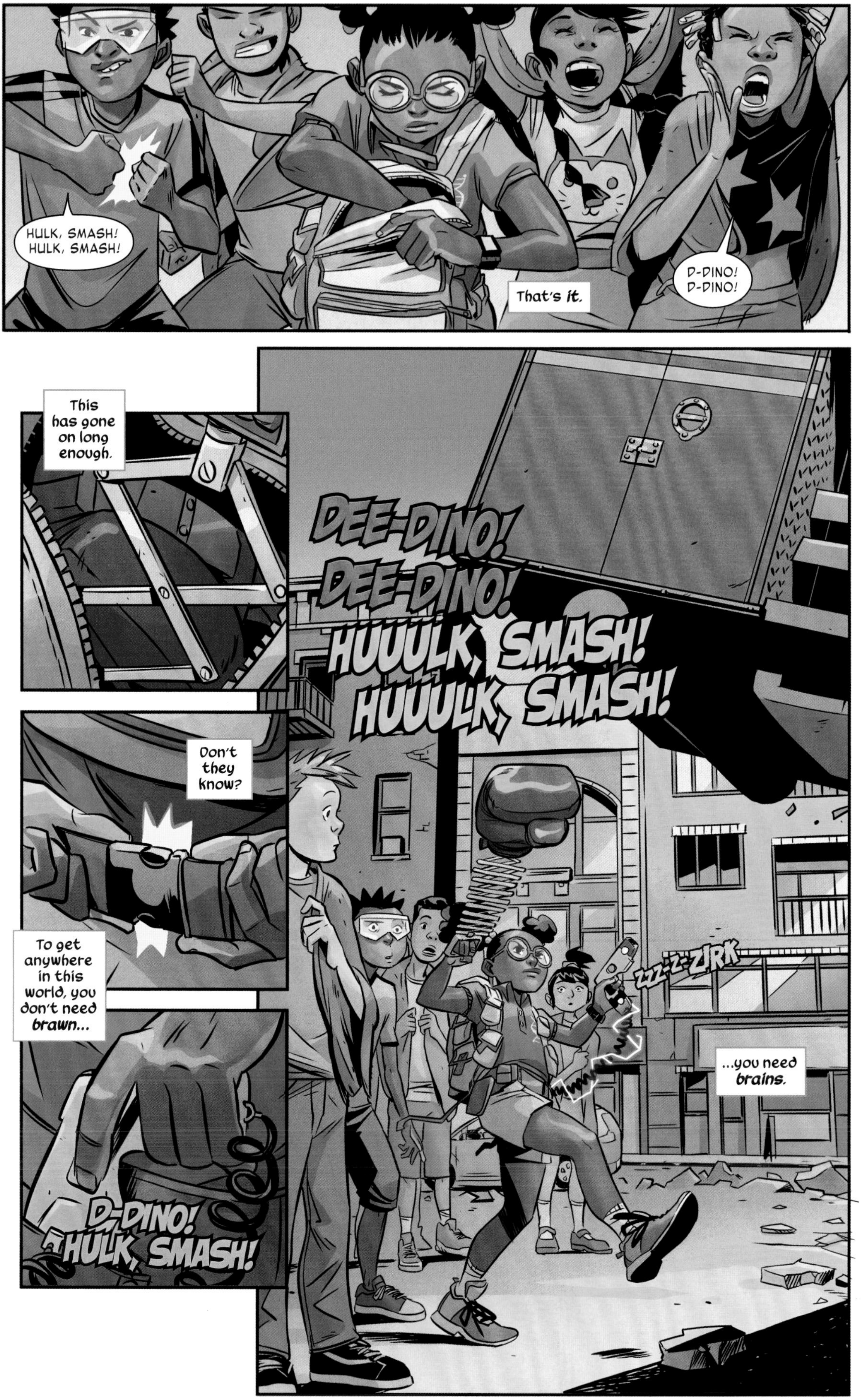
HULK, SMASH!
HULK, SMASH!
That's it.
D-DINO!
D-DINO!
This has gone on long enough.
DEE-DINO!
DEE-DINO!
HUUULK, SMASH!
HUUULK, SMASH!
Don't they know?
To get anywhere in this world, you don't need brawn...
D-DINO!
HULK, SMASH!
ZZZ-Z-ZIRK
...you need brains.

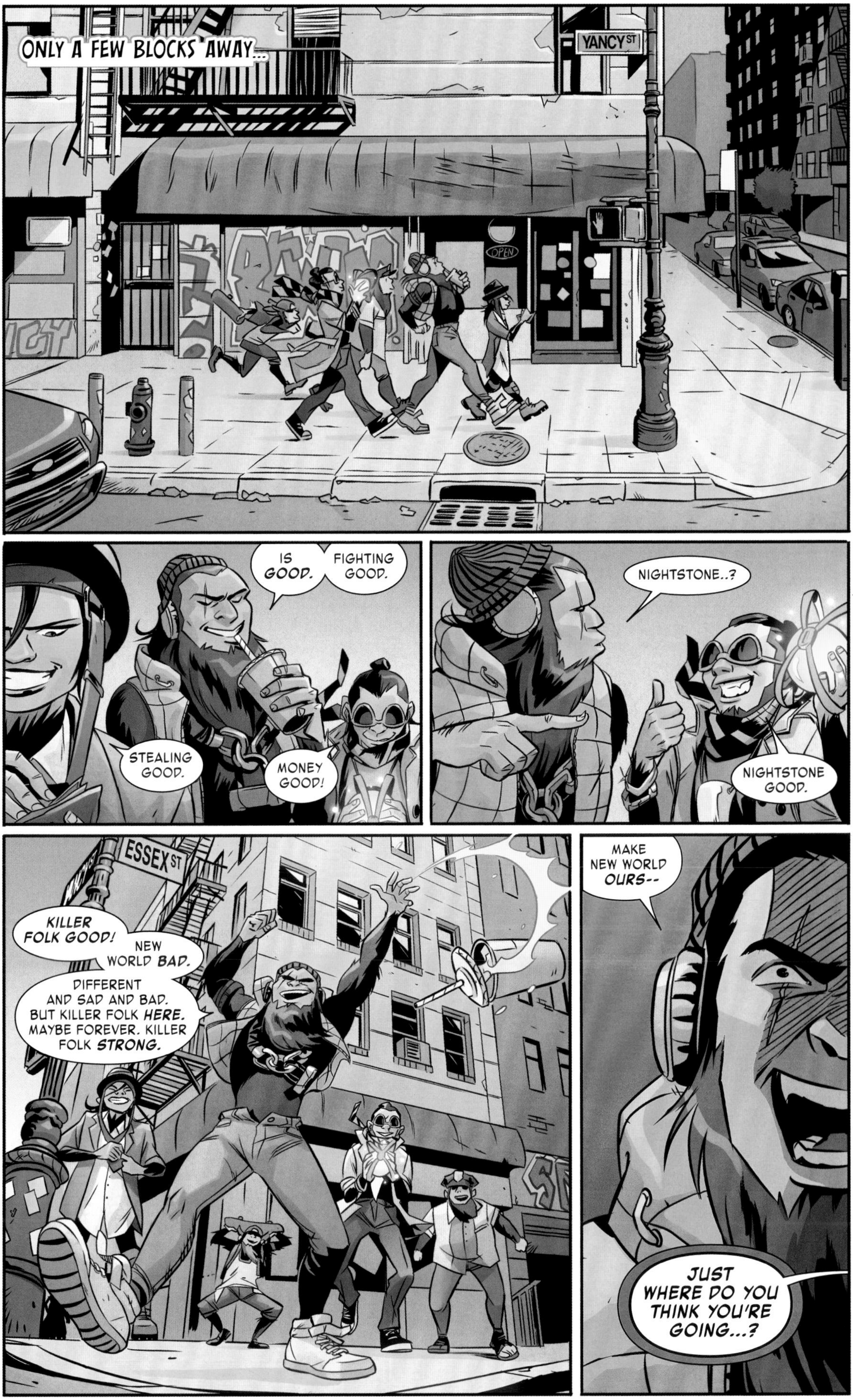
ONLY A FEW BLOCKS AWAY...
YANCY ST
OPEN
IS GOOD.
FIGHTING GOOD.
STEALING GOOD.
MONEY GOOD!
NIGHTSTONE..?
NIGHTSTONE GOOD.
ESSEX ST
KILLER FOLK GOOD!
NEW WORLD BAD.
DIFFERENT AND SAD AND BAD. BUT KILLER FOLK HERE. MAYBE FOREVER. KILLER FOLK STRONG.
MAKE NEW WORLD OURS--
JUST WHERE DO YOU THINK YOU'RE GOING...?

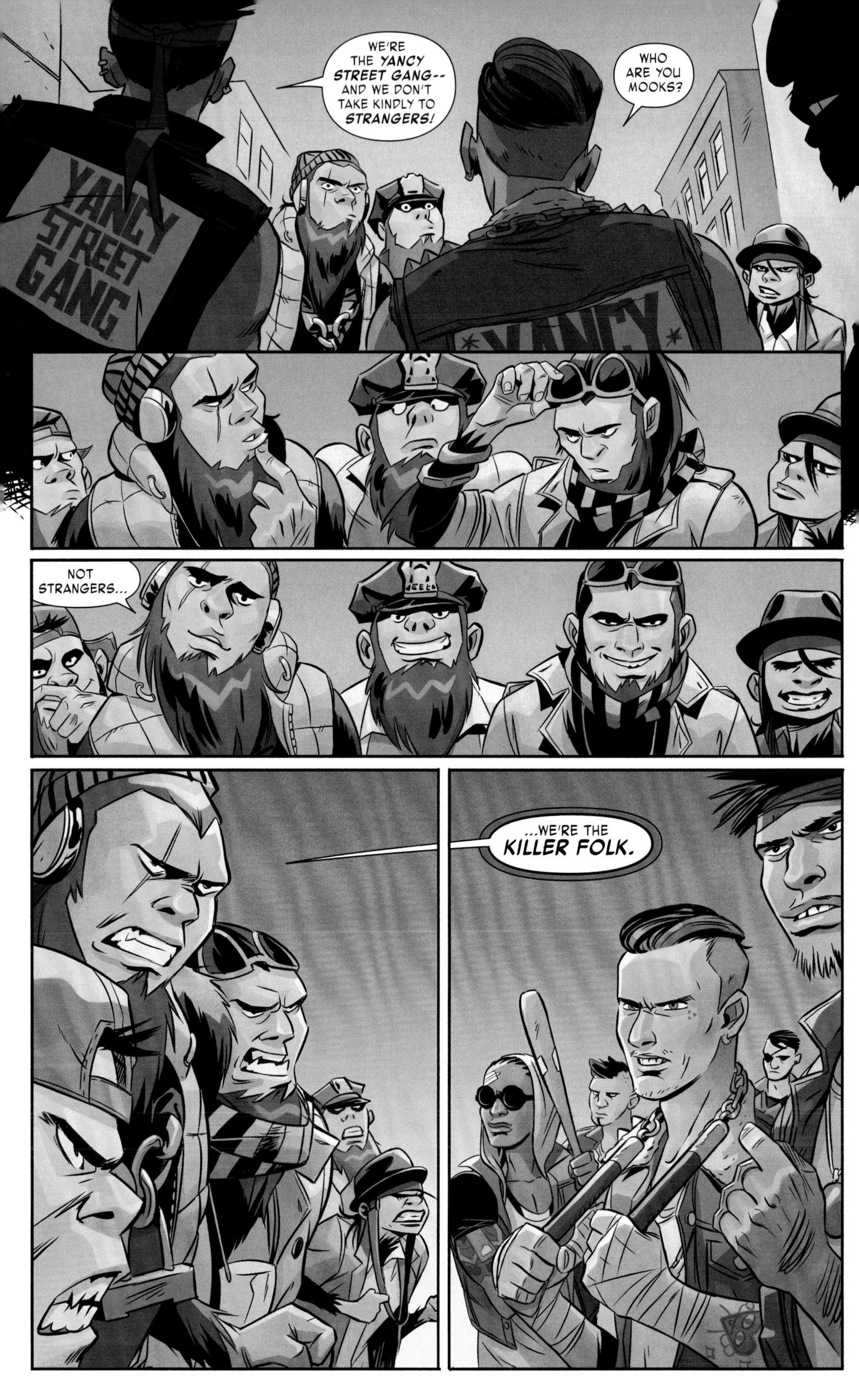
YANCY STREET GANG
WE'RE THE YANCY STREET GANG-- AND WE DON'T TAKE KINDLY TO STRANGERS!
WHO ARE YOU MOOKS?
NOT STRANGERS...
...WE'RE THE KILLER FOLK.

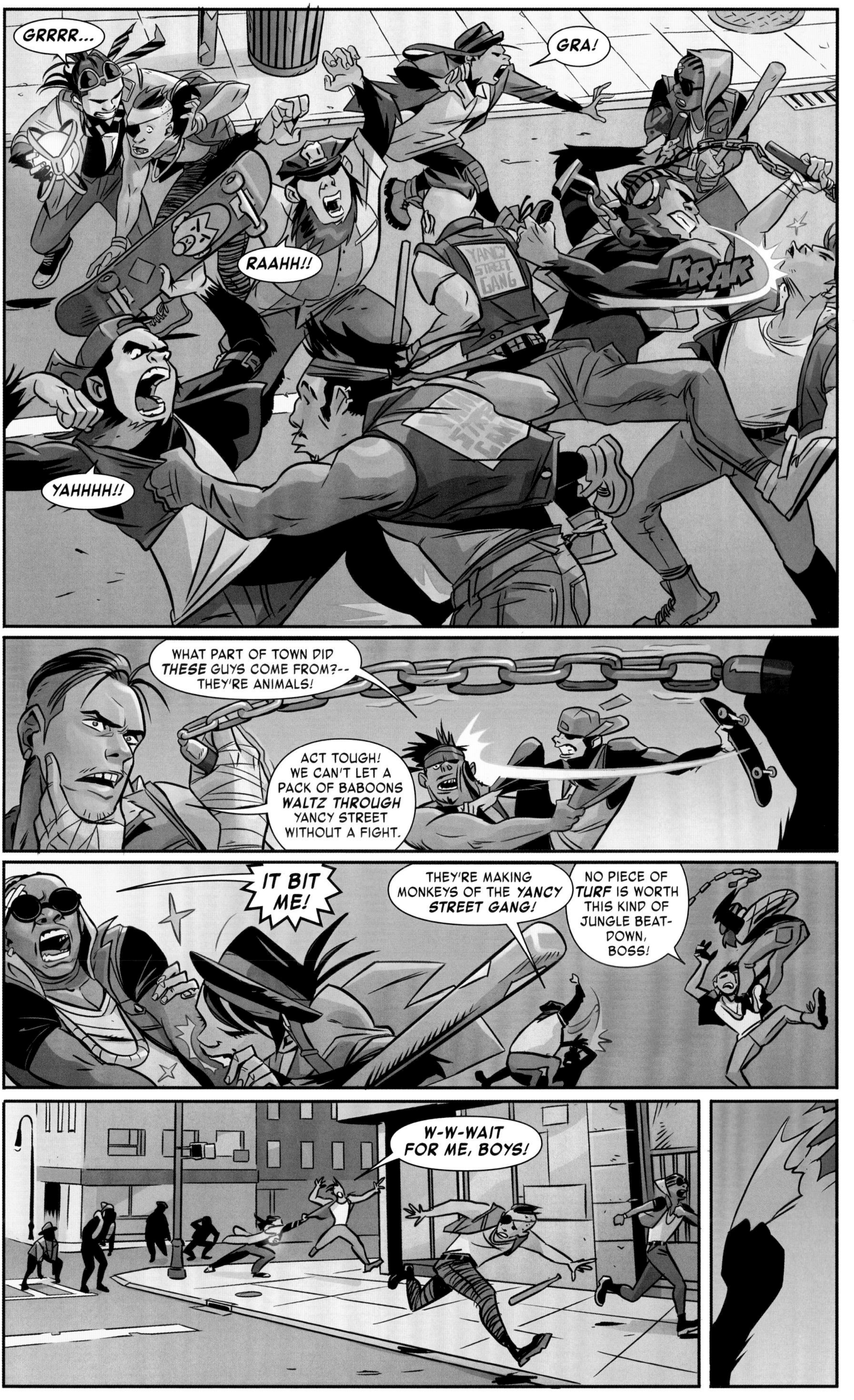
GRRRR...
GRA!
RAAHH!!
KRAK
YAHHHH!!
WHAT PART OF TOWN DID THESE GUYS COME FROM?-- THEY'RE ANIMALS!
ACT TOUGH! WE CAN'T LET A PACK OF BABOONS WALTZ THROUGH YANCY STREET WITHOUT A FIGHT.
IT BIT ME!
THEY'RE MAKING MONKEYS OF THE YANCY STREET GANG!
NO PIECE OF TURF IS WORTH THIS KIND OF JUNGLE BEAT-DOWN, BOSS!
W-W-WAIT FOR ME, BOYS!

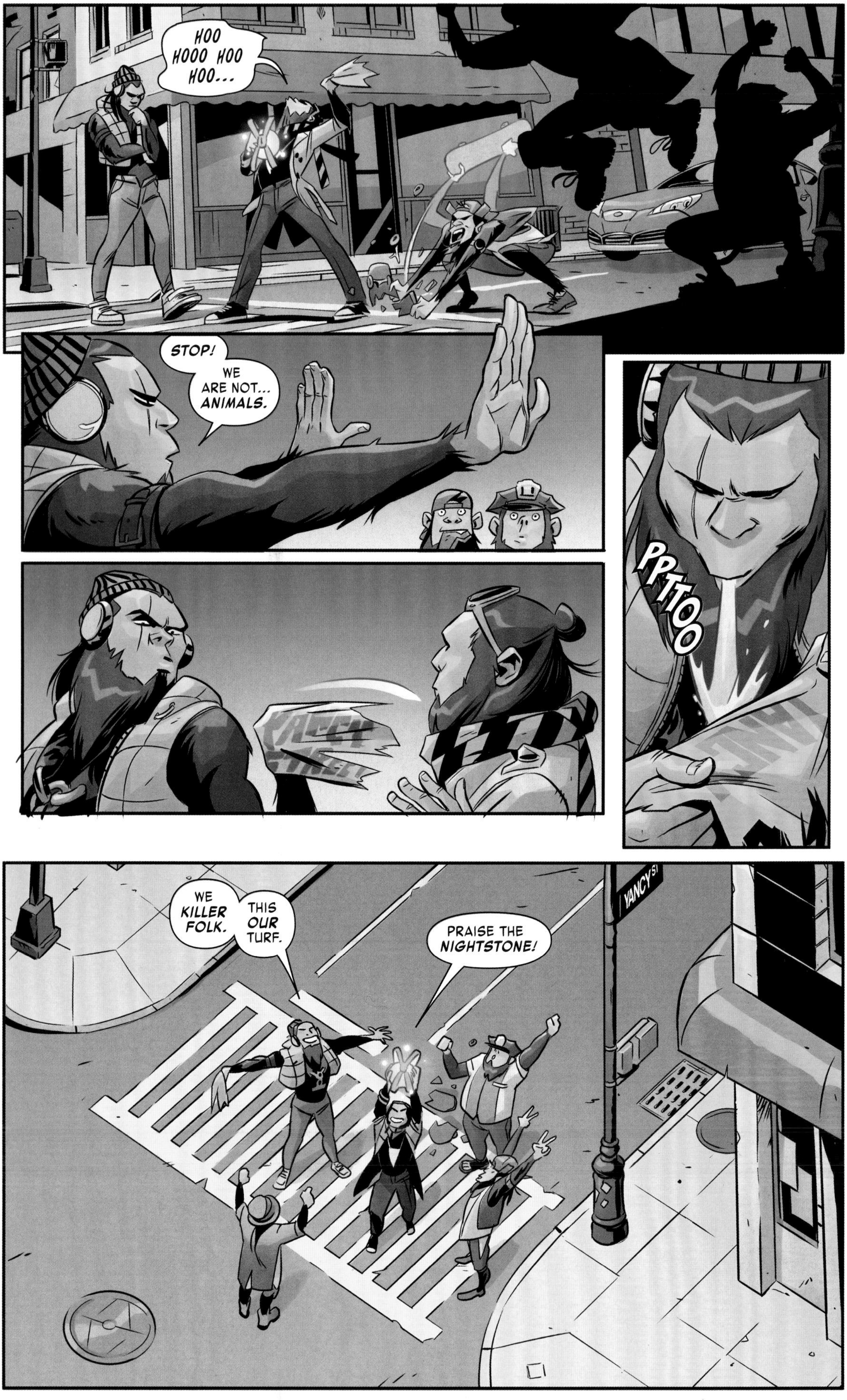
HOO HOOO HOO HOO...
STOP!
WE ARE NOT... ANIMALS.
PPTTOO
WE KILLER FOLK.
THIS OUR TURF.
PRAISE THE NIGHTSTONE!
YANCY ST

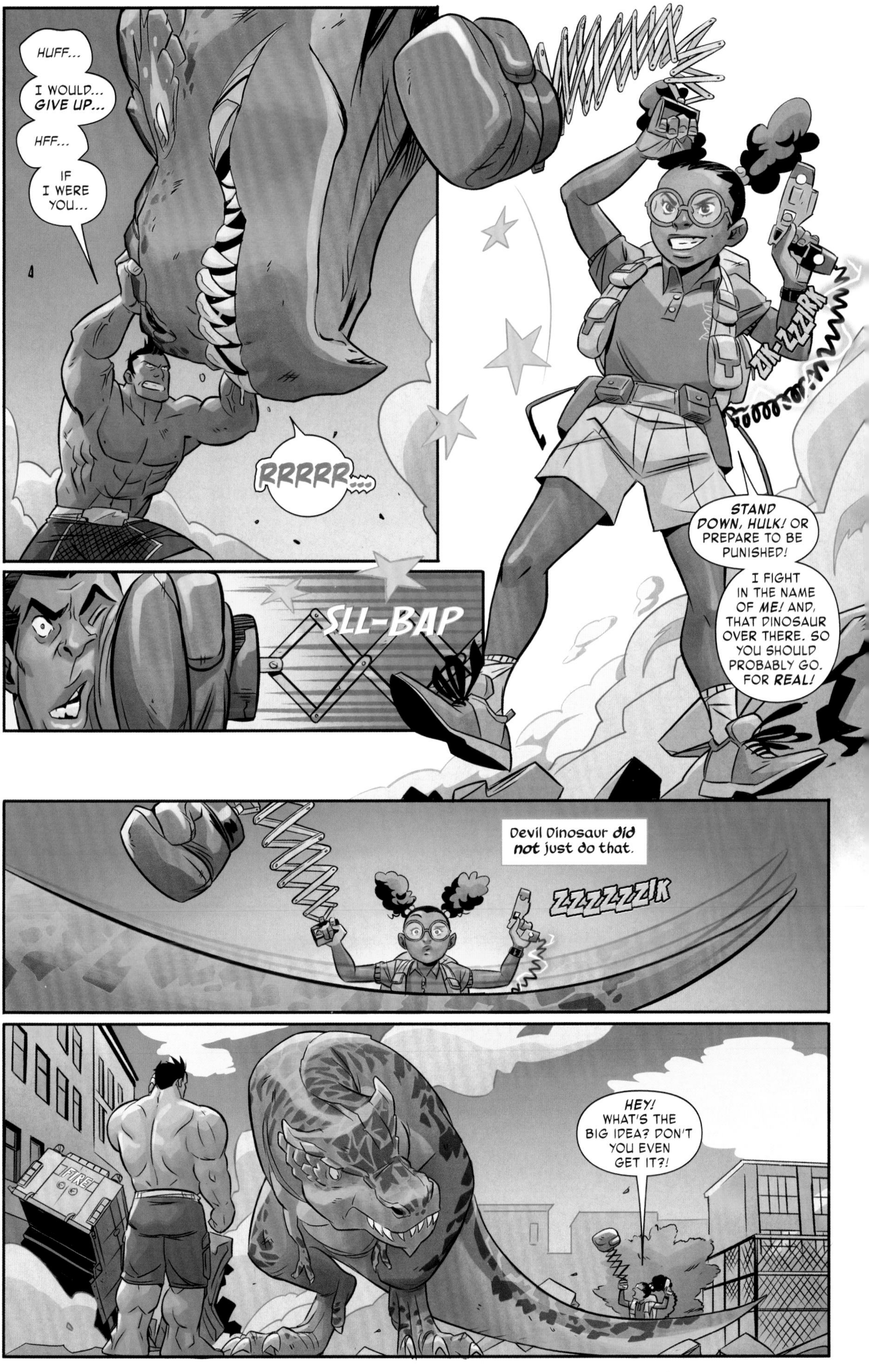

HUFF...
I WOULD... GIVE UP...
HFF...
IF I WERE YOU...
RRRRR...
SLL-BAP
ZIK-ZZZIRK
STAND DOWN, HULK! OR PREPARE TO BE PUNISHED!
I FIGHT IN THE NAME OF ME! AND, THAT DINOSAUR OVER THERE. SO YOU SHOULD PROBABLY GO. FOR REAL!
Devil Dinosaur did not just do that.
ZZZZZZIK
HEY! WHAT'S THE BIG IDEA? DON'T YOU EVEN GET IT?!
FIRE

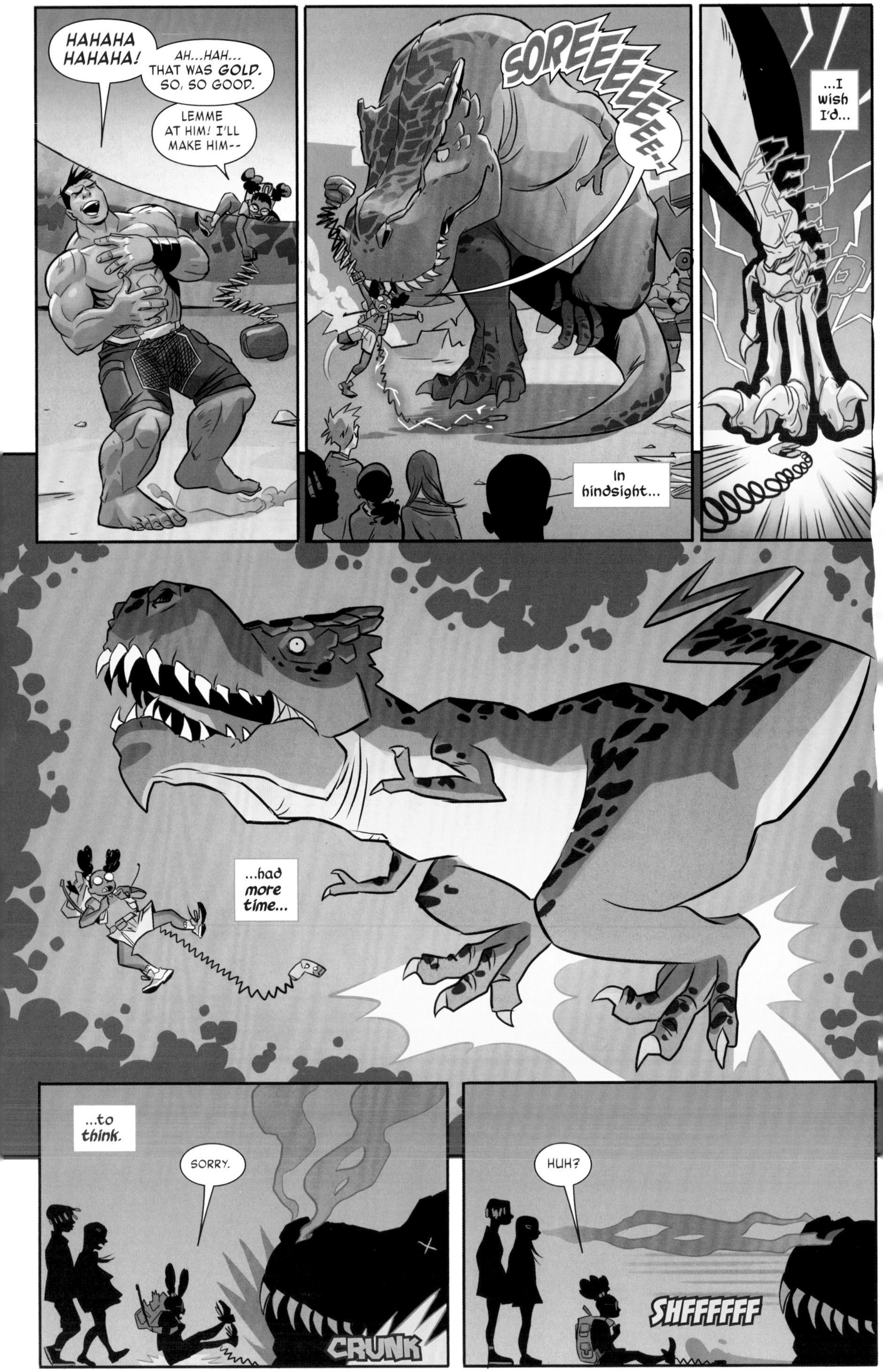
HAHAHA HAHAHA!
AH...HAH... THAT WAS GOLD. SO, SO GOOD.
LEMME AT HIM! I'LL MAKE HIM--
SOREEEEEEEE--
In hindsight...
...I wish I'd...
...had more time...
...to think.
SORRY.
CRUNK
HUH?
SHFFFFFF

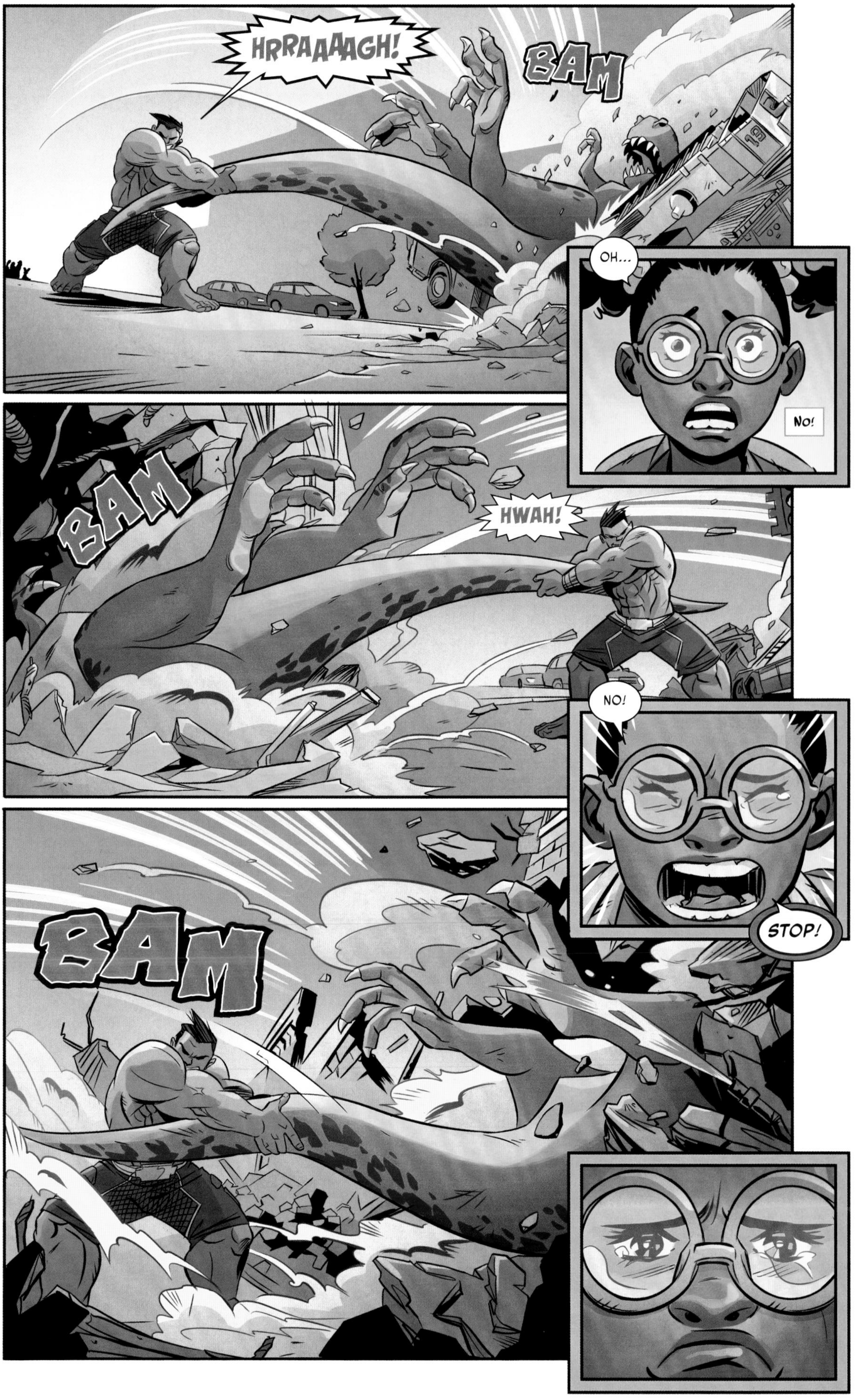
HRRAAAAGH!
BAM
OH...
NO!
BAM
HWAH!
NO!
STOP!
BAM

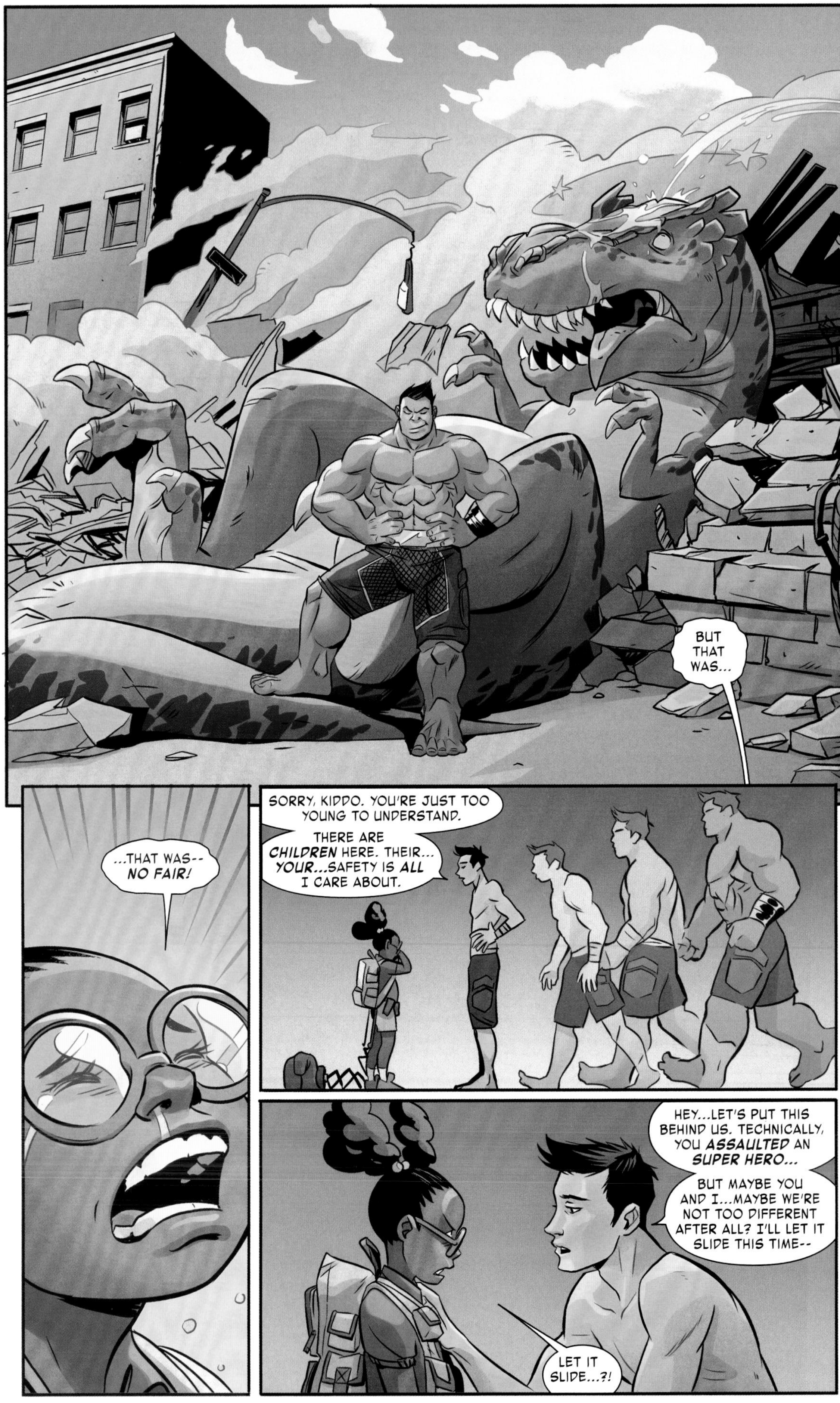
BUT THAT WAS...
...THAT WAS-- NO FAIR!
SORRY, KIDDO. YOU'RE JUST TOO YOUNG TO UNDERSTAND.
THERE ARE CHILDREN HERE. THEIR... YOUR...SAFETY IS ALL I CARE ABOUT.
HEY...LET'S PUT THIS BEHIND US. TECHNICALLY, YOU ASSAULTED AN SUPER HERO...
BUT MAYBE YOU AND I...MAYBE WE'RE NOT TOO DIFFERENT AFTER ALL? I'LL LET IT SLIDE THIS TIME--
LET IT SLIDE...?!

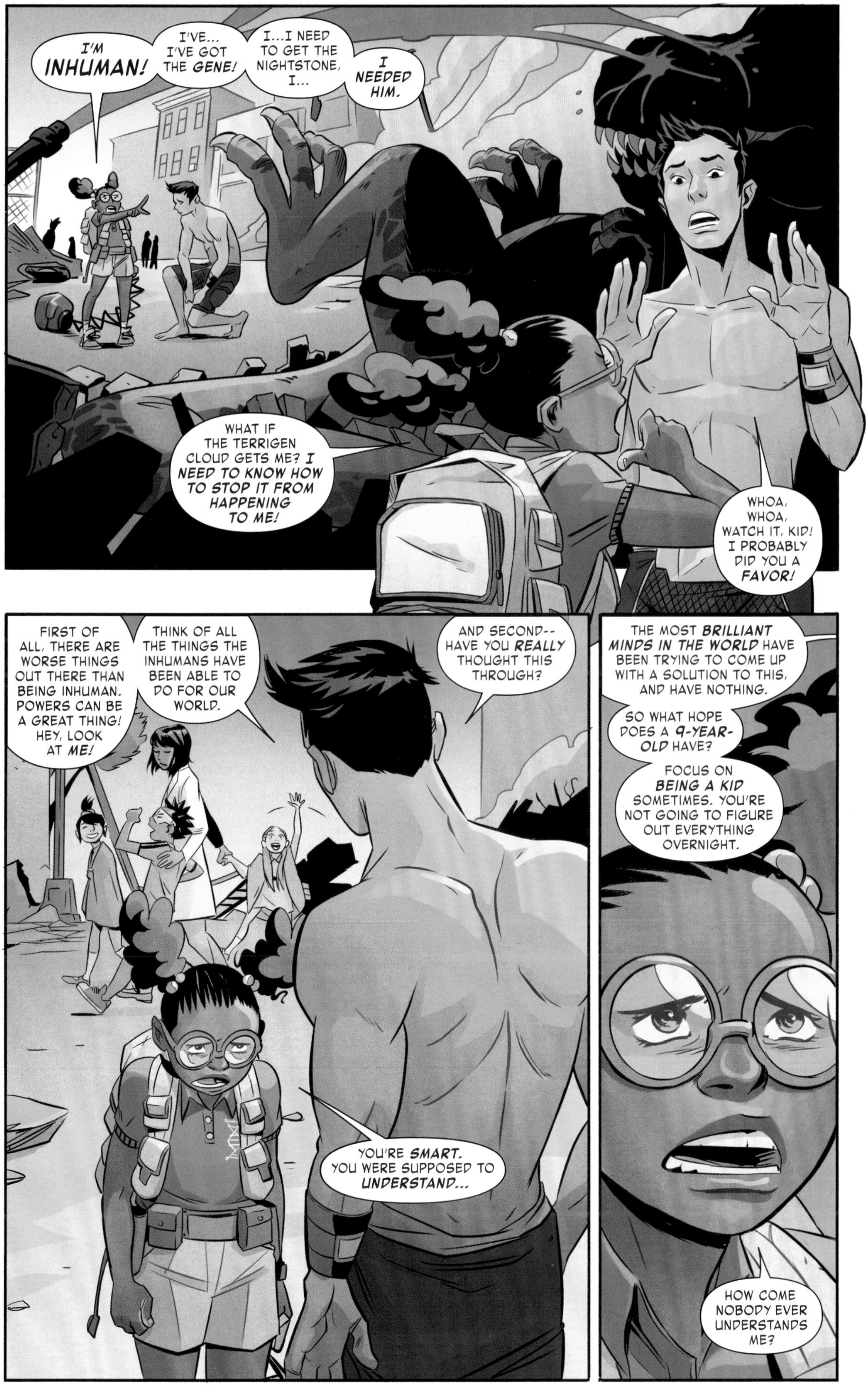
I'M INHUMAN!
I'VE... I'VE GOT THE GENE!
I...I NEED TO GET THE NIGHTSTONE, I...
I NEEDED HIM.
WHAT IF THE TERRIGEN CLOUD GETS ME? I NEED TO KNOW HOW TO STOP IT FROM HAPPENING TO ME!
WHOA, WHOA, WATCH IT, KID! I PROBABLY DID YOU A FAVOR!
FIRST OF ALL, THERE ARE WORSE THINGS OUT THERE THAN BEING INHUMAN. POWERS CAN BE A GREAT THING! HEY, LOOK AT ME!
THINK OF ALL THE THINGS THE INHUMANS HAVE BEEN ABLE TO DO FOR OUR WORLD.
AND SECOND-- HAVE YOU REALLY THOUGHT THIS THROUGH?
YOU'RE SMART. YOU WERE SUPPOSED TO UNDERSTAND...
THE MOST BRILLIANT MINDS IN THE WORLD HAVE BEEN TRYING TO COME UP WITH A SOLUTION TO THIS, AND HAVE NOTHING.
SO WHAT HOPE DOES A 9-YEAR-OLD HAVE?
FOCUS ON BEING A KID SOMETIMES. YOU'RE NOT GOING TO FIGURE OUT EVERYTHING OVERNIGHT.
HOW COME NOBODY EVER UNDERSTANDS ME?

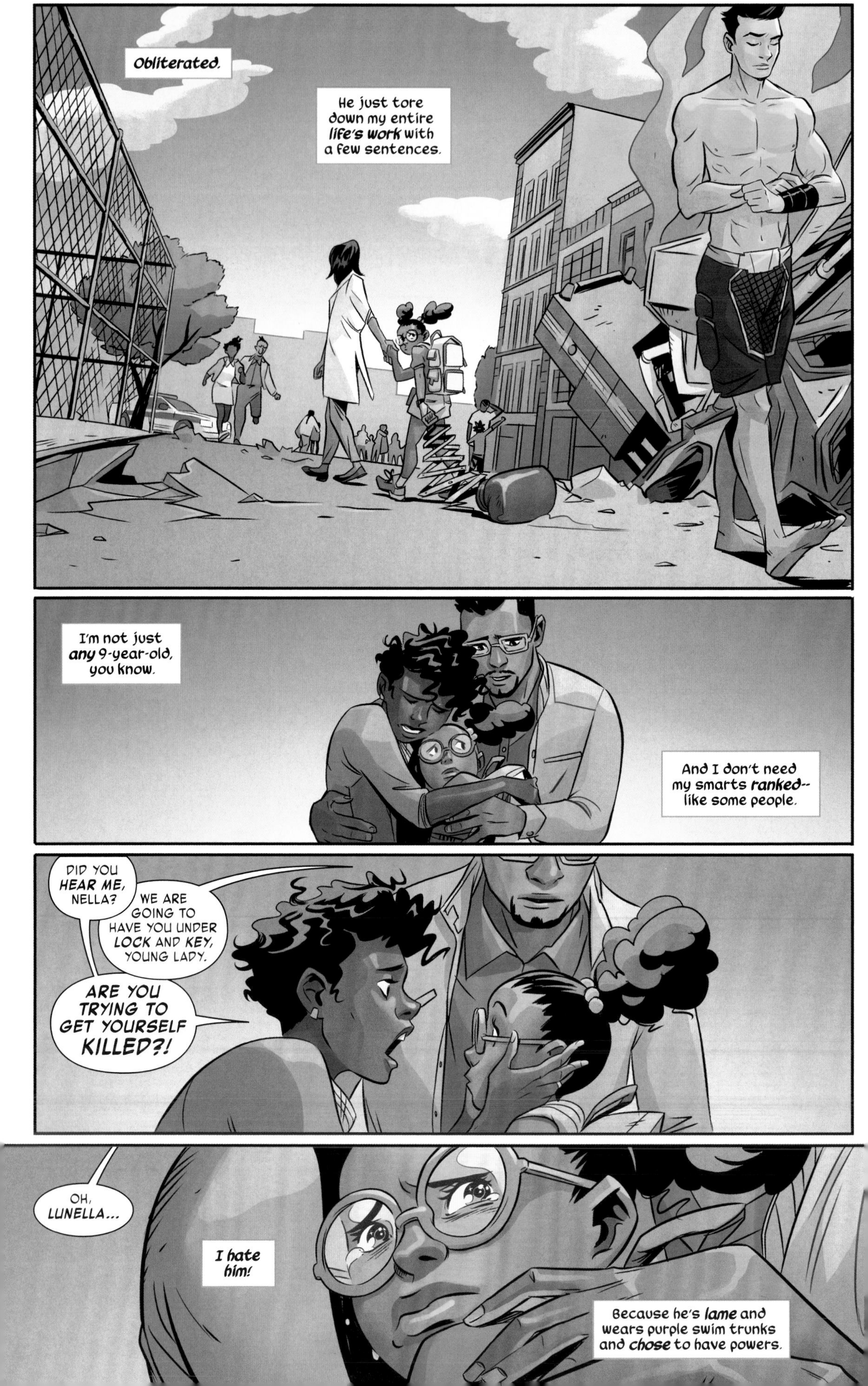
Obliterated.
He just tore down my entire life's work with a few sentences.
I'm not just any 9-year-old, you know.
And I don't need my smarts ranked-- like some people.
DID YOU HEAR ME, NELLA?
WE ARE GOING TO HAVE YOU UNDER LOCK AND KEY, YOUNG LADY.
ARE YOU TRYING TO GET YOURSELF KILLED?!
OH, LUNELLA...
I hate him!
Because he's lame and wears purple swim trunks and chose to have powers.

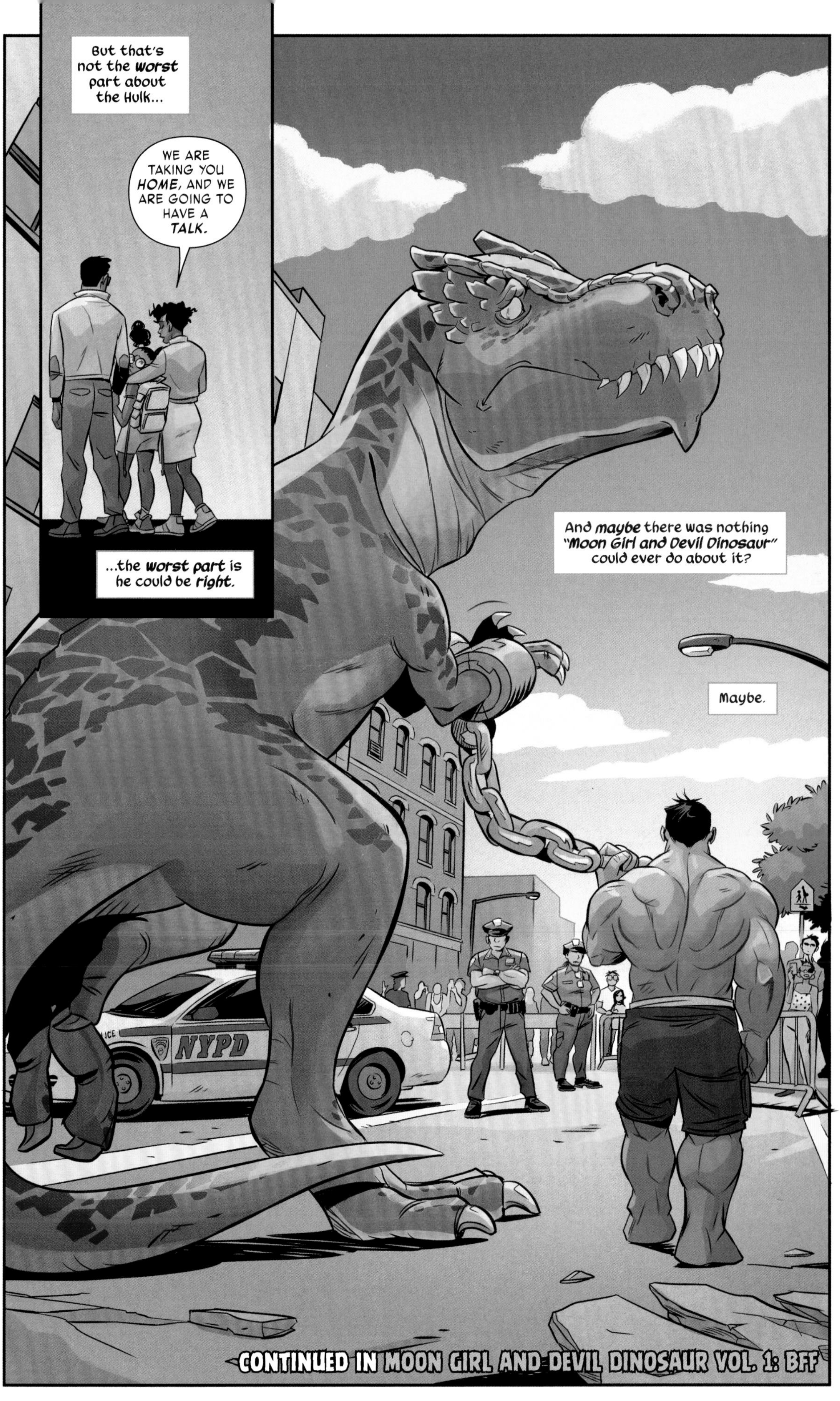
But that's not the worst part about the Hulk...
WE ARE TAKING YOU HOME, AND WE ARE GOING TO HAVE A TALK.
...the worst part is he could be right.
And maybe there was nothing "Moon Girl and Devil Dinosaur" could ever do about it?
Maybe.
NYPD
CONTINUED IN MOON GIRL AND DEVIL DINOSAUR VOL. 1: BFF

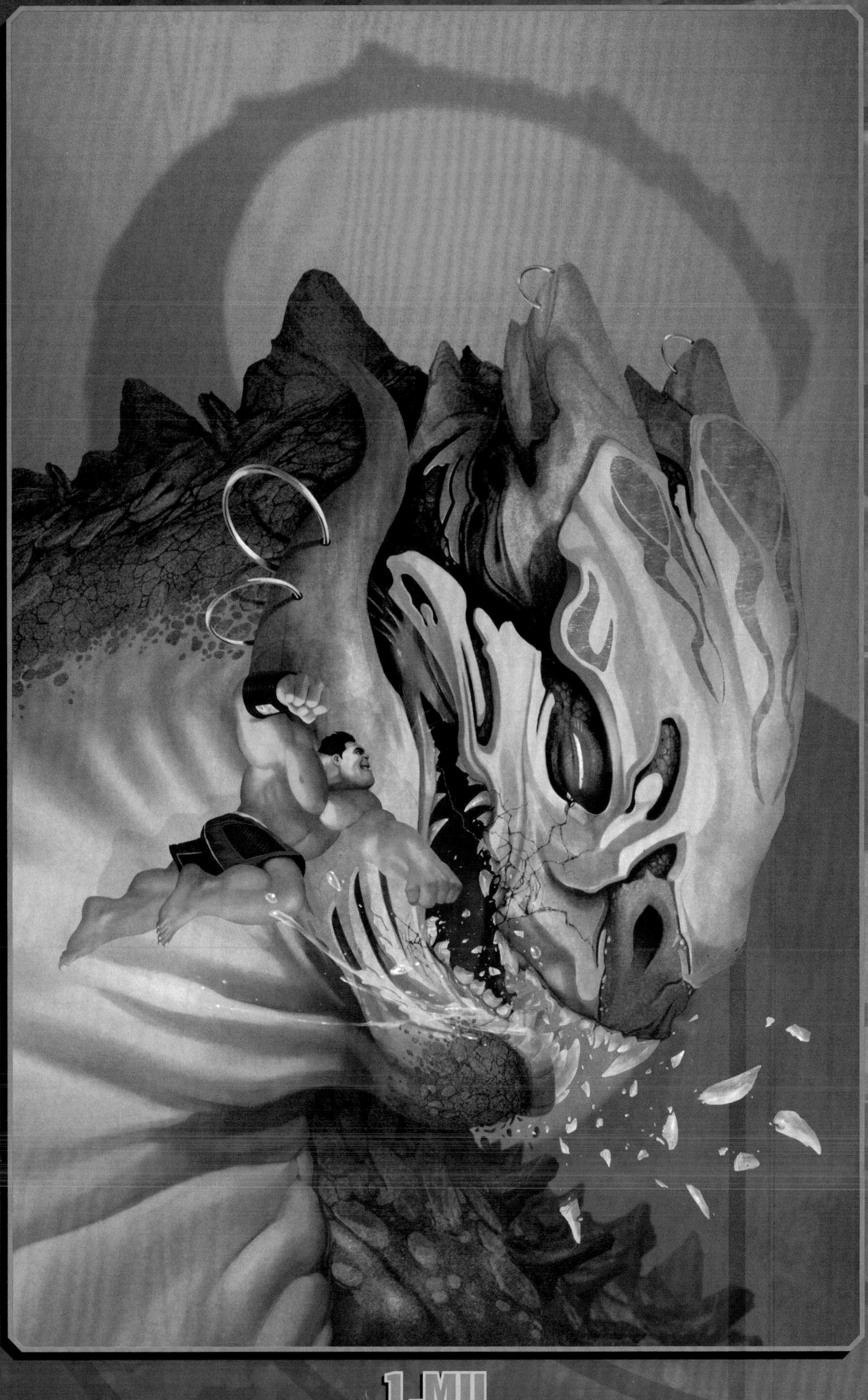

1.MU

THE TOTALLY AWESOME HULK

MONSTERS UNLEASHED!

SUPER-GENIUS TEENAGER AMADEUS CHO CURED BRUCE BANNER AND TOOK ON THE POWERS AND MANTLE OF THE HULK!

WAVES OF GIANT MONSTERS KNOWN AS LEVIATHONS ARE APPROACHING EARTH, INTENT ON RAZING THE WORLD. WHILE THE THREAT IS NOT YET FULLY UNDERSTOOD, SOMETIMES IT TAKES A MONSTER TO FIGHT MONSTERS...

[THIS STORY TAKES PLACE JUST BEFORE THE EVENTS OF MONSTERS UNLEASHED #1]

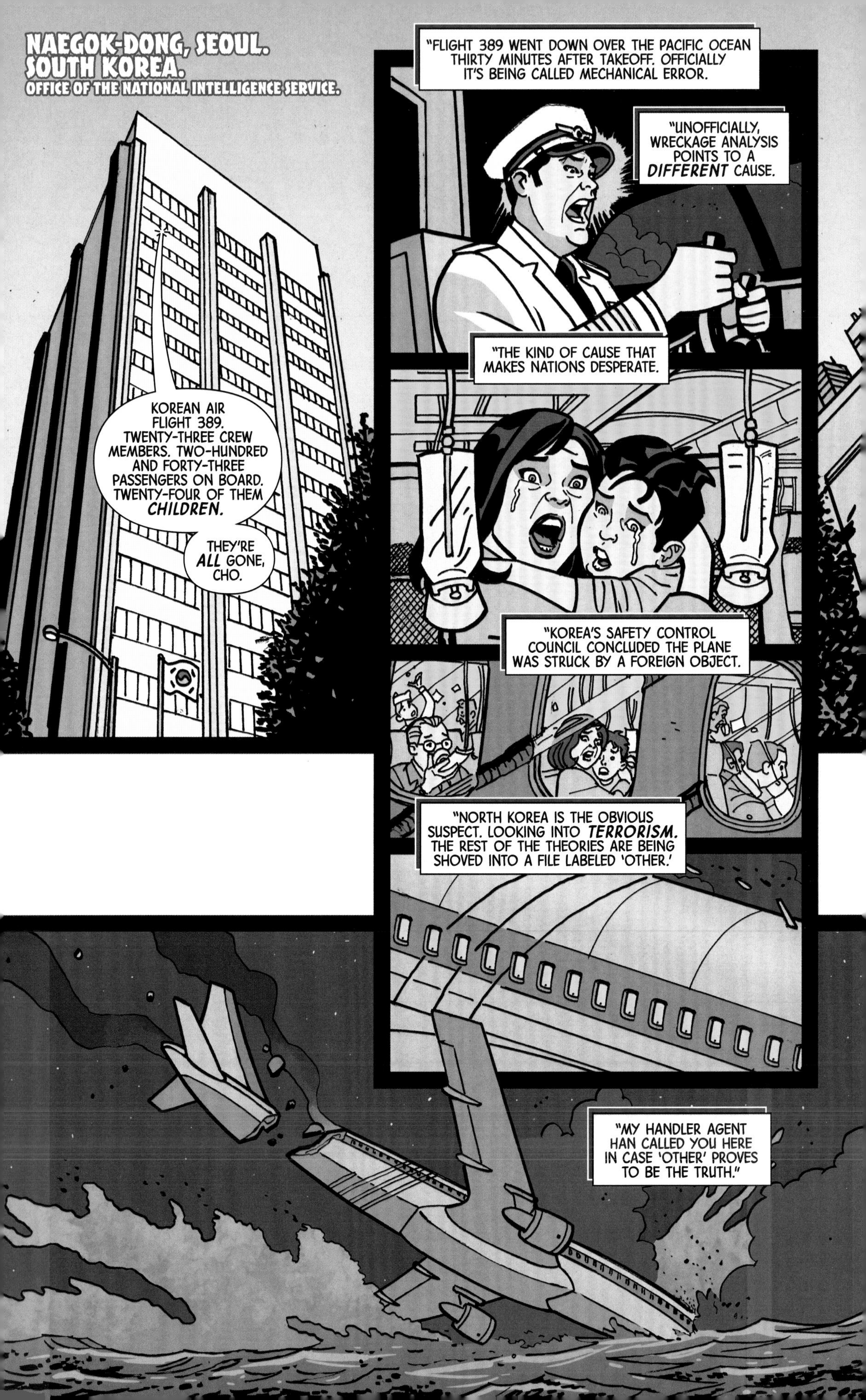
NAEGOK-DONG, SEOUL. SOUTH KOREA.
OFFICE OF THE NATIONAL INTELLIGENCE SERVICE.
KOREAN AIR FLIGHT 389. TWENTY-THREE CREW MEMBERS. TWO-HUNDRED AND FORTY-THREE PASSENGERS ON BOARD. TWENTY-FOUR OF THEM CHILDREN.
THEY'RE ALL GONE, CHO.
"FLIGHT 389 WENT DOWN OVER THE PACIFIC OCEAN THIRTY MINUTES AFTER TAKEOFF. OFFICIALLY IT'S BEING CALLED MECHANICAL ERROR.
"UNOFFICIALLY, WRECKAGE ANALYSIS POINTS TO A DIFFERENT CAUSE.
"THE KIND OF CAUSE THAT MAKES NATIONS DESPERATE.
"KOREA'S SAFETY CONTROL COUNCIL CONCLUDED THE PLANE WAS STRUCK BY A FOREIGN OBJECT.
"NORTH KOREA IS THE OBVIOUS SUSPECT. LOOKING INTO TERRORISM. THE REST OF THE THEORIES ARE BEING SHOVED INTO A FILE LABELED 'OTHER.'
"MY HANDLER AGENT HAN CALLED YOU HERE IN CASE 'OTHER' PROVES TO BE THE TRUTH."

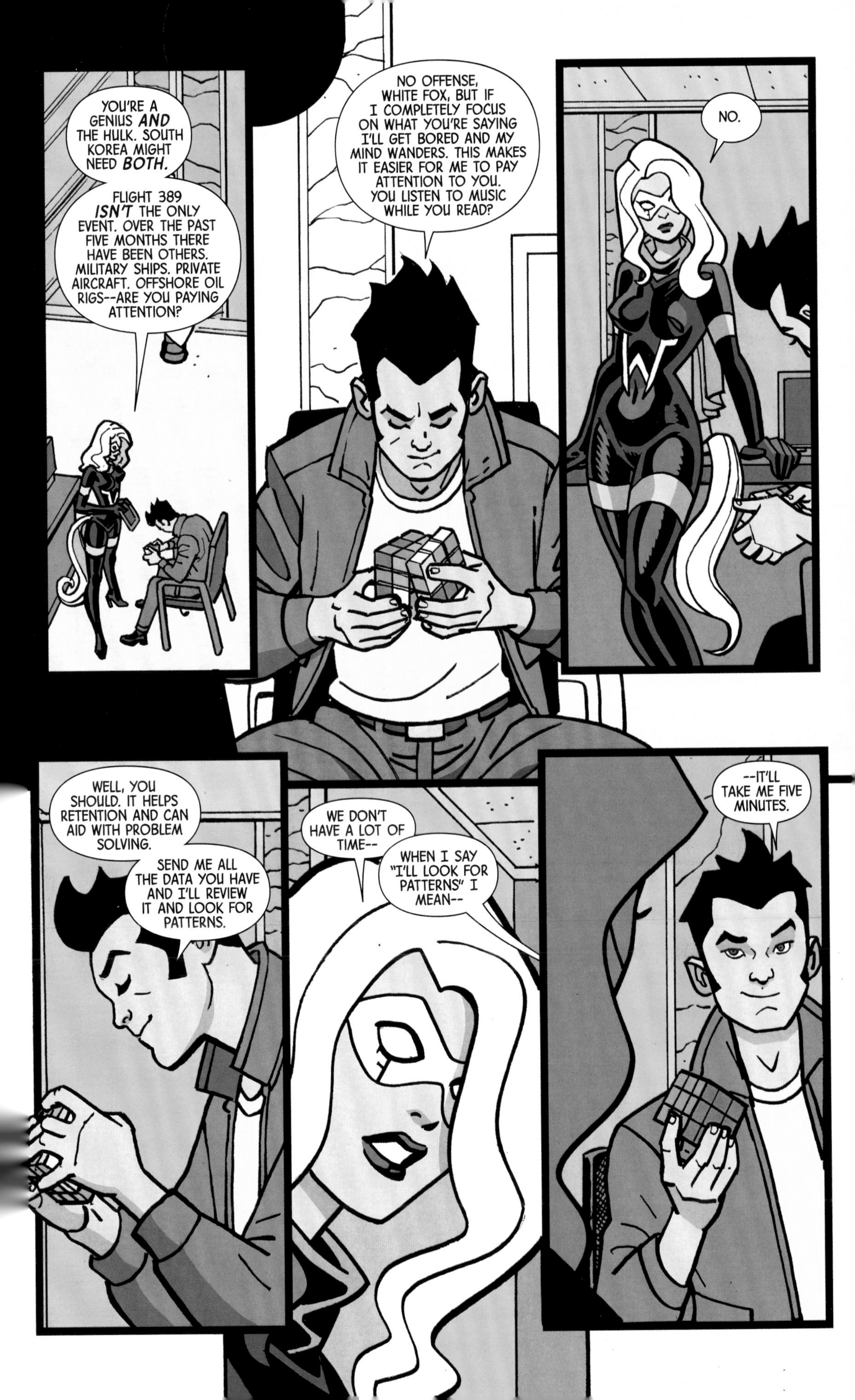
YOU'RE A GENIUS AND THE HULK. SOUTH KOREA MIGHT NEED BOTH.
FLIGHT 389 ISN'T THE ONLY EVENT. OVER THE PAST FIVE MONTHS THERE HAVE BEEN OTHERS. MILITARY SHIPS. PRIVATE AIRCRAFT. OFFSHORE OIL RIGS--ARE YOU PAYING ATTENTION?
NO OFFENSE, WHITE FOX, BUT IF I COMPLETELY FOCUS ON WHAT YOU'RE SAYING I'LL GET BORED AND MY MIND WANDERS. THIS MAKES IT EASIER FOR ME TO PAY ATTENTION TO YOU. YOU LISTEN TO MUSIC WHILE YOU READ?
NO.
WELL, YOU SHOULD. IT HELPS RETENTION AND CAN AID WITH PROBLEM SOLVING.
SEND ME ALL THE DATA YOU HAVE AND I'LL REVIEW IT AND LOOK FOR PATTERNS.
WE DON'T HAVE A LOT OF TIME--
WHEN I SAY "I'LL LOOK FOR PATTERNS" I MEAN--
--IT'LL TAKE ME FIVE MINUTES.

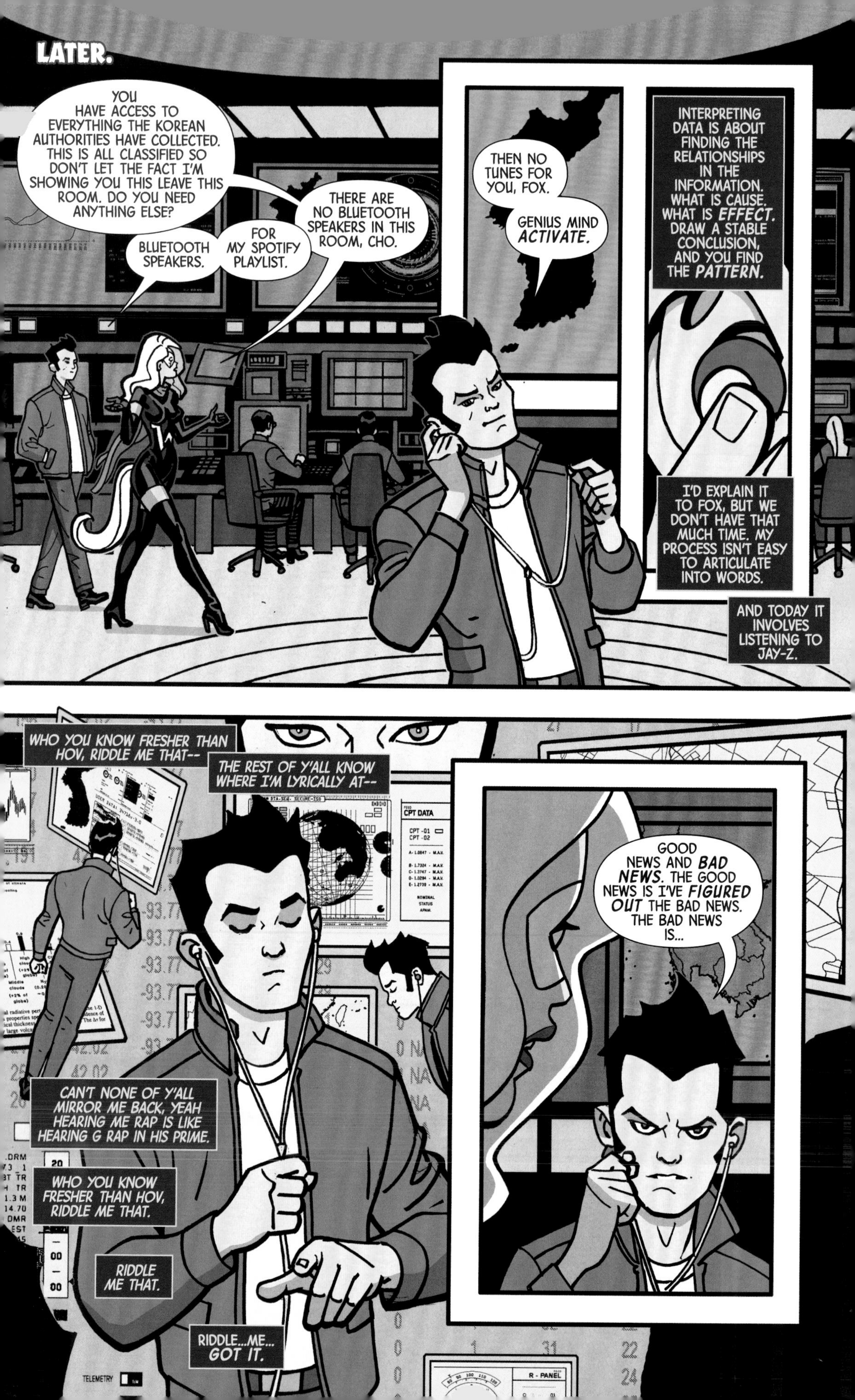
LATER.
YOU HAVE ACCESS TO EVERYTHING THE KOREAN AUTHORITIES HAVE COLLECTED. THIS IS ALL CLASSIFIED SO DON'T LET THE FACT I'M SHOWING YOU THIS LEAVE THIS ROOM. DO YOU NEED ANYTHING ELSE?
BLUETOOTH SPEAKERS.
FOR MY SPOTIFY PLAYLIST.
THERE ARE NO BLUETOOTH SPEAKERS IN THIS ROOM, CHO.
THEN NO TUNES FOR YOU, FOX.
GENIUS MIND ACTIVATE.
INTERPRETING DATA IS ABOUT FINDING THE RELATIONSHIPS IN THE INFORMATION. WHAT IS CAUSE. WHAT IS EFFECT. DRAW A STABLE CONCLUSION, AND YOU FIND THE PATTERN.
I'D EXPLAIN IT TO FOX, BUT WE DON'T HAVE THAT MUCH TIME. MY PROCESS ISN'T EASY TO ARTICULATE INTO WORDS.
AND TODAY IT INVOLVES LISTENING TO JAY-Z.
WHO YOU KNOW FRESHER THAN HOV, RIDDLE ME THAT--
THE REST OF Y'ALL KNOW WHERE I'M LYRICALLY AT--
CAN'T NONE OF Y'ALL MIRROR ME BACK, YEAH HEARING ME RAP IS LIKE HEARING G RAP IN HIS PRIME.
WHO YOU KNOW FRESHER THAN HOV, RIDDLE ME THAT.
RIDDLE ME THAT.
RIDDLE...ME... GOT IT.
GOOD NEWS AND BAD NEWS. THE GOOD NEWS IS I'VE FIGURED OUT THE BAD NEWS. THE BAD NEWS IS...

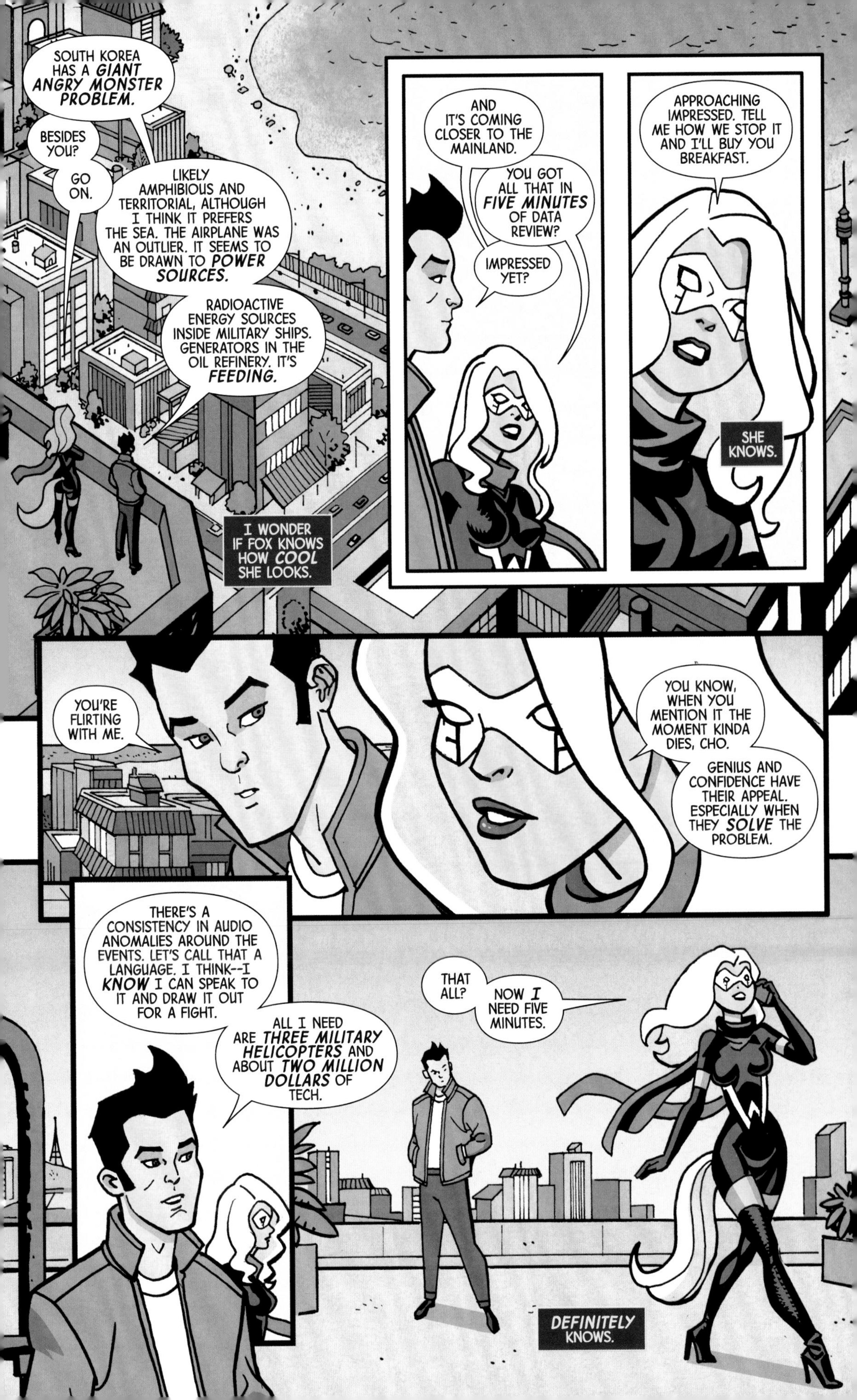

SOUTH KOREA HAS A GIANT ANGRY MONSTER PROBLEM.
BESIDES YOU?
GO ON.
LIKELY AMPHIBIOUS AND TERRITORIAL, ALTHOUGH I THINK IT PREFERS THE SEA. THE AIRPLANE WAS AN OUTLIER. IT SEEMS TO BE DRAWN TO POWER SOURCES.
RADIOACTIVE ENERGY SOURCES INSIDE MILITARY SHIPS. GENERATORS IN THE OIL REFINERY. IT'S FEEDING.
I WONDER IF FOX KNOWS HOW COOL SHE LOOKS.
AND IT'S COMING CLOSER TO THE MAINLAND.
YOU GOT ALL THAT IN FIVE MINUTES OF DATA REVIEW?
IMPRESSED YET?
APPROACHING IMPRESSED. TELL ME HOW WE STOP IT AND I'LL BUY YOU BREAKFAST.
SHE KNOWS.
YOU'RE FLIRTING WITH ME.
YOU KNOW, WHEN YOU MENTION IT THE MOMENT KINDA DIES, CHO.
GENIUS AND CONFIDENCE HAVE THEIR APPEAL. ESPECIALLY WHEN THEY SOLVE THE PROBLEM.
THERE'S A CONSISTENCY IN AUDIO ANOMALIES AROUND THE EVENTS. LET'S CALL THAT A LANGUAGE. I THINK--I KNOW I CAN SPEAK TO IT AND DRAW IT OUT FOR A FIGHT.
ALL I NEED ARE THREE MILITARY HELICOPTERS AND ABOUT TWO MILLION DOLLARS OF TECH.
THAT ALL?
NOW I NEED FIVE MINUTES.
DEFINITELY KNOWS.

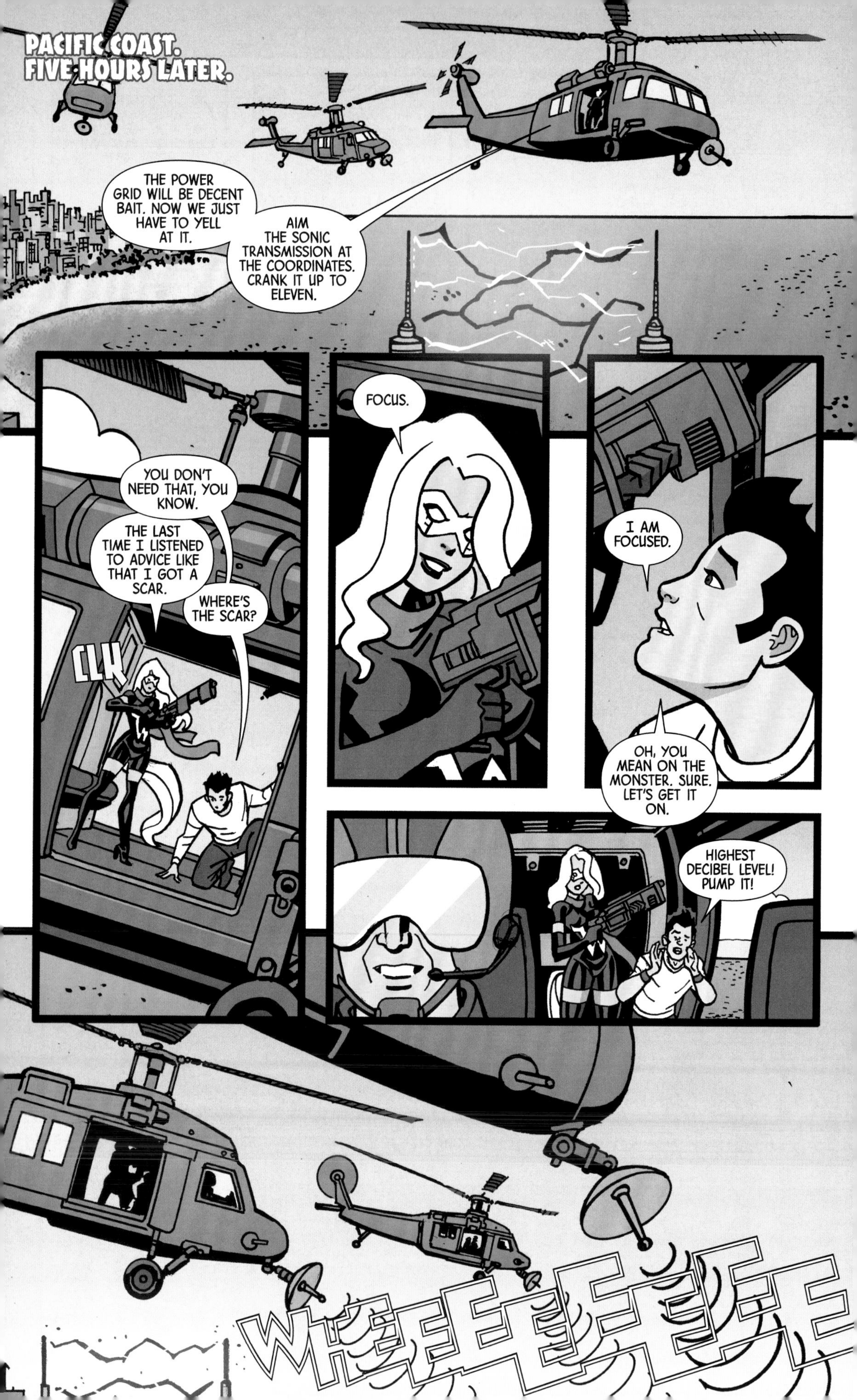
PACIFIC COAST. FIVE HOURS LATER.
THE POWER GRID WILL BE DECENT BAIT. NOW WE JUST HAVE TO YELL AT IT.
AIM THE SONIC TRANSMISSION AT THE COORDINATES. CRANK IT UP TO ELEVEN.
YOU DON'T NEED THAT, YOU KNOW.
THE LAST TIME I LISTENED TO ADVICE LIKE THAT I GOT A SCAR.
WHERE'S THE SCAR?
CLK
FOCUS.
I AM FOCUSED.
OH, YOU MEAN ON THE MONSTER. SURE. LET'S GET IT ON.
HIGHEST DECIBEL LEVEL! PUMP IT!
WHEEEEEEEEE

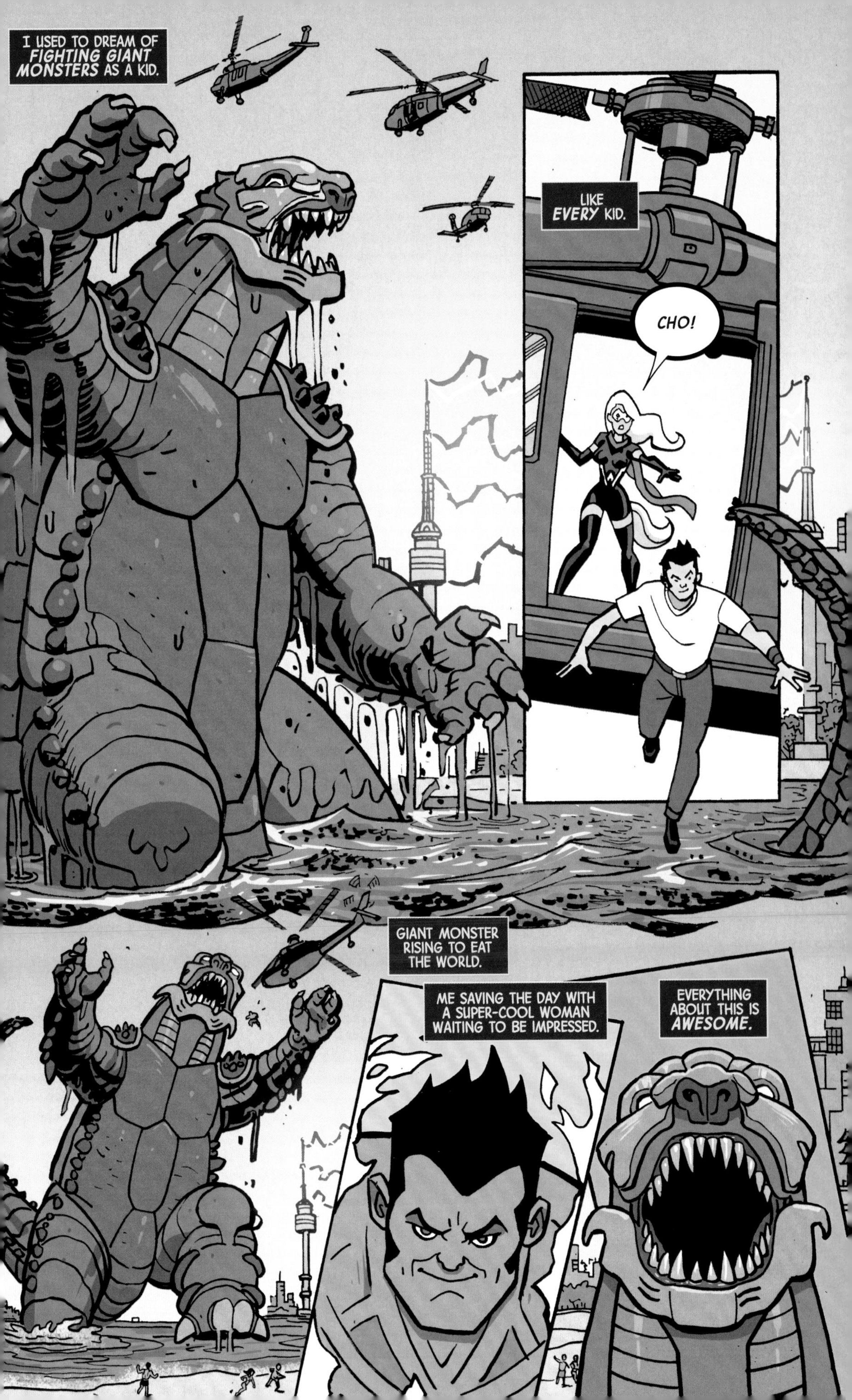
I USED TO DREAM OF *FIGHTING GIANT MONSTERS* AS A KID.
LIKE *EVERY* KID.
CHO!
GIANT MONSTER RISING TO EAT THE WORLD.
ME SAVING THE DAY WITH A SUPER-COOL WOMAN WAITING TO BE IMPRESSED.
EVERYTHING ABOUT THIS IS *AWESOME.*

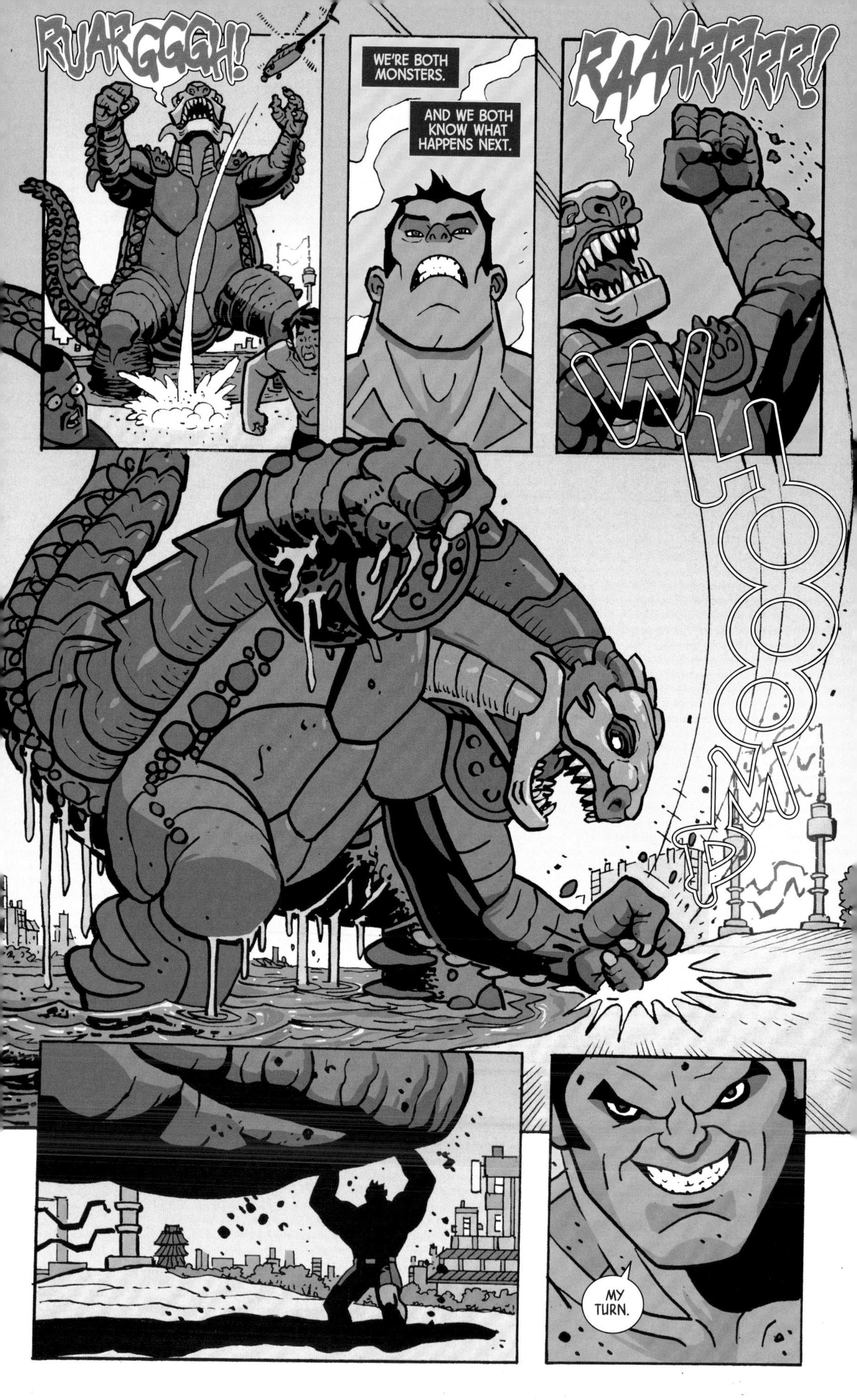
RUARGGGH!
WE'RE BOTH MONSTERS.
AND WE BOTH KNOW WHAT HAPPENS NEXT.
RAAARRRR!
WHOOOOMP
MY TURN.

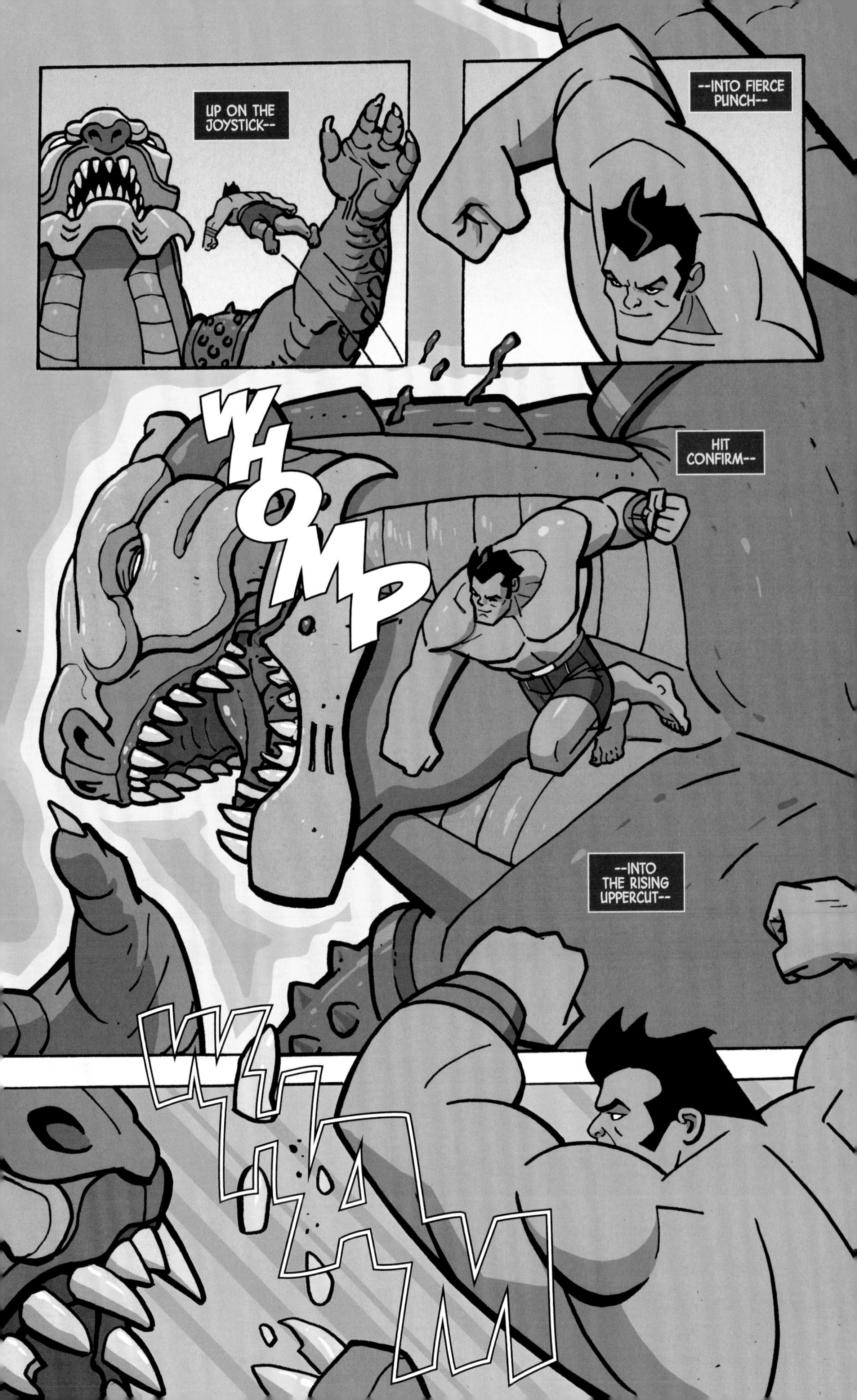
UP ON THE JOYSTICK--
--INTO FIERCE PUNCH--
WHOMP
HIT CONFIRM--
--INTO THE RISING UPPERCUT--
WHAM

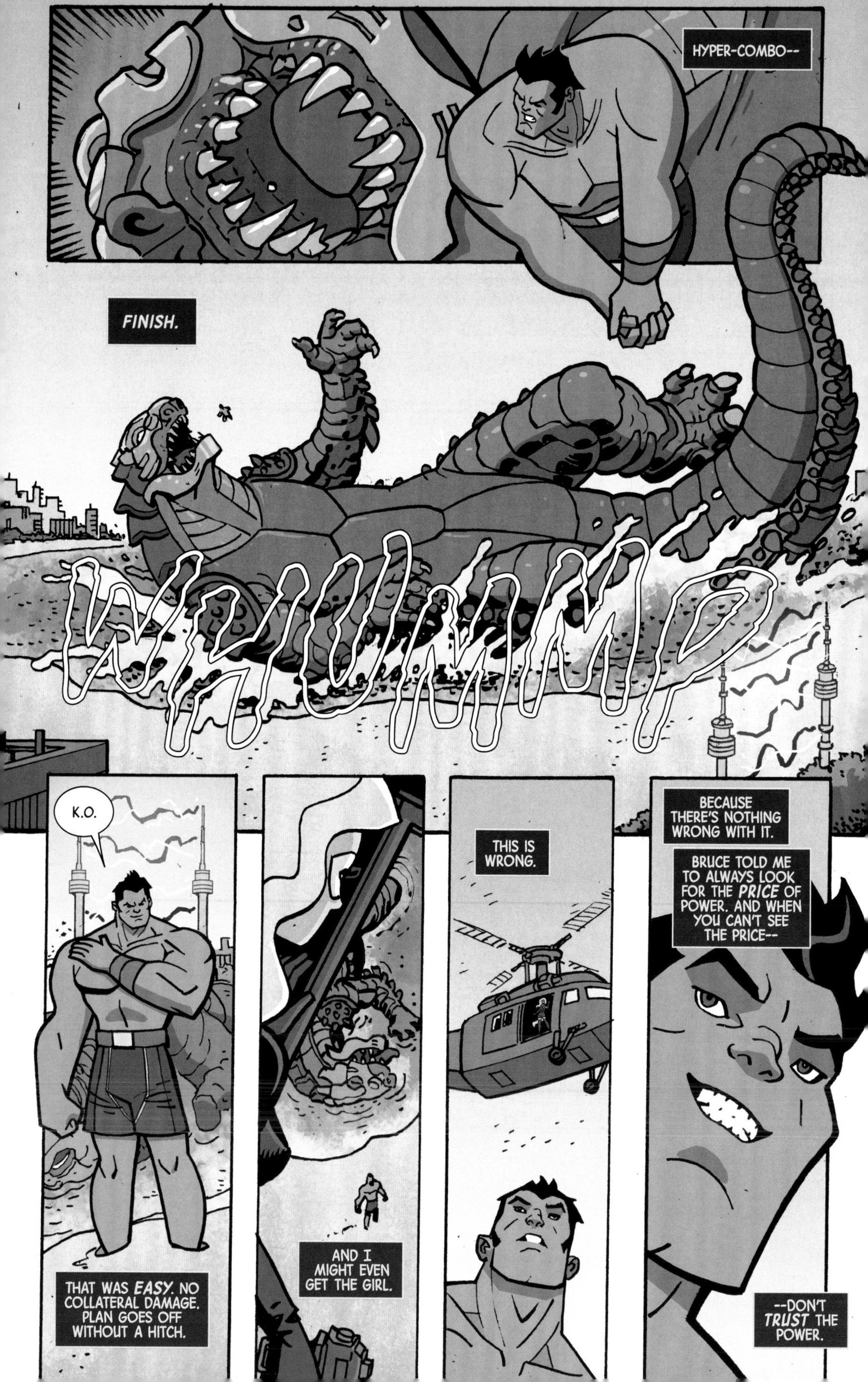

HYPER-COMBO--
FINISH.
WHUMMP
K.O.
THAT WAS EASY. NO COLLATERAL DAMAGE. PLAN GOES OFF WITHOUT A HITCH.
AND I MIGHT EVEN GET THE GIRL.
THIS IS WRONG.
BECAUSE THERE'S NOTHING WRONG WITH IT.
BRUCE TOLD ME TO ALWAYS LOOK FOR THE PRICE OF POWER. AND WHEN YOU CAN'T SEE THE PRICE--
--DON'T TRUST THE POWER.

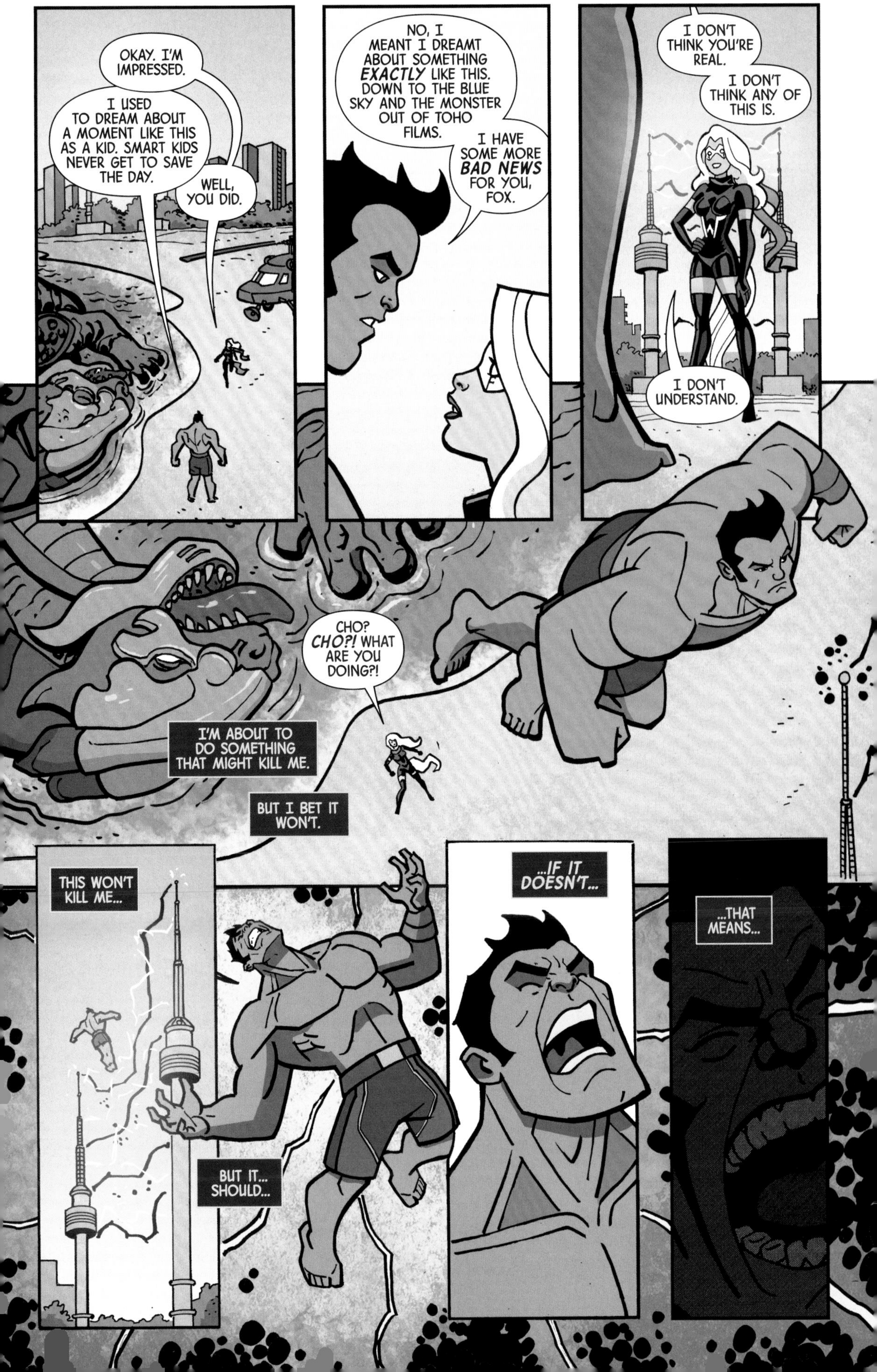

OKAY. I'M IMPRESSED.
I USED TO DREAM ABOUT A MOMENT LIKE THIS AS A KID. SMART KIDS NEVER GET TO SAVE THE DAY.
WELL, YOU DID.
NO, I MEANT I DREAMT ABOUT SOMETHING EXACTLY LIKE THIS. DOWN TO THE BLUE SKY AND THE MONSTER OUT OF TOHO FILMS.
I HAVE SOME MORE BAD NEWS FOR YOU, FOX.
I DON'T THINK YOU'RE REAL.
I DON'T THINK ANY OF THIS IS.
I DON'T UNDERSTAND.
CHO? CHO?! WHAT ARE YOU DOING?!
I'M ABOUT TO DO SOMETHING THAT MIGHT KILL ME.
BUT I BET IT WON'T.
THIS WON'T KILL ME...
BUT IT... SHOULD...
...IF IT DOESN'T...
...THAT MEANS...

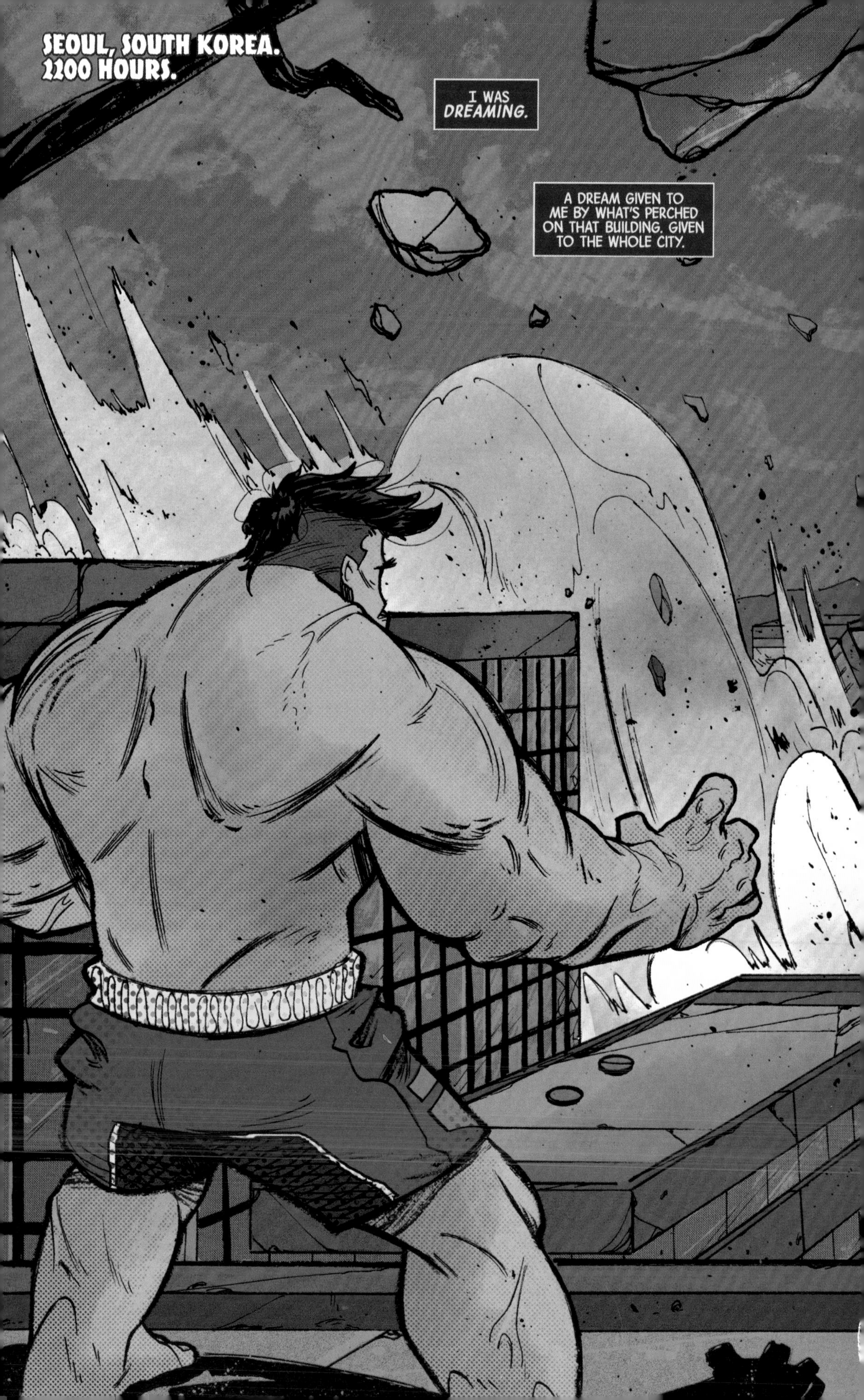
SEOUL, SOUTH KOREA.
2200 HOURS.
I WAS DREAMING.
A DREAM GIVEN TO ME BY WHAT'S PERCHED ON THAT BUILDING. GIVEN TO THE WHOLE CITY.

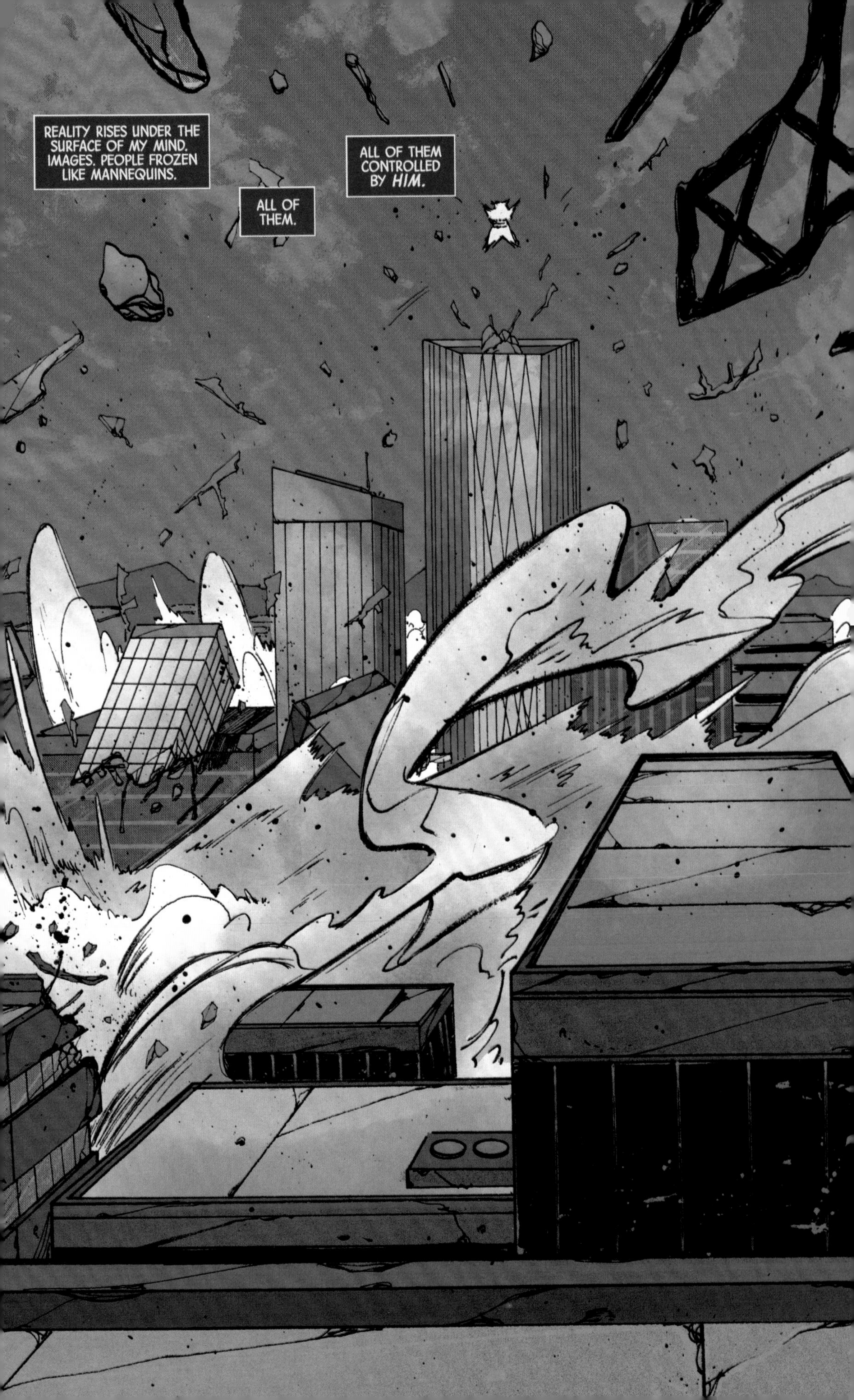
REALITY RISES UNDER THE SURFACE OF MY MIND. IMAGES. PEOPLE FROZEN LIKE MANNEQUINS.
ALL OF THEM.
ALL OF THEM CONTROLLED BY *HIM*.

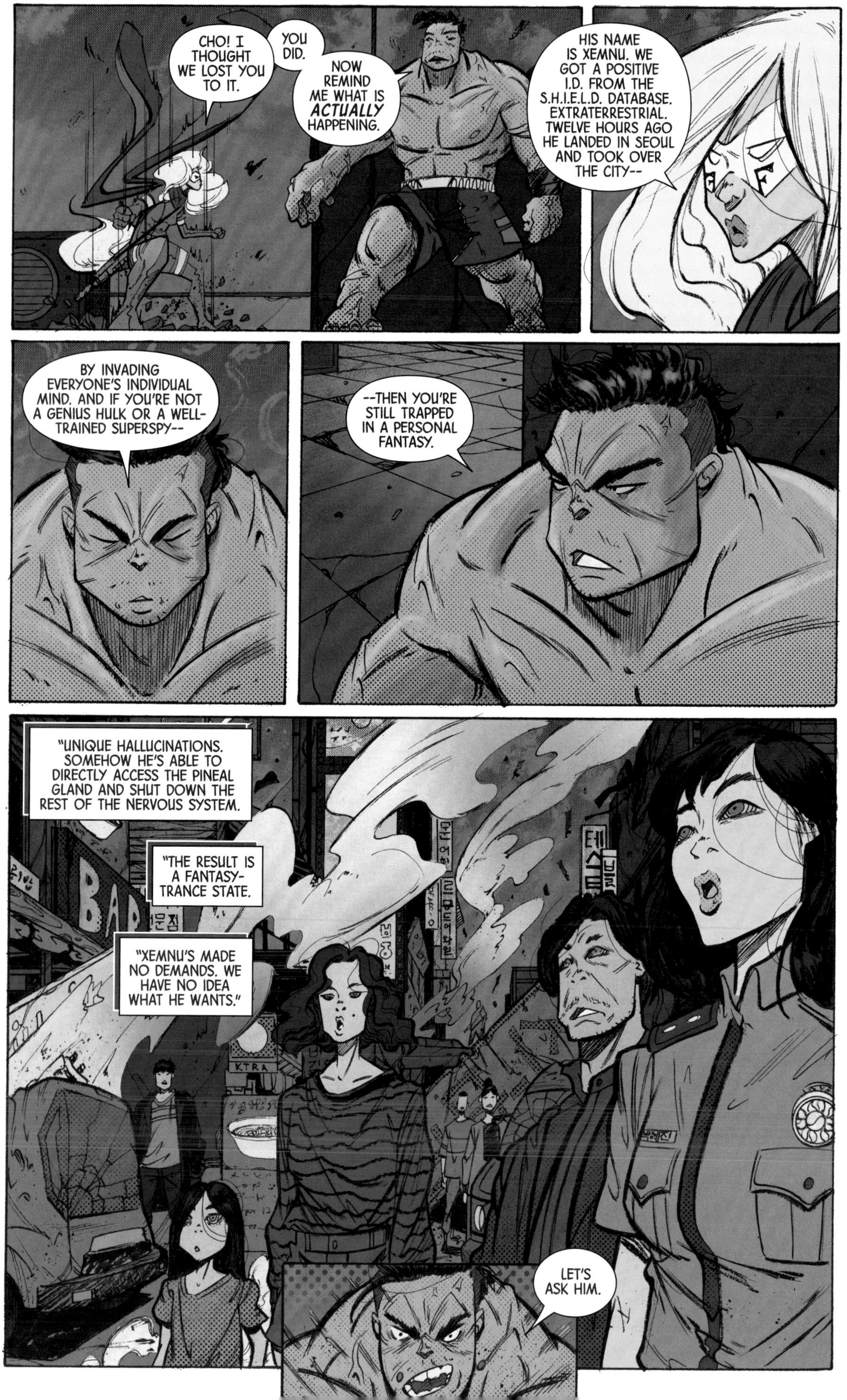
CHO! I THOUGHT WE LOST YOU TO IT.
YOU DID.
NOW REMIND ME WHAT IS *ACTUALLY* HAPPENING.
HIS NAME IS XEMNU. WE GOT A POSITIVE I.D. FROM THE S.H.I.E.L.D. DATABASE. EXTRATERRESTRIAL. TWELVE HOURS AGO HE LANDED IN SEOUL AND TOOK OVER THE CITY--
BY INVADING EVERYONE'S INDIVIDUAL MIND. AND IF YOU'RE NOT A GENIUS HULK OR A WELL-TRAINED SUPERSPY--
--THEN YOU'RE STILL TRAPPED IN A PERSONAL FANTASY.
"UNIQUE HALLUCINATIONS. SOMEHOW HE'S ABLE TO DIRECTLY ACCESS THE PINEAL GLAND AND SHUT DOWN THE REST OF THE NERVOUS SYSTEM.
"THE RESULT IS A FANTASY-TRANCE STATE.
"XEMNU'S MADE NO DEMANDS. WE HAVE NO IDEA WHAT HE WANTS."
LET'S ASK HIM.

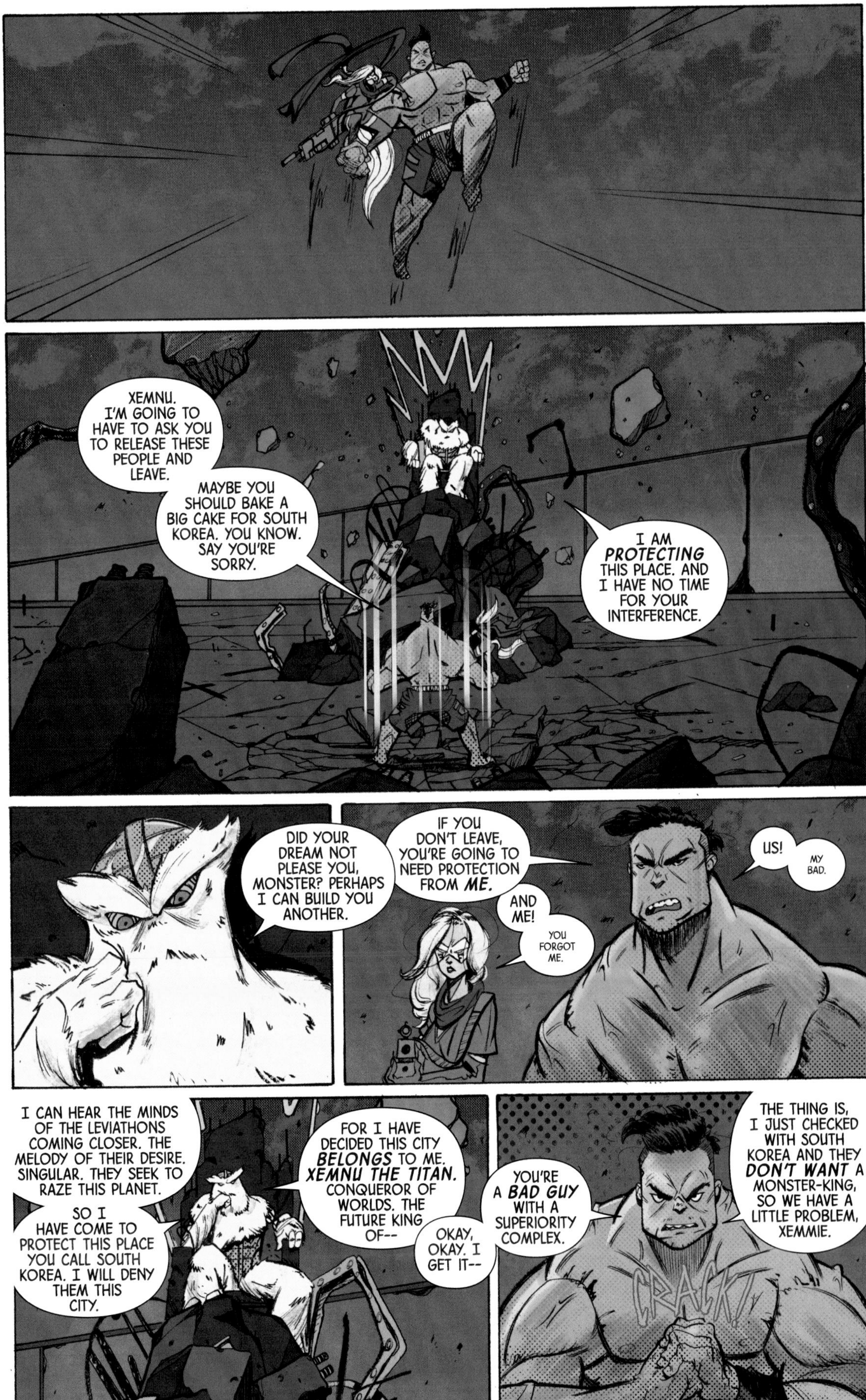
XEMNU. I'M GOING TO HAVE TO ASK YOU TO RELEASE THESE PEOPLE AND LEAVE.
MAYBE YOU SHOULD BAKE A BIG CAKE FOR SOUTH KOREA. YOU KNOW. SAY YOU'RE SORRY.
I AM *PROTECTING* THIS PLACE. AND I HAVE NO TIME FOR YOUR INTERFERENCE.
DID YOUR DREAM NOT PLEASE YOU, MONSTER? PERHAPS I CAN BUILD YOU ANOTHER.
IF YOU DON'T LEAVE, YOU'RE GOING TO NEED PROTECTION FROM *ME.*
AND ME!
YOU FORGOT ME.
US!
MY BAD.
I CAN HEAR THE MINDS OF THE LEVIATHONS COMING CLOSER. THE MELODY OF THEIR DESIRE. SINGULAR. THEY SEEK TO RAZE THIS PLANET.
SO I HAVE COME TO PROTECT THIS PLACE YOU CALL SOUTH KOREA. I WILL DENY THEM THIS CITY.
FOR I HAVE DECIDED THIS CITY *BELONGS* TO ME. *XEMNU THE TITAN.* CONQUEROR OF WORLDS. THE FUTURE KING OF--
OKAY, OKAY. I GET IT--
YOU'RE A *BAD GUY* WITH A SUPERIORITY COMPLEX.
THE THING IS, I JUST CHECKED WITH SOUTH KOREA AND THEY *DON'T WANT* A MONSTER-KING, SO WE HAVE A LITTLE PROBLEM, XEMMIE.
CRACK!

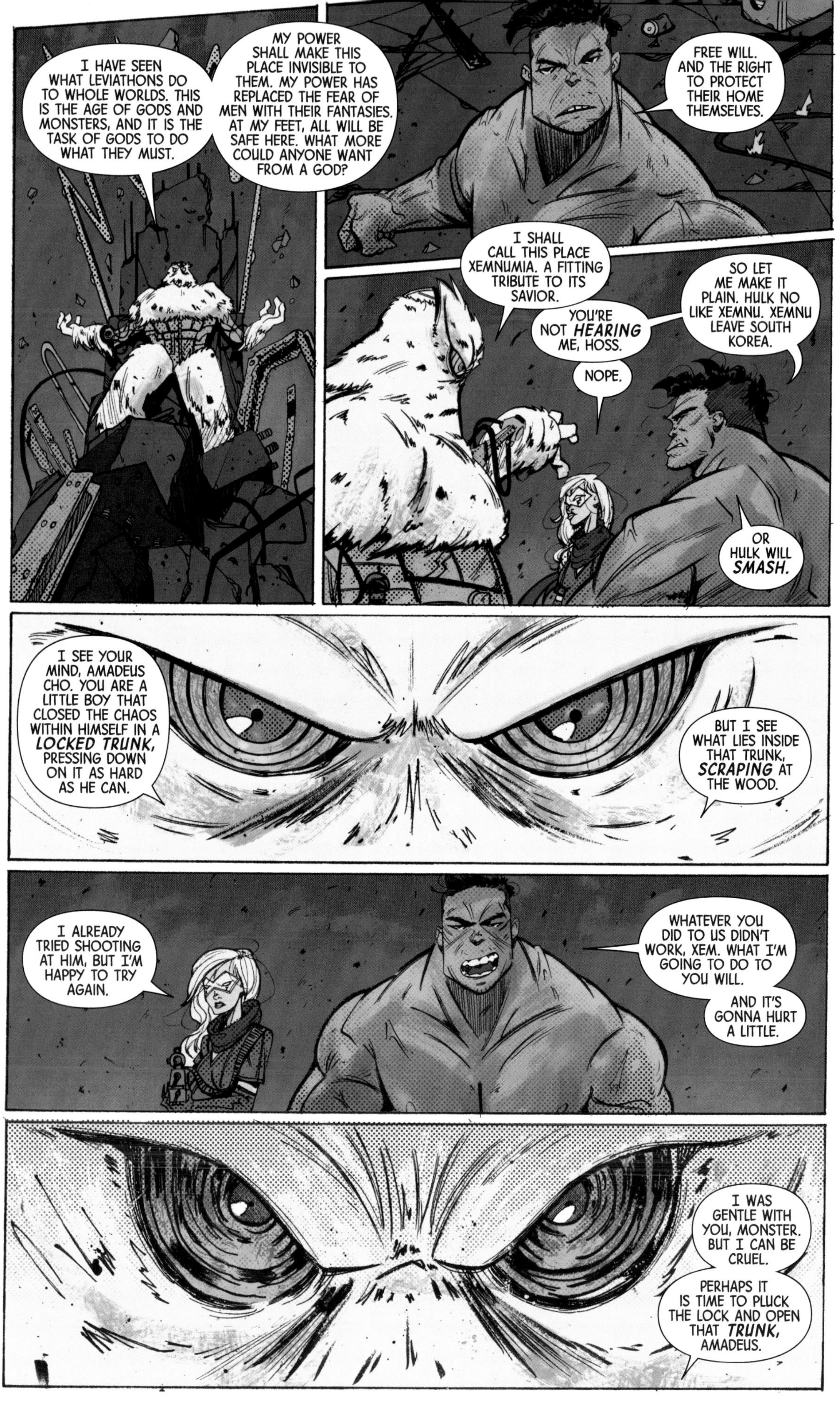
I HAVE SEEN WHAT LEVIATHONS DO TO WHOLE WORLDS. THIS IS THE AGE OF GODS AND MONSTERS, AND IT IS THE TASK OF GODS TO DO WHAT THEY MUST.
MY POWER SHALL MAKE THIS PLACE INVISIBLE TO THEM. MY POWER HAS REPLACED THE FEAR OF MEN WITH THEIR FANTASIES. AT MY FEET, ALL WILL BE SAFE HERE. WHAT MORE COULD ANYONE WANT FROM A GOD?
FREE WILL. AND THE RIGHT TO PROTECT THEIR HOME THEMSELVES.
I SHALL CALL THIS PLACE XEMNUMIA. A FITTING TRIBUTE TO ITS SAVIOR.
YOU'RE NOT HEARING ME, HOSS.
NOPE.
SO LET ME MAKE IT PLAIN. HULK NO LIKE XEMNU. XEMNU LEAVE SOUTH KOREA.
OR HULK WILL SMASH.
I SEE YOUR MIND, AMADEUS CHO. YOU ARE A LITTLE BOY THAT CLOSED THE CHAOS WITHIN HIMSELF IN A LOCKED TRUNK, PRESSING DOWN ON IT AS HARD AS HE CAN.
BUT I SEE WHAT LIES INSIDE THAT TRUNK, SCRAPING AT THE WOOD.
I ALREADY TRIED SHOOTING AT HIM, BUT I'M HAPPY TO TRY AGAIN.
WHATEVER YOU DID TO US DIDN'T WORK, XEM. WHAT I'M GOING TO DO TO YOU WILL.
AND IT'S GONNA HURT A LITTLE.
I WAS GENTLE WITH YOU, MONSTER. BUT I CAN BE CRUEL.
PERHAPS IT IS TIME TO PLUCK THE LOCK AND OPEN THAT TRUNK, AMADEUS.

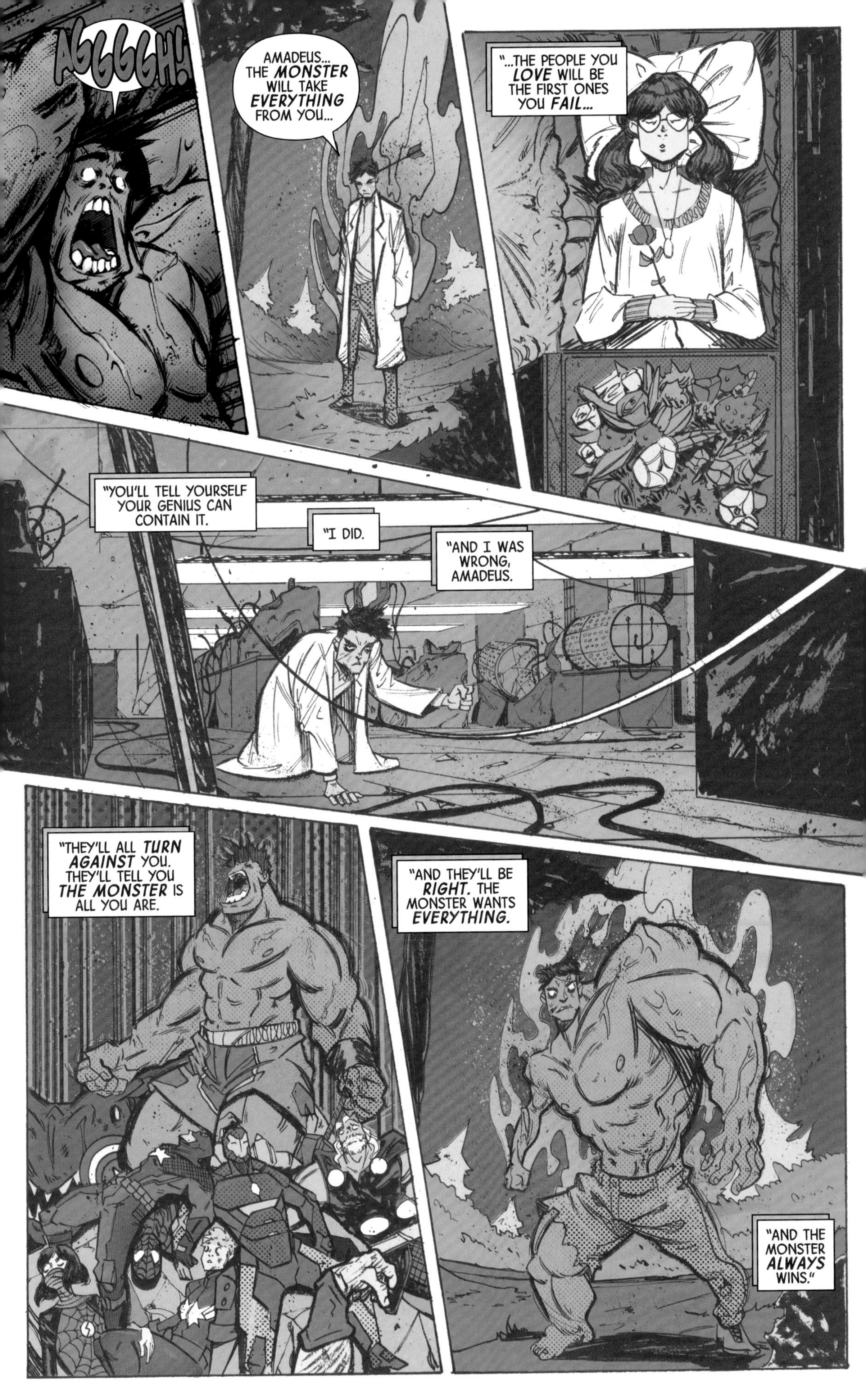
AGGGGH!
AMADEUS... THE MONSTER WILL TAKE EVERYTHING FROM YOU...
"...THE PEOPLE YOU LOVE WILL BE THE FIRST ONES YOU FAIL...
"YOU'LL TELL YOURSELF YOUR GENIUS CAN CONTAIN IT.
"I DID.
"AND I WAS WRONG, AMADEUS.
"THEY'LL ALL TURN AGAINST YOU. THEY'LL TELL YOU THE MONSTER IS ALL YOU ARE.
"AND THEY'LL BE RIGHT. THE MONSTER WANTS EVERYTHING.
"AND THE MONSTER ALWAYS WINS."

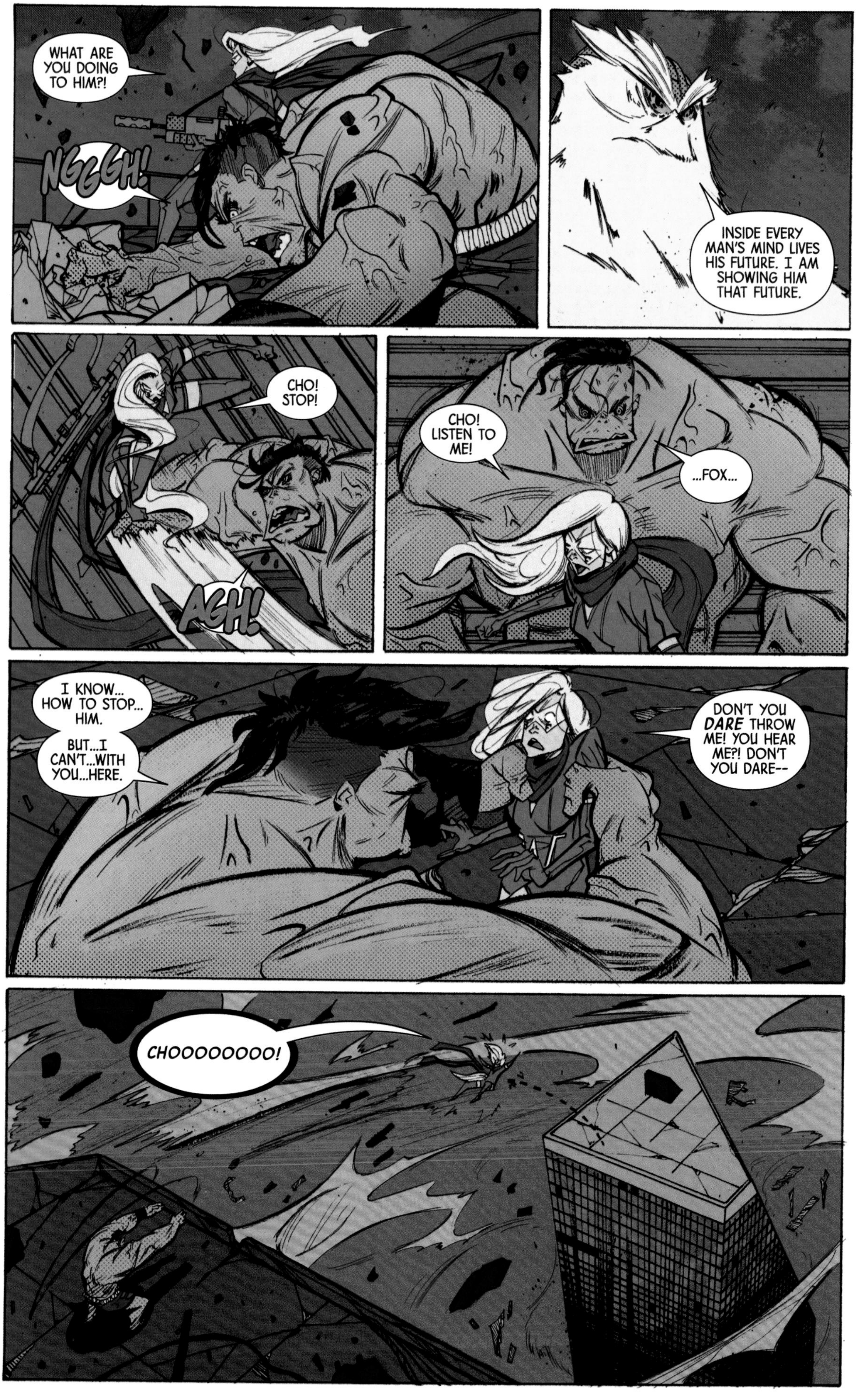
WHAT ARE YOU DOING TO HIM?!
NGGGH!
INSIDE EVERY MAN'S MIND LIVES HIS FUTURE. I AM SHOWING HIM THAT FUTURE.
CHO! STOP!
AGH!
CHO! LISTEN TO ME!
...FOX...
I KNOW... HOW TO STOP... HIM.
BUT...I CAN'T...WITH YOU...HERE.
DON'T YOU DARE THROW ME! YOU HEAR ME?! DON'T YOU DARE--
CHOOOOOOOO!

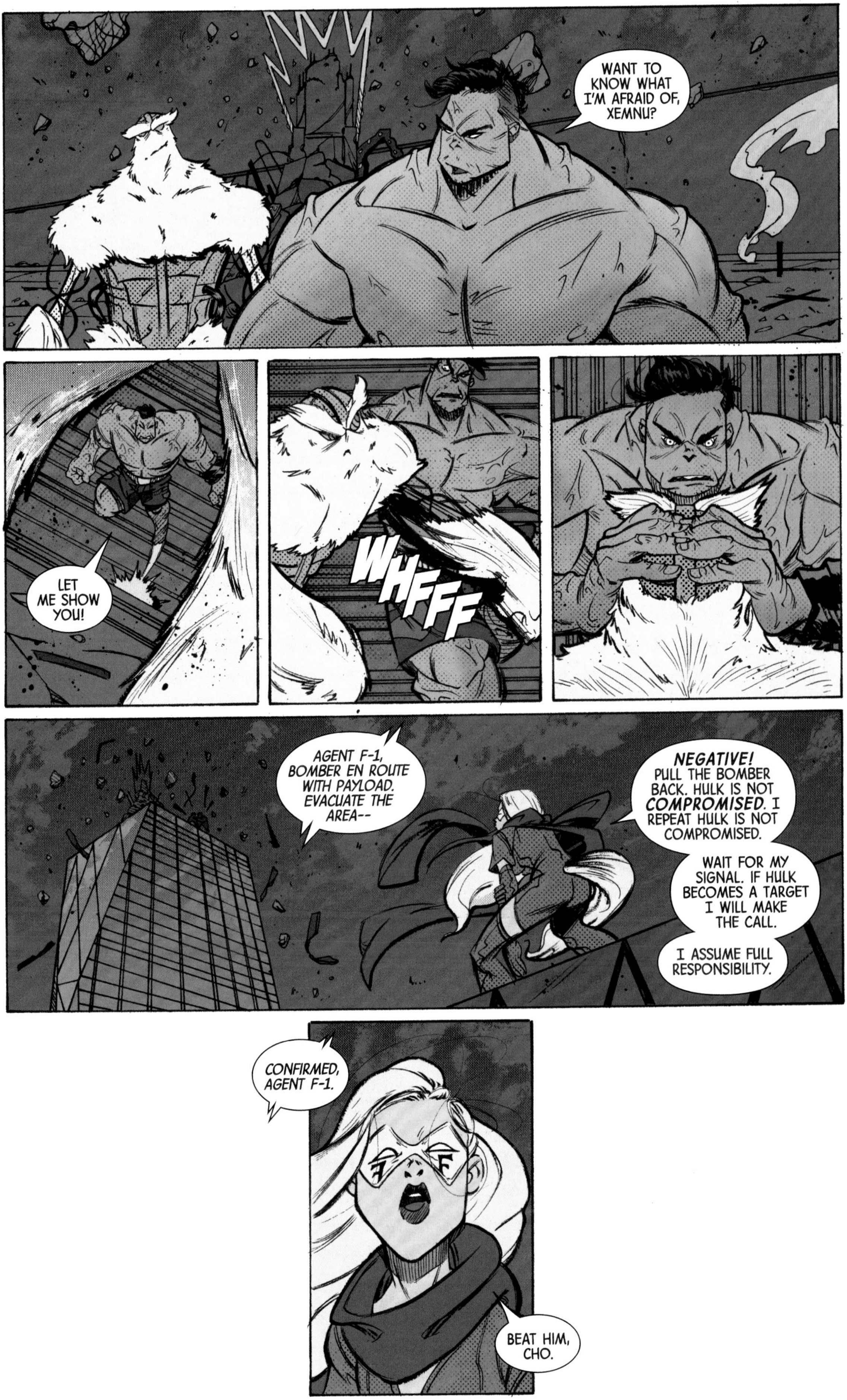
WANT TO KNOW WHAT I'M AFRAID OF, XEMNU?
LET ME SHOW YOU!
WHFFFF
AGENT F-1, BOMBER EN ROUTE WITH PAYLOAD. EVACUATE THE AREA--
NEGATIVE! PULL THE BOMBER BACK. HULK IS NOT COMPROMISED. I REPEAT HULK IS NOT COMPROMISED.
WAIT FOR MY SIGNAL. IF HULK BECOMES A TARGET I WILL MAKE THE CALL.
I ASSUME FULL RESPONSIBILITY.
CONFIRMED, AGENT F-1.
BEAT HIM, CHO.

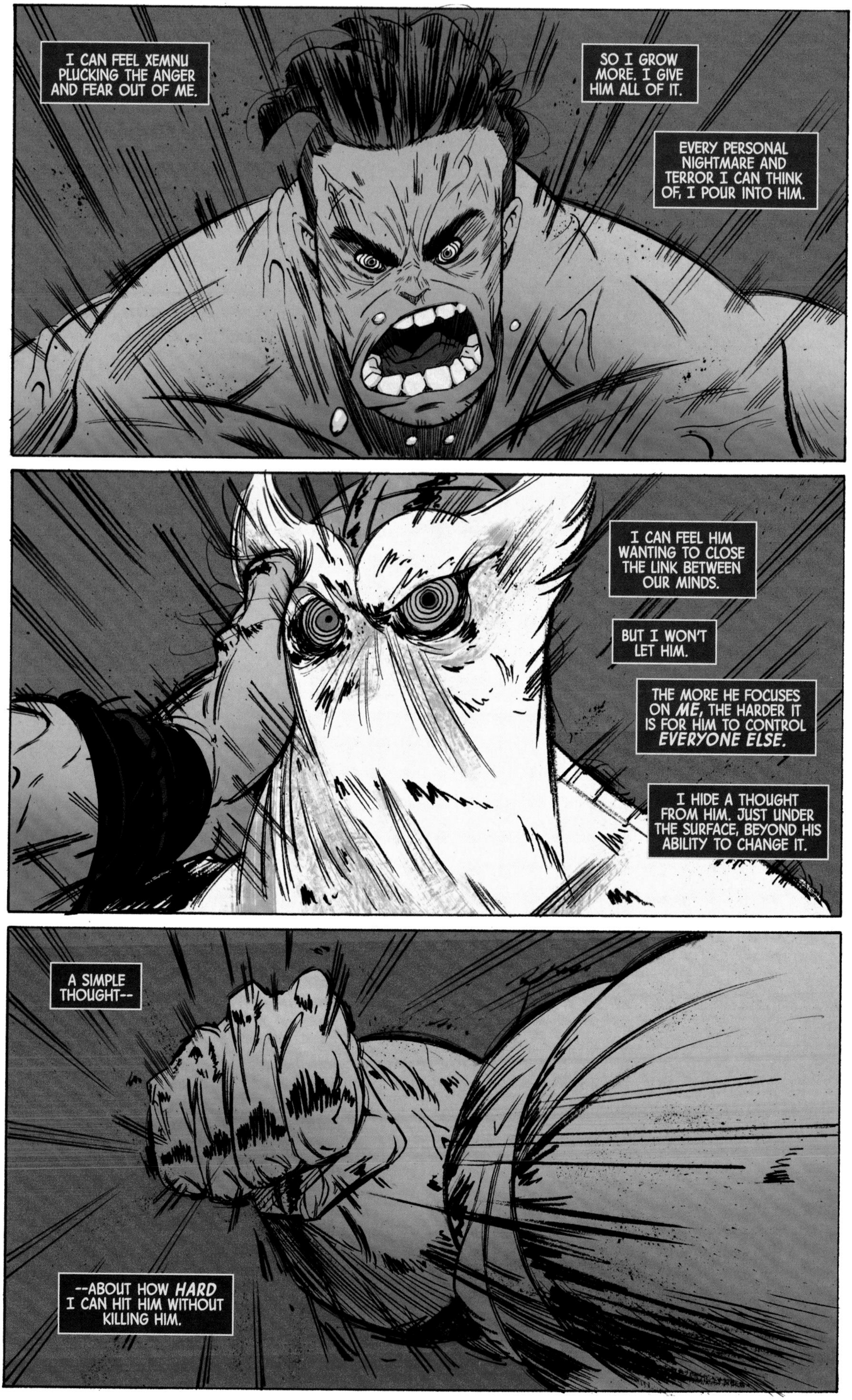
I CAN FEEL XEMNU PLUCKING THE ANGER AND FEAR OUT OF ME.
SO I GROW MORE. I GIVE HIM ALL OF IT.
EVERY PERSONAL NIGHTMARE AND TERROR I CAN THINK OF, I POUR INTO HIM.
I CAN FEEL HIM WANTING TO CLOSE THE LINK BETWEEN OUR MINDS.
BUT I WON'T LET HIM.
THE MORE HE FOCUSES ON *ME,* THE HARDER IT IS FOR HIM TO CONTROL *EVERYONE ELSE.*
I HIDE A THOUGHT FROM HIM. JUST UNDER THE SURFACE, BEYOND HIS ABILITY TO CHANGE IT.
A SIMPLE THOUGHT--
--ABOUT HOW *HARD* I CAN HIT HIM WITHOUT KILLING HIM.

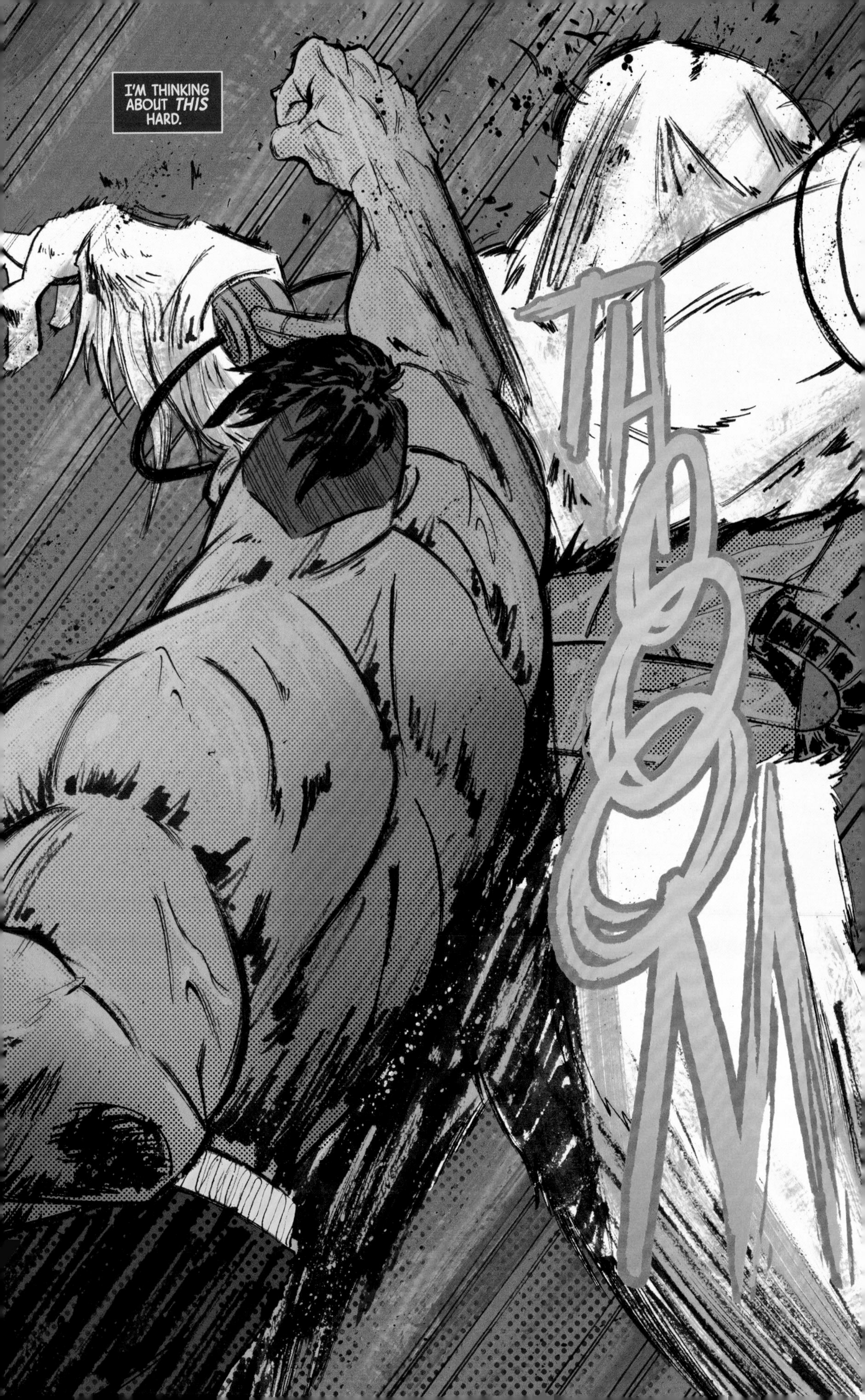
I'M THINKING ABOUT THIS HARD.
THOOOM

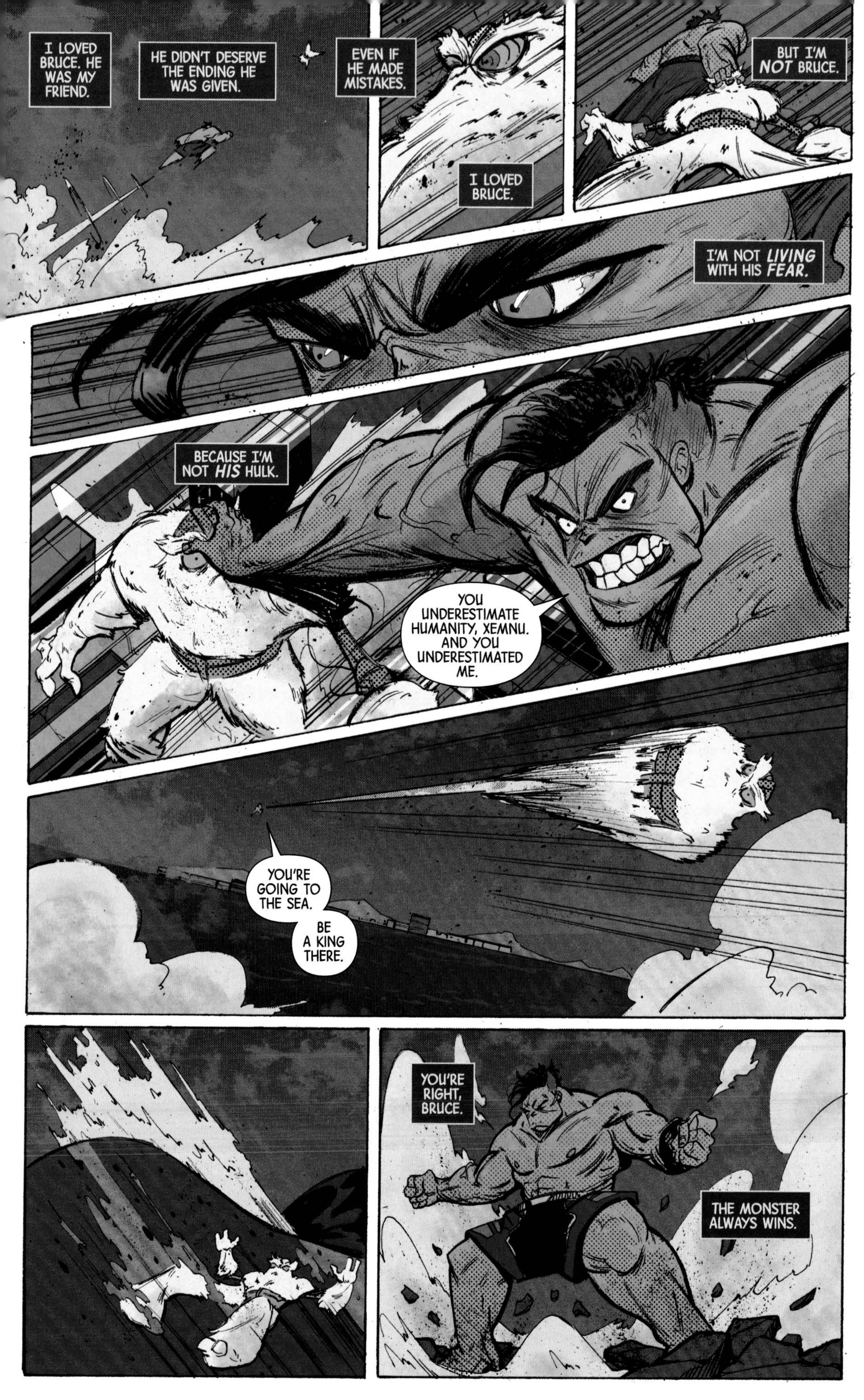
I LOVED BRUCE. HE WAS MY FRIEND.
HE DIDN'T DESERVE THE ENDING HE WAS GIVEN.
EVEN IF HE MADE MISTAKES.
I LOVED BRUCE.
BUT I'M NOT BRUCE.
I'M NOT LIVING WITH HIS FEAR.
BECAUSE I'M NOT HIS HULK.
YOU UNDERESTIMATE HUMANITY, XEMNU. AND YOU UNDERESTIMATED ME.
YOU'RE GOING TO THE SEA.
BE A KING THERE.
YOU'RE RIGHT, BRUCE.
THE MONSTER ALWAYS WINS.

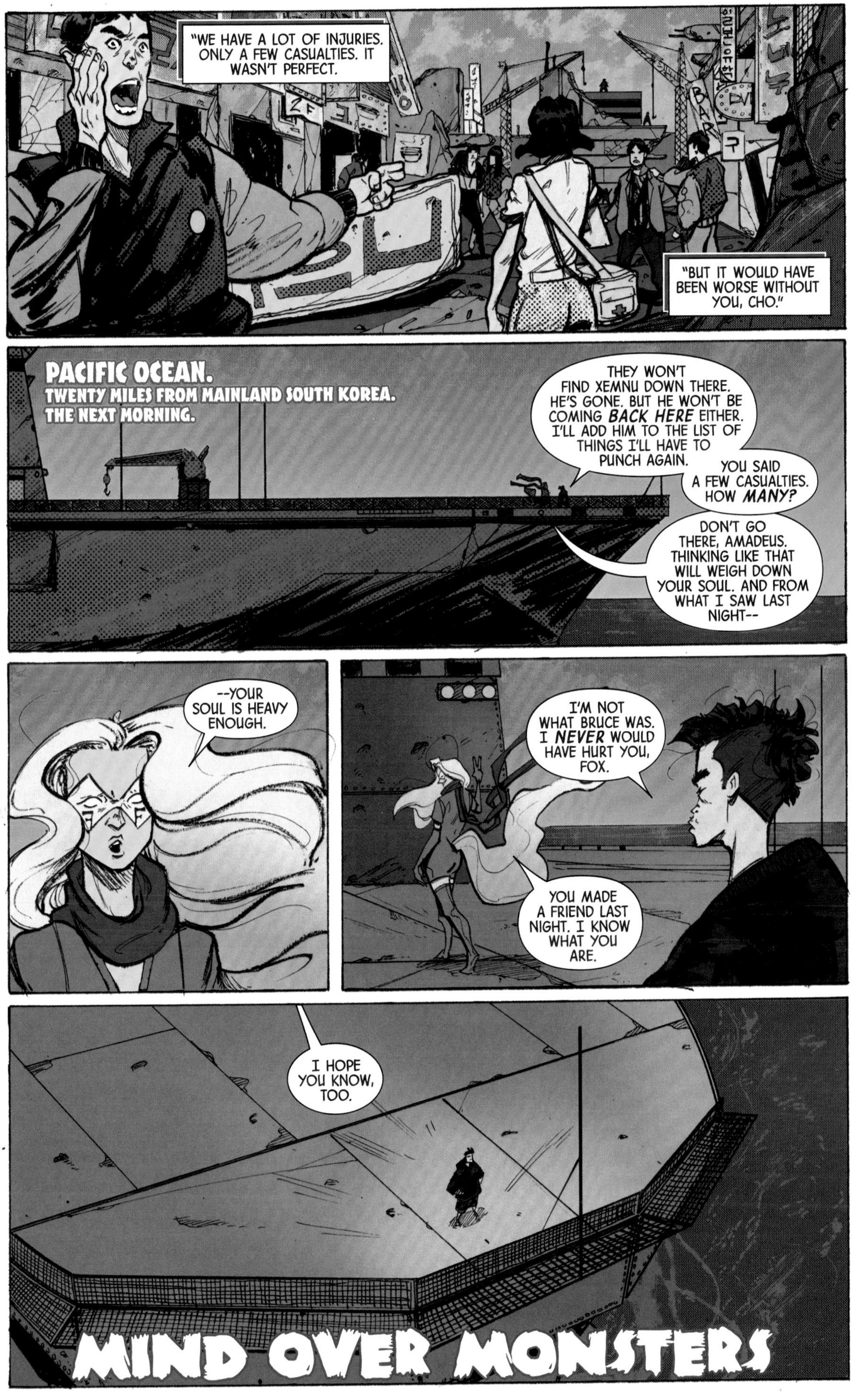
"WE HAVE A LOT OF INJURIES. ONLY A FEW CASUALTIES. IT WASN'T PERFECT.
"BUT IT WOULD HAVE BEEN WORSE WITHOUT YOU, CHO."
PACIFIC OCEAN.
TWENTY MILES FROM MAINLAND SOUTH KOREA.
THE NEXT MORNING.
THEY WON'T FIND XEMNU DOWN THERE. HE'S GONE. BUT HE WON'T BE COMING BACK HERE EITHER. I'LL ADD HIM TO THE LIST OF THINGS I'LL HAVE TO PUNCH AGAIN.
YOU SAID A FEW CASUALTIES. HOW MANY?
DON'T GO THERE, AMADEUS. THINKING LIKE THAT WILL WEIGH DOWN YOUR SOUL. AND FROM WHAT I SAW LAST NIGHT--
--YOUR SOUL IS HEAVY ENOUGH.
I'M NOT WHAT BRUCE WAS. I NEVER WOULD HAVE HURT YOU, FOX.
YOU MADE A FRIEND LAST NIGHT. I KNOW WHAT YOU ARE.
I HOPE YOU KNOW, TOO.
MIND OVER MONSTERS

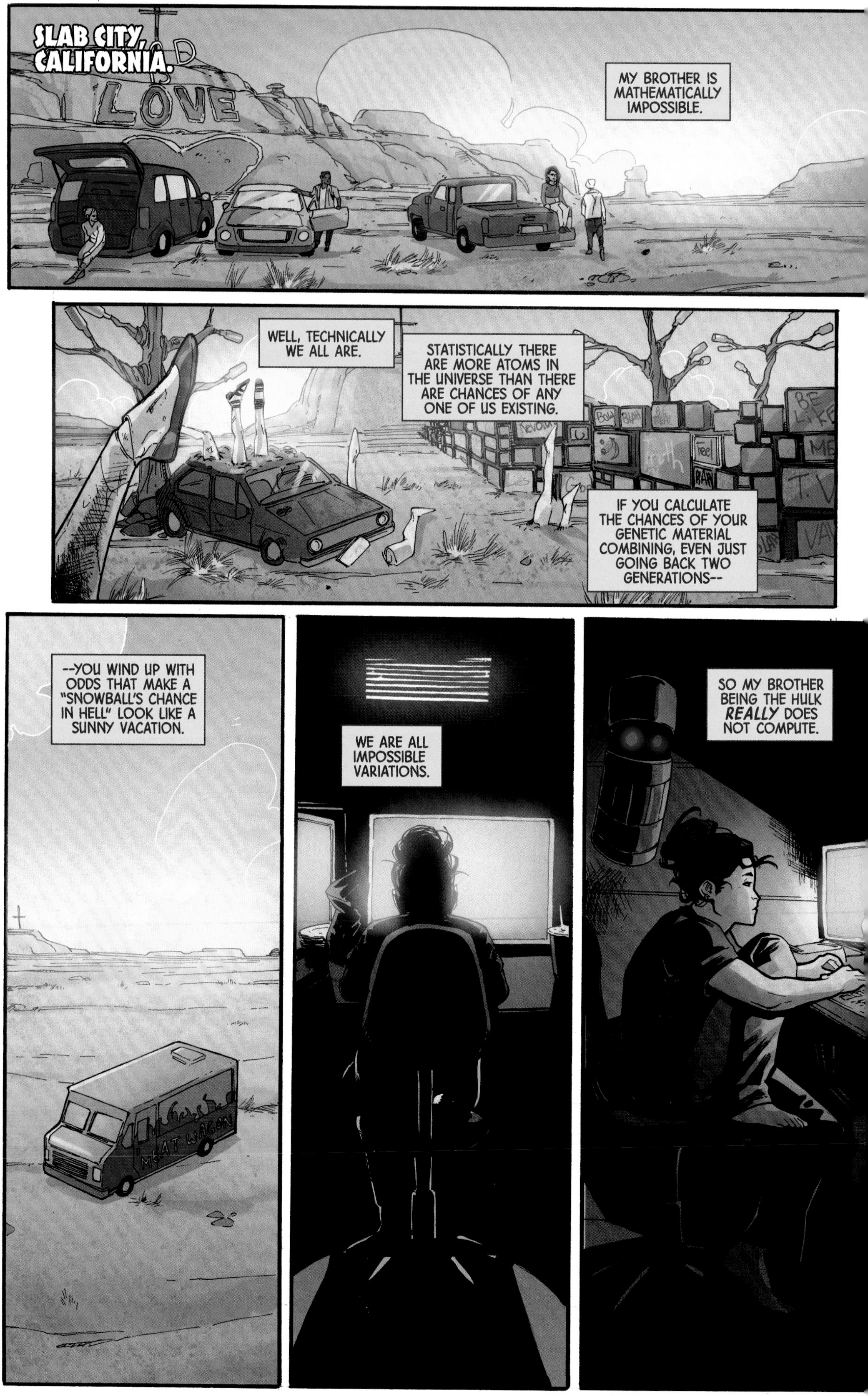

SLAB CITY, CALIFORNIA.
LOVE
MY BROTHER IS MATHEMATICALLY IMPOSSIBLE.
WELL, TECHNICALLY WE ALL ARE.
STATISTICALLY THERE ARE MORE ATOMS IN THE UNIVERSE THAN THERE ARE CHANCES OF ANY ONE OF US EXISTING.
IF YOU CALCULATE THE CHANCES OF YOUR GENETIC MATERIAL COMBINING, EVEN JUST GOING BACK TWO GENERATIONS--
--YOU WIND UP WITH ODDS THAT MAKE A "SNOWBALL'S CHANCE IN HELL" LOOK LIKE A SUNNY VACATION.
MEAT WAGON
WE ARE ALL IMPOSSIBLE VARIATIONS.
SO MY BROTHER BEING THE HULK *REALLY* DOES NOT COMPUTE.

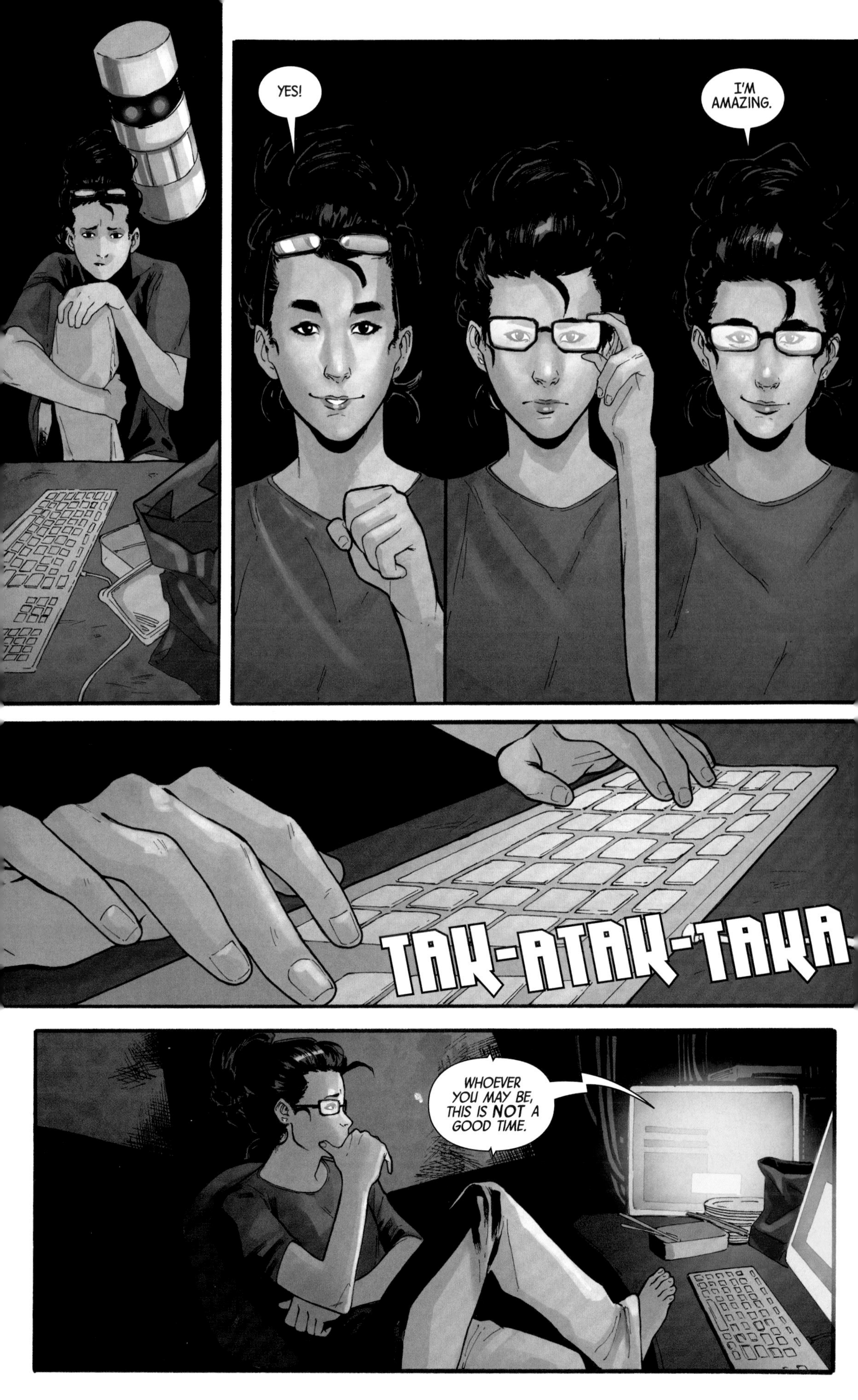
YES!
I'M AMAZING.
TAK-ATAK-TAKA
WHOEVER YOU MAY BE, THIS IS NOT A GOOD TIME.

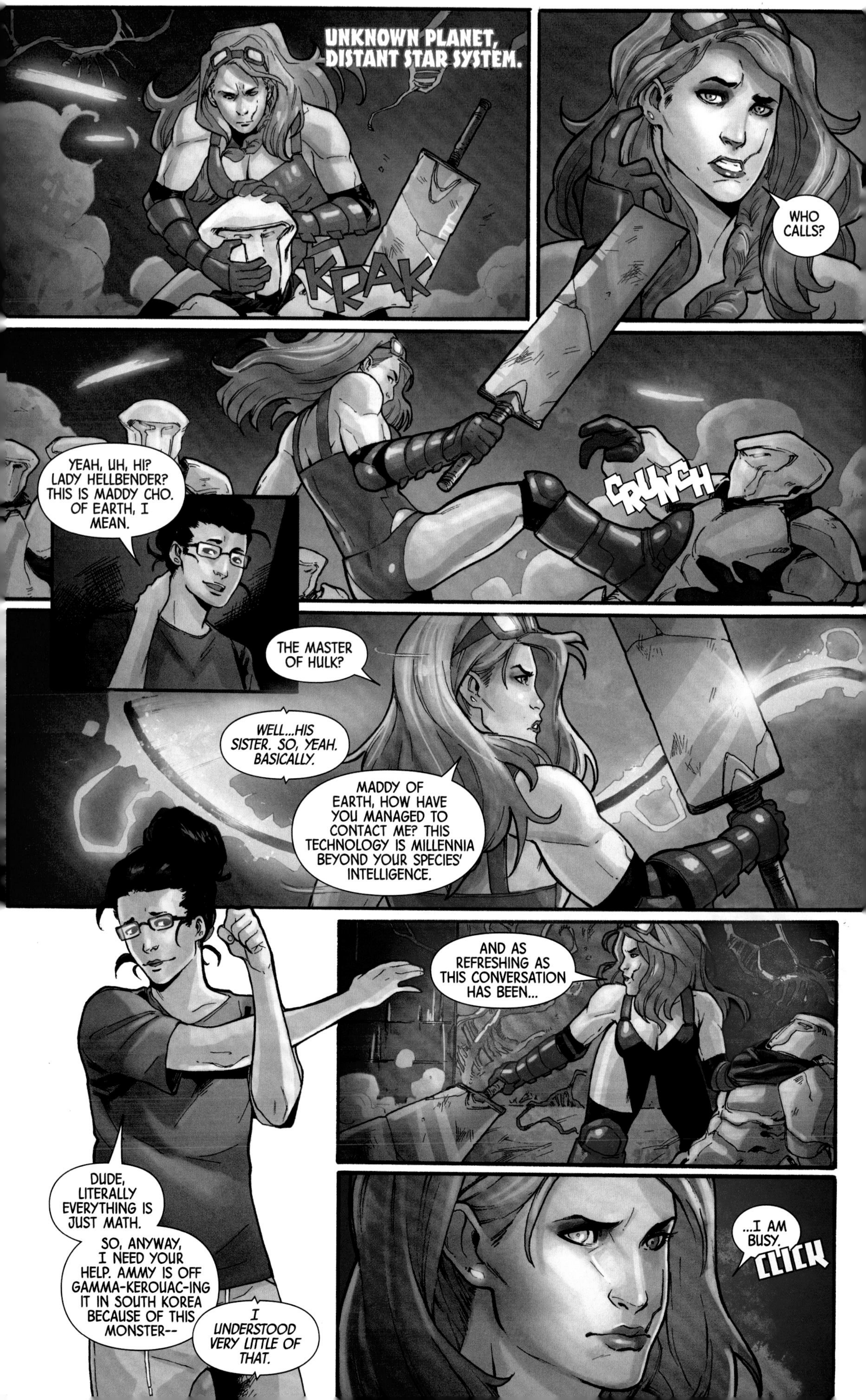
UNKNOWN PLANET, DISTANT STAR SYSTEM.
KRAK
WHO CALLS?
YEAH, UH, HI? LADY HELLBENDER? THIS IS MADDY CHO. OF EARTH, I MEAN.
CRUNCH
THE MASTER OF HULK?
WELL...HIS SISTER. SO, YEAH. BASICALLY.
MADDY OF EARTH, HOW HAVE YOU MANAGED TO CONTACT ME? THIS TECHNOLOGY IS MILLENNIA BEYOND YOUR SPECIES' INTELLIGENCE.
AND AS REFRESHING AS THIS CONVERSATION HAS BEEN...
DUDE, LITERALLY EVERYTHING IS JUST MATH.
SO, ANYWAY, I NEED YOUR HELP. AMMY IS OFF GAMMA-KEROUAC-ING IT IN SOUTH KOREA BECAUSE OF THIS MONSTER--
I UNDERSTOOD VERY LITTLE OF THAT.
...I AM BUSY.
CLICK

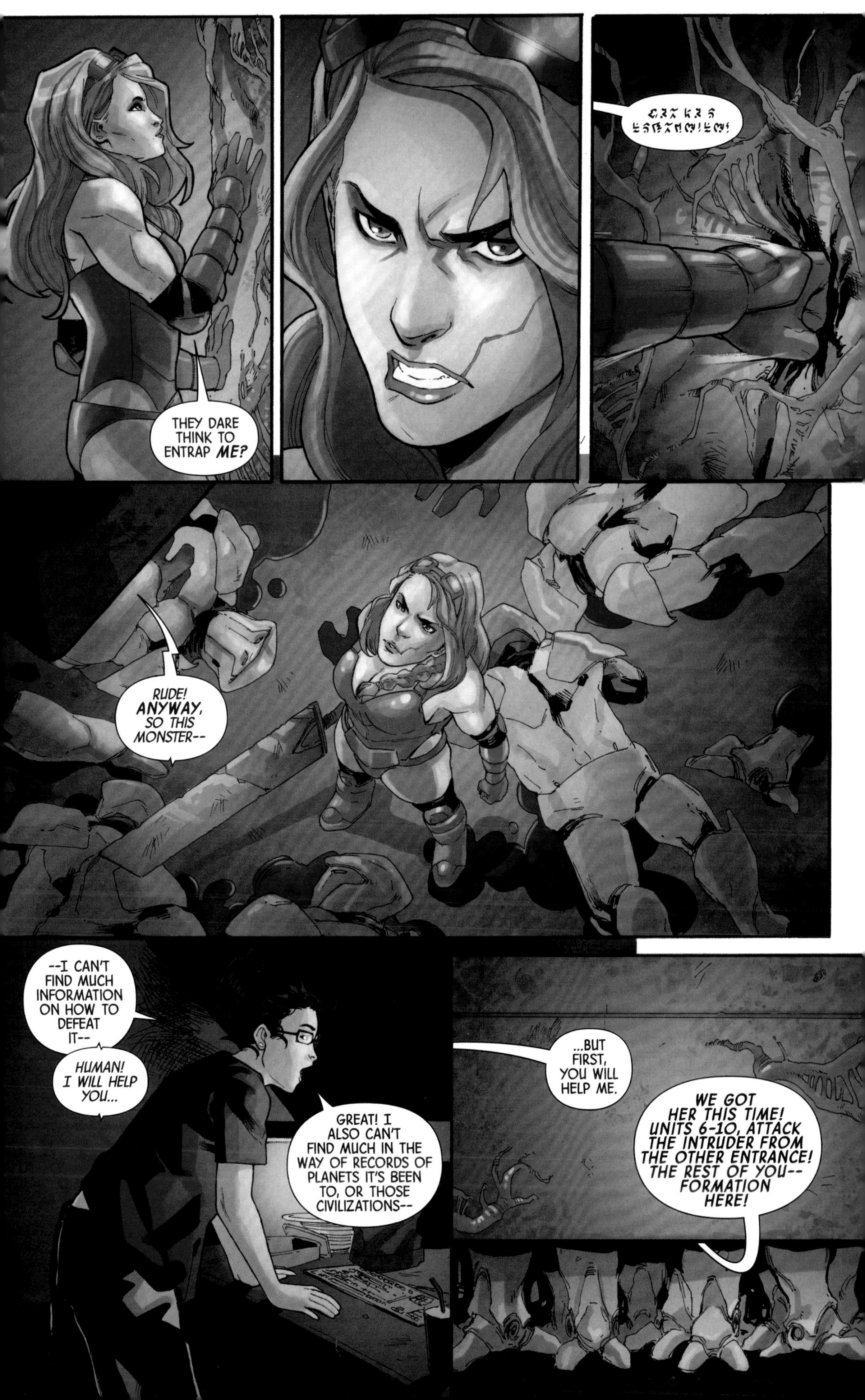
THEY DARE THINK TO ENTRAP ME?
RUDE! ANYWAY, SO THIS MONSTER--
--I CAN'T FIND MUCH INFORMATION ON HOW TO DEFEAT IT--
HUMAN! I WILL HELP YOU...
GREAT! I ALSO CAN'T FIND MUCH IN THE WAY OF RECORDS OF PLANETS IT'S BEEN TO, OR THOSE CIVILIZATIONS--
...BUT FIRST, YOU WILL HELP ME.
WE GOT HER THIS TIME! UNITS 6-10, ATTACK THE INTRUDER FROM THE OTHER ENTRANCE! THE REST OF YOU-- FORMATION HERE!

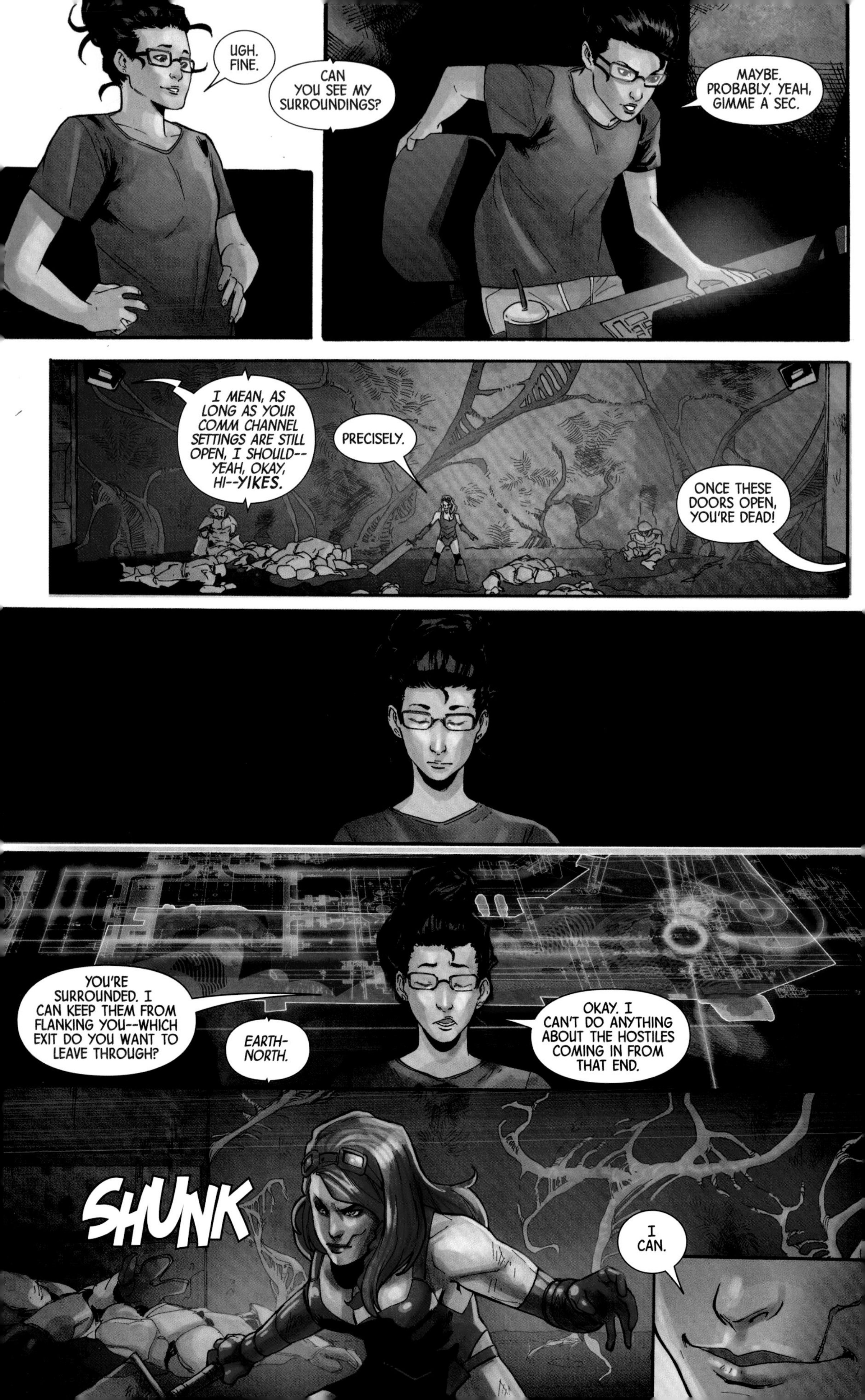
UGH. FINE.
CAN YOU SEE MY SURROUNDINGS?
MAYBE. PROBABLY. YEAH, GIMME A SEC.
I MEAN, AS LONG AS YOUR COMM CHANNEL SETTINGS ARE STILL OPEN, I SHOULD-- YEAH, OKAY, HI--YIKES.
PRECISELY.
ONCE THESE DOORS OPEN, YOU'RE DEAD!
YOU'RE SURROUNDED. I CAN KEEP THEM FROM FLANKING YOU--WHICH EXIT DO YOU WANT TO LEAVE THROUGH?
EARTH-NORTH.
OKAY. I CAN'T DO ANYTHING ABOUT THE HOSTILES COMING IN FROM THAT END.
SHUNK
I CAN.

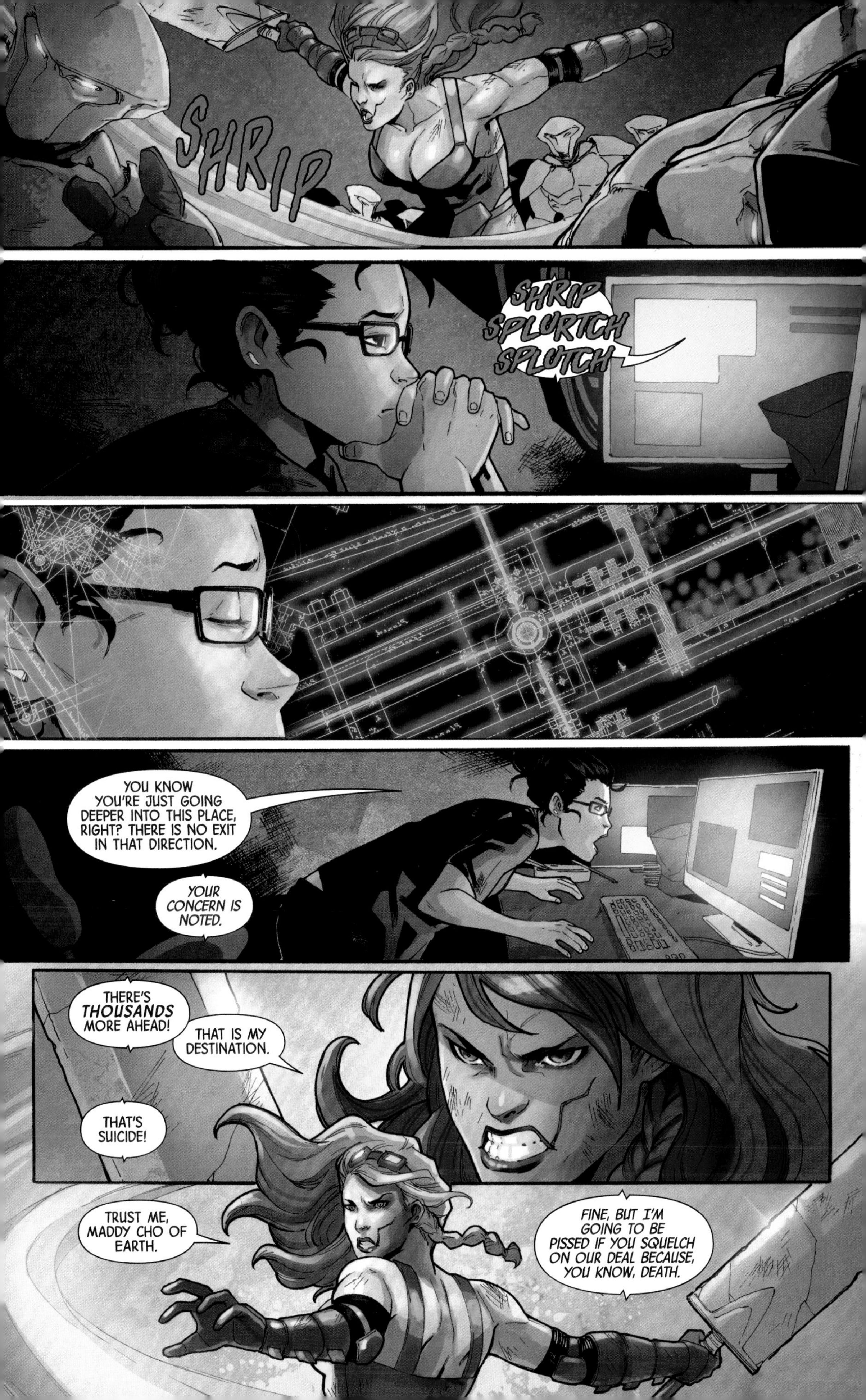
SHRIP
SHRIP SPLURTCH SPLUTCH
YOU KNOW YOU'RE JUST GOING DEEPER INTO THIS PLACE, RIGHT? THERE IS NO EXIT IN THAT DIRECTION.
YOUR CONCERN IS NOTED.
THERE'S *THOUSANDS* MORE AHEAD!
THAT IS MY DESTINATION.
THAT'S SUICIDE!
TRUST ME, MADDY CHO OF EARTH.
FINE, BUT I'M GOING TO BE PISSED IF YOU SQUELCH ON OUR DEAL BECAUSE, YOU KNOW, DEATH.

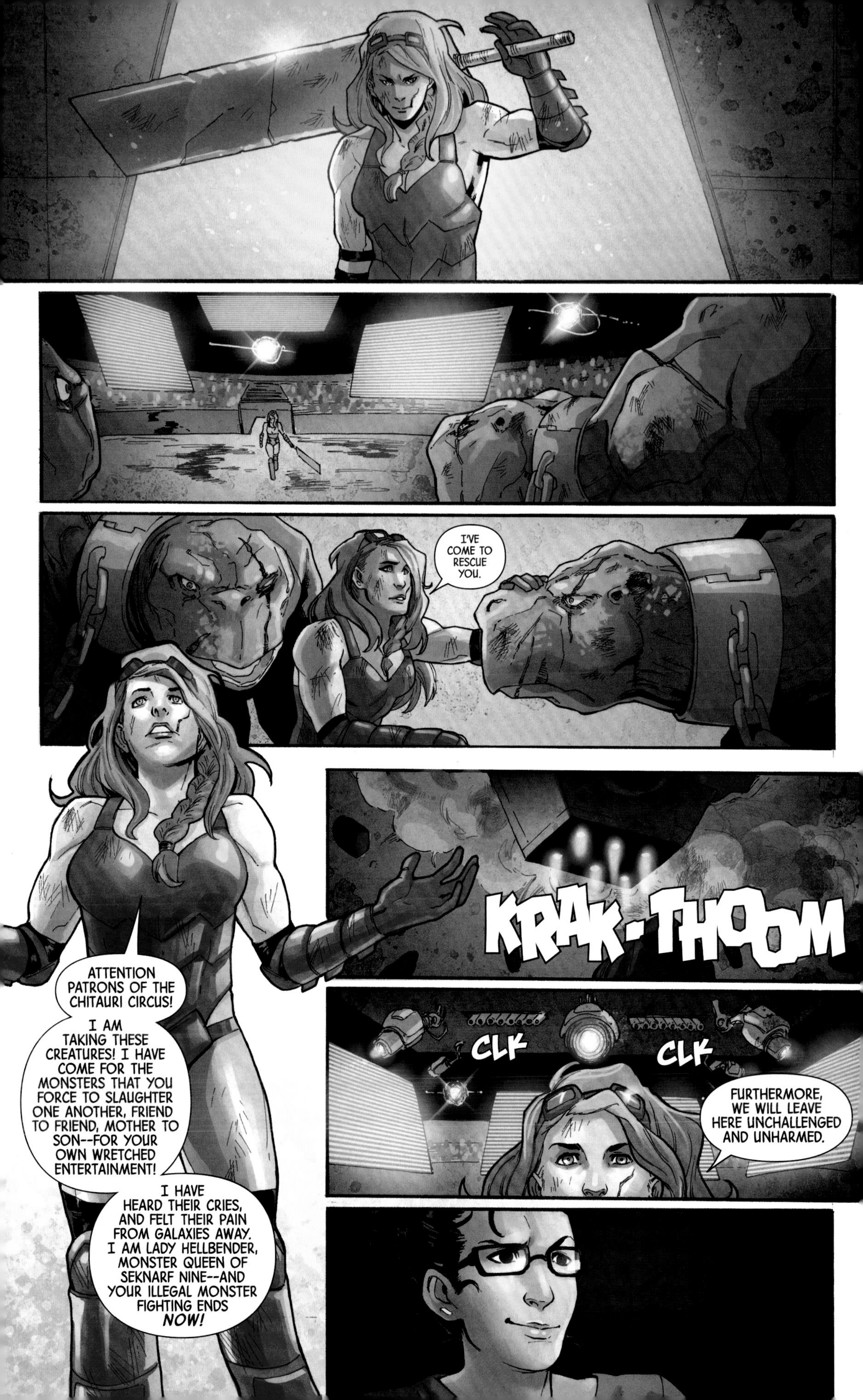
I'VE COME TO RESCUE YOU.
ATTENTION PATRONS OF THE CHITAURI CIRCUS!
I AM TAKING THESE CREATURES! I HAVE COME FOR THE MONSTERS THAT YOU FORCE TO SLAUGHTER ONE ANOTHER, FRIEND TO FRIEND, MOTHER TO SON--FOR YOUR OWN WRETCHED ENTERTAINMENT!
I HAVE HEARD THEIR CRIES, AND FELT THEIR PAIN FROM GALAXIES AWAY. I AM LADY HELLBENDER, MONSTER QUEEN OF SEKNARF NINE--AND YOUR ILLEGAL MONSTER FIGHTING ENDS *NOW!*
KRAK-THOOM
CLK
CLK
FURTHERMORE, WE WILL LEAVE HERE UNCHALLENGED AND UNHARMED.

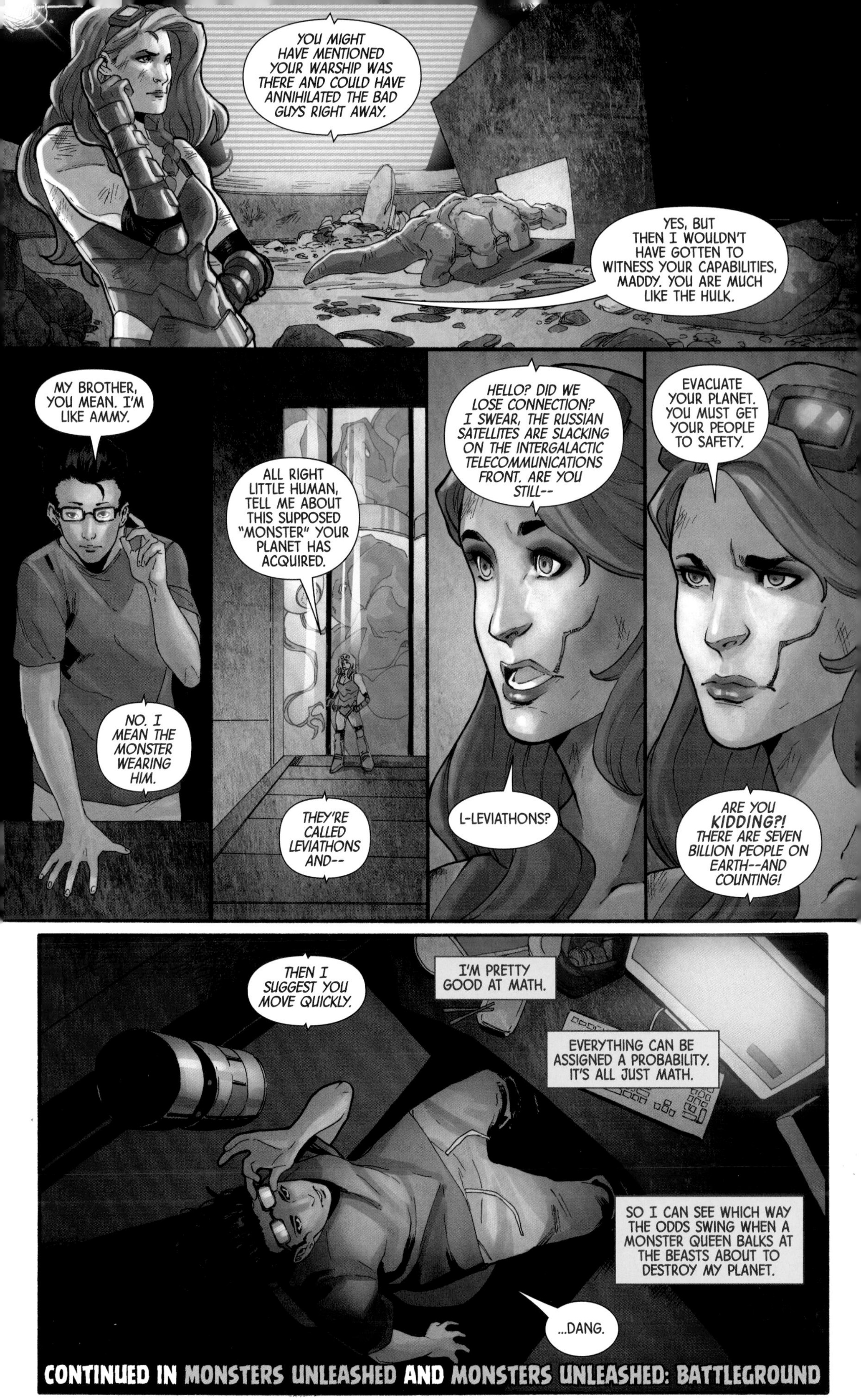

YOU MIGHT HAVE MENTIONED YOUR WARSHIP WAS THERE AND COULD HAVE ANNIHILATED THE BAD GUYS RIGHT AWAY.
YES, BUT THEN I WOULDN'T HAVE GOTTEN TO WITNESS YOUR CAPABILITIES, MADDY. YOU ARE MUCH LIKE THE HULK.
MY BROTHER, YOU MEAN. I'M LIKE AMMY.
NO. I MEAN THE MONSTER WEARING HIM.
ALL RIGHT LITTLE HUMAN, TELL ME ABOUT THIS SUPPOSED "MONSTER" YOUR PLANET HAS ACQUIRED.
THEY'RE CALLED LEVIATHONS AND--
HELLO? DID WE LOSE CONNECTION? I SWEAR, THE RUSSIAN SATELLITES ARE SLACKING ON THE INTERGALACTIC TELECOMMUNICATIONS FRONT. ARE YOU STILL--
L-LEVIATHONS?
EVACUATE YOUR PLANET. YOU MUST GET YOUR PEOPLE TO SAFETY.
ARE YOU KIDDING?! THERE ARE SEVEN BILLION PEOPLE ON EARTH--AND COUNTING!
THEN I SUGGEST YOU MOVE QUICKLY.
I'M PRETTY GOOD AT MATH.
EVERYTHING CAN BE ASSIGNED A PROBABILITY. IT'S ALL JUST MATH.
SO I CAN SEE WHICH WAY THE ODDS SWING WHEN A MONSTER QUEEN BALKS AT THE BEASTS ABOUT TO DESTROY MY PLANET.
...DANG.

CONTINUED IN MONSTERS UNLEASHED AND MONSTERS UNLEASHED: BATTLEGROUND

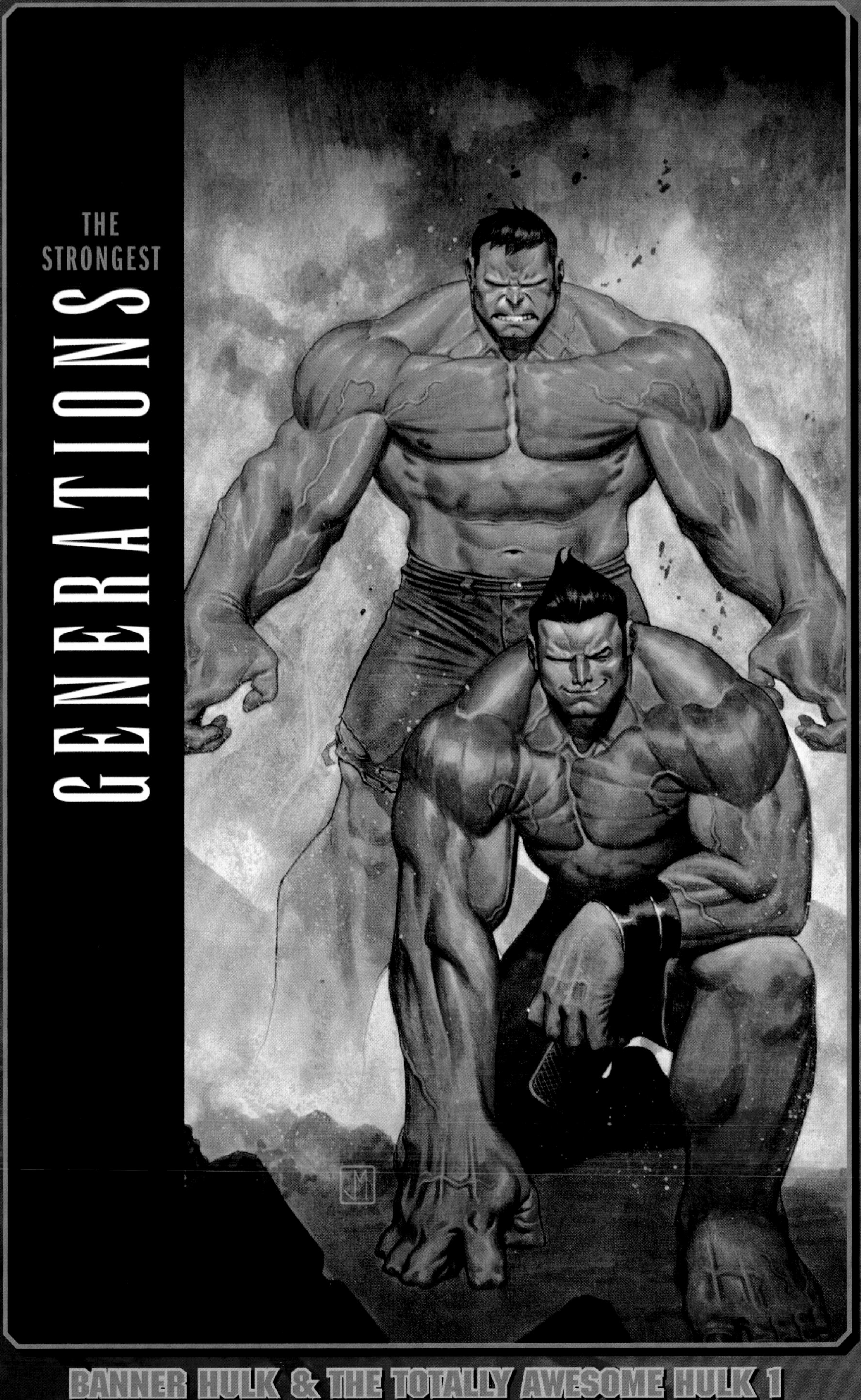
THE STRONGEST
GENERATIONS

BANNER HULK & THE TOTALLY AWESOME HULK 1

THE VANISHING POINT

AN INSTANT APART!

A MOMENT BEYOND!

LOOSED FROM THE SHACKLES OF PAST, PRESENT, FUTURE— A PLACE WHERE TIME HAS NO MEANING!

BUT WHERE TRUE INSIGHT CAN BE GAINED!

MAKE YOUR CHOICE! SELECT YOUR DESTINATION!

THIS JOURNEY IS A GIFT...

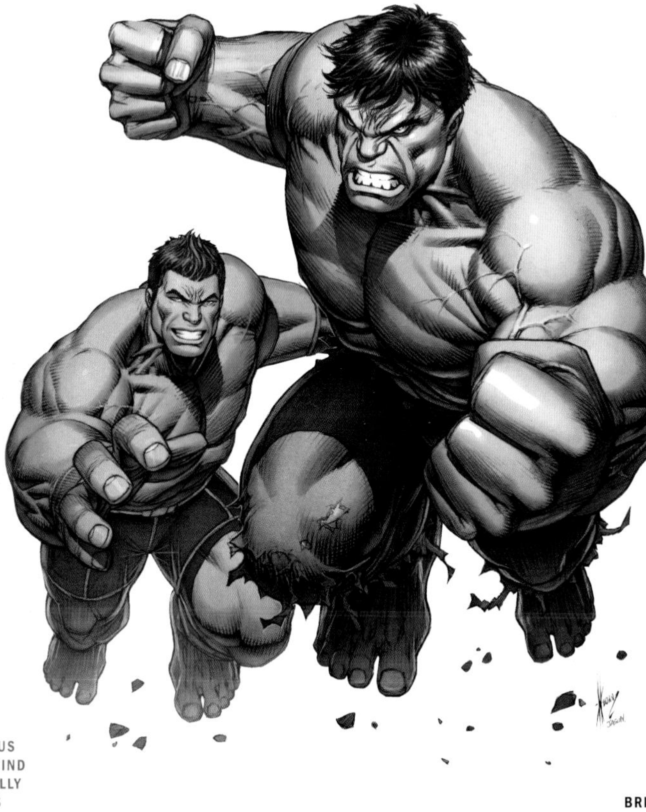

AMADEUS CHO IS A SUPER-GENIUS TEENAGER GIFTED WITH A HYPERMIND THAT ALLOWS HIM TO RUN VIRTUALLY INFINITE CALCULATIONS IN HIS HEAD. USING HIS BRAINS, AMADEUS CREATED SPECIAL NANOBOTS TO CURE BRUCE BANNER AND TAKE ON THE POWERS AND MANTLE OF THE HULK! NOW, WITH INCREDIBLE BRAWN TO MATCH HIS INFINITE BRAINS, AMADEUS DOES GOOD DEEDS ALL OVER THE WORLD.

TOTALLY AWESOME HULK

BRILLIANT GAMMA SCIENTIST BRUCE BANNER CREATED WEAPONS OF MASS DESTRUCTION FOR THE ARMY UNTIL HE WAS THE VICTIM OF ONE OF HIS CREATIONS. EXPOSURE TO HIS GAMMA BOMB MADE BRUCE TRANSFORM INTO THE MONSTROUS HULK WHEN STRESSED. HE SEARCHES FOR SOLITUDE IN THE WORLD TO KEEP THE POWER OF THIS TERRIBLE CURSE OUT OF THE WRONG HANDS.

BANNER HULK

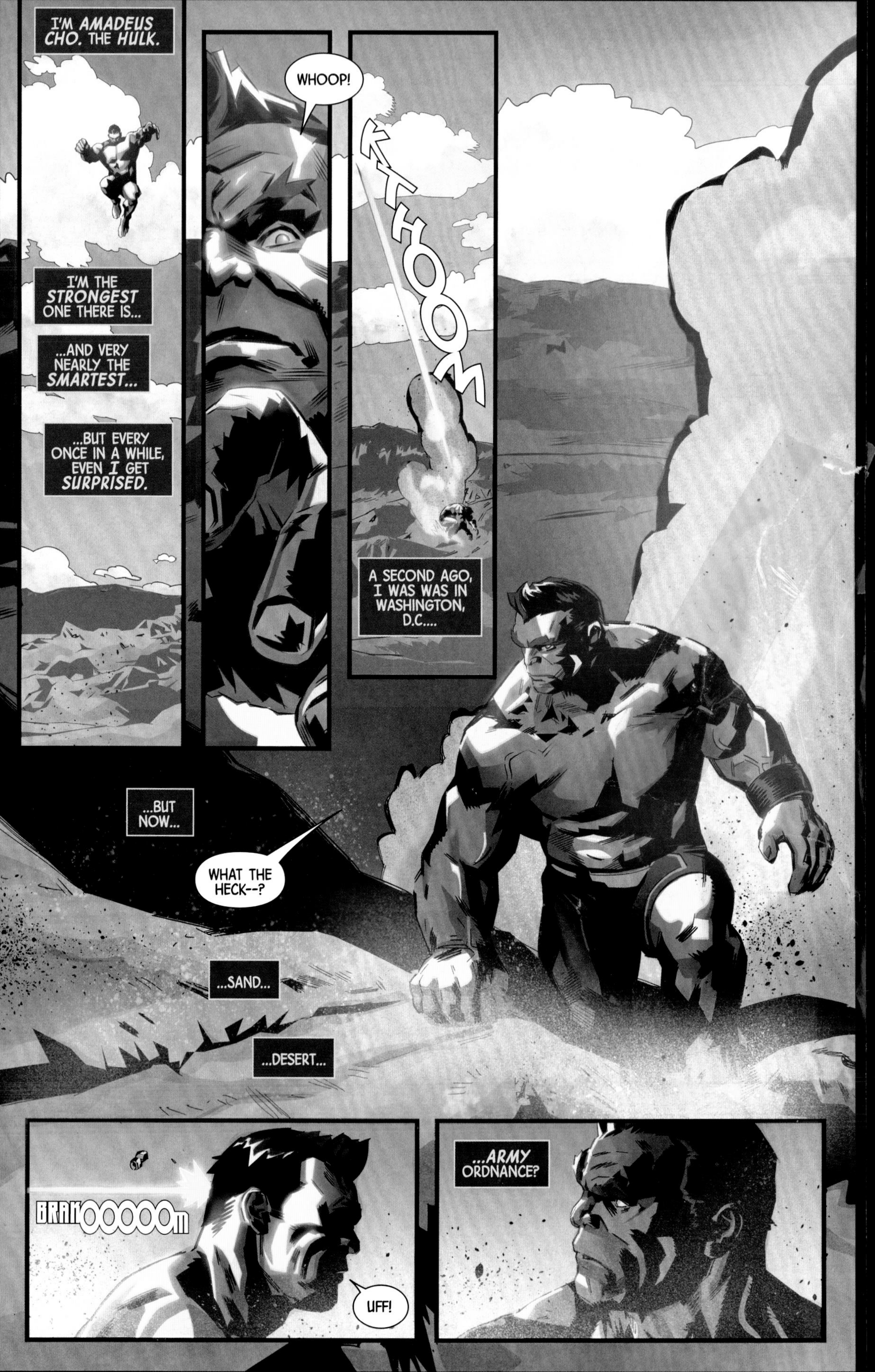

I'M AMADEUS CHO. THE HULK.
I'M THE STRONGEST ONE THERE IS...
...AND VERY NEARLY THE SMARTEST...
...BUT EVERY ONCE IN A WHILE, EVEN I GET SURPRISED.
WHOOP!
KTHOOOM
A SECOND AGO, I WAS WAS IN WASHINGTON, D.C....
...BUT NOW...
WHAT THE HECK--?
...SAND...
...DESERT...
BRAKOOOOOm
UFF!
...ARMY ORDNANCE?

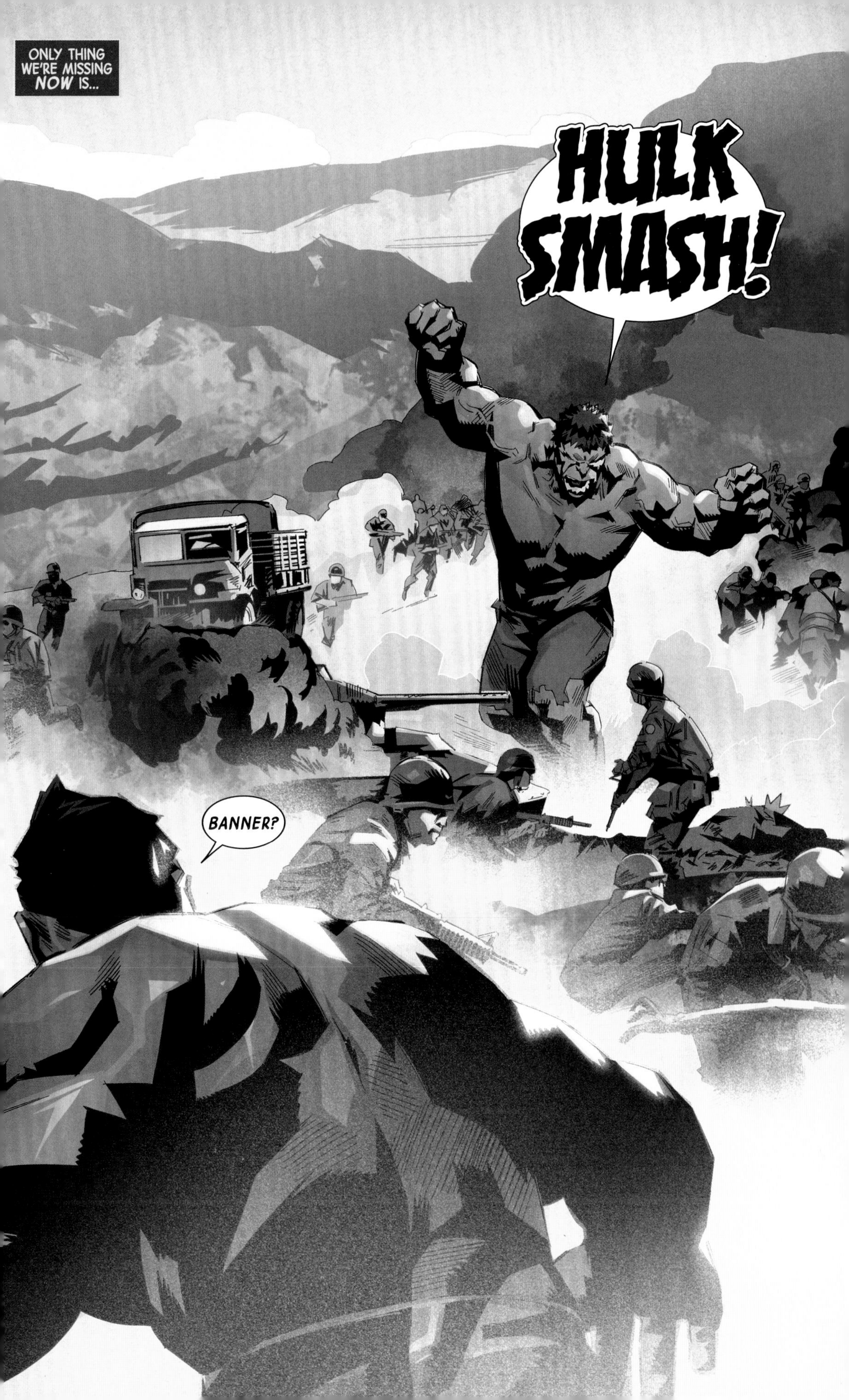
ONLY THING WE'RE MISSING NOW IS...
HULK SMASH!
BANNER?

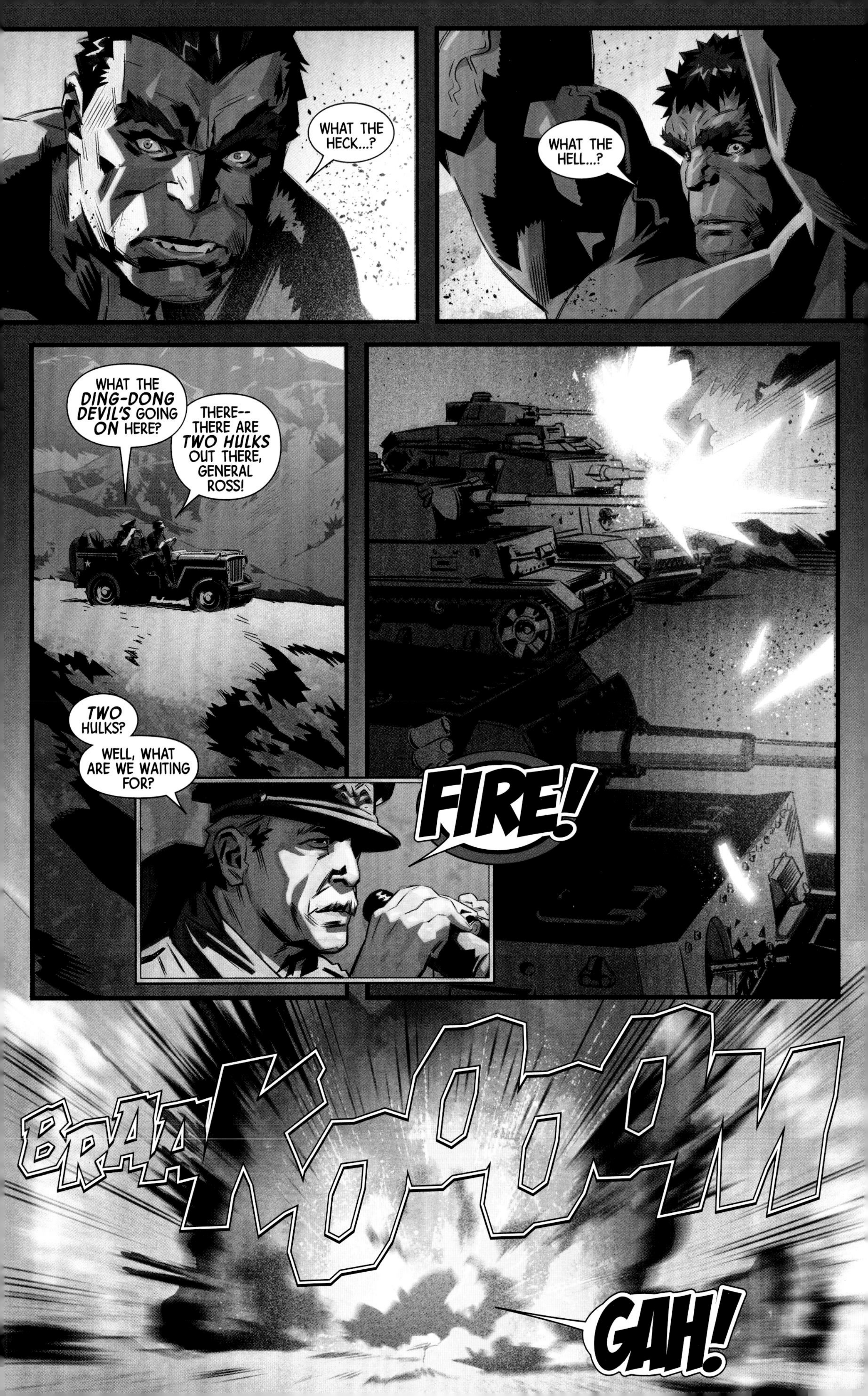
WHAT THE HECK...?
WHAT THE HELL...?
WHAT THE DING-DONG DEVIL'S GOING ON HERE?
THERE-- THERE ARE TWO HULKS OUT THERE, GENERAL ROSS!
TWO HULKS?
WELL, WHAT ARE WE WAITING FOR?
FIRE!
BRAAKOOOOM
GAH!

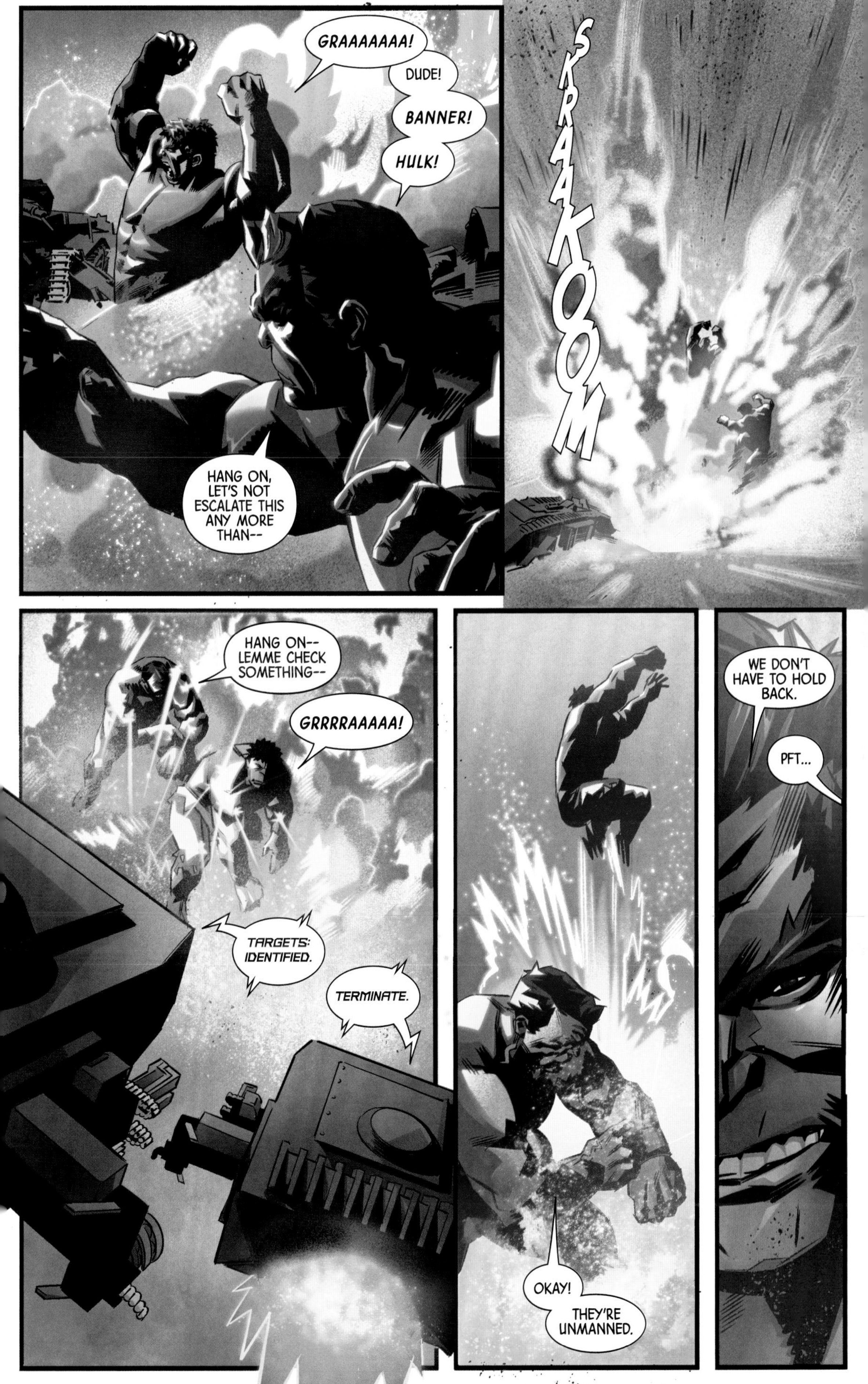
GRAAAAAAA!
DUDE!
BANNER!
HULK!
HANG ON, LET'S NOT ESCALATE THIS ANY MORE THAN--
SKRAAKOOM
HANG ON-- LEMME CHECK SOMETHING--
GRRRRAAAAA!
TARGETS: IDENTIFIED.
TERMINATE.
OKAY!
THEY'RE UNMANNED.
WE DON'T HAVE TO HOLD BACK.
PFT...

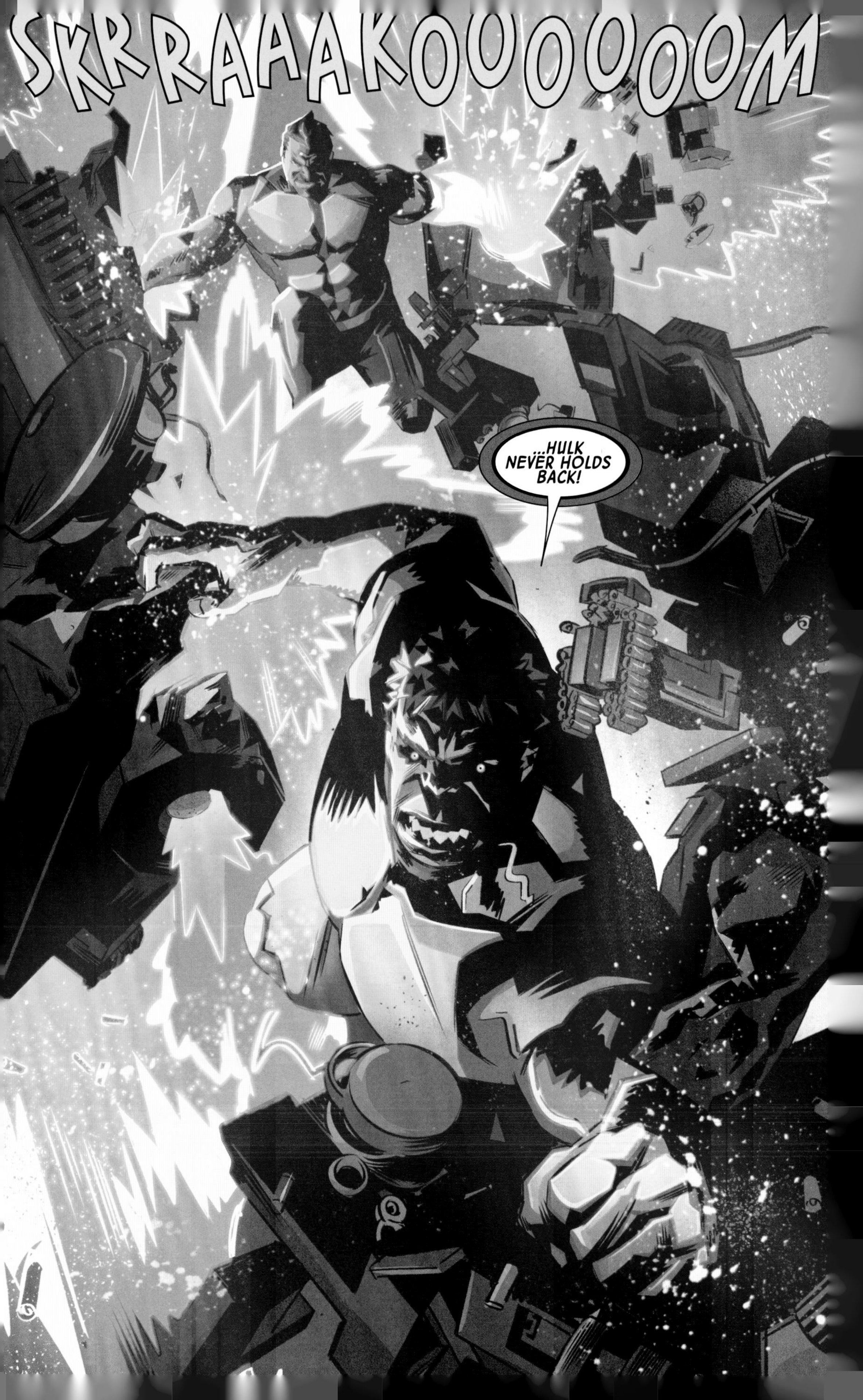
SKRRAAAKOOOOOOM
...HULK NEVER HOLDS BACK!

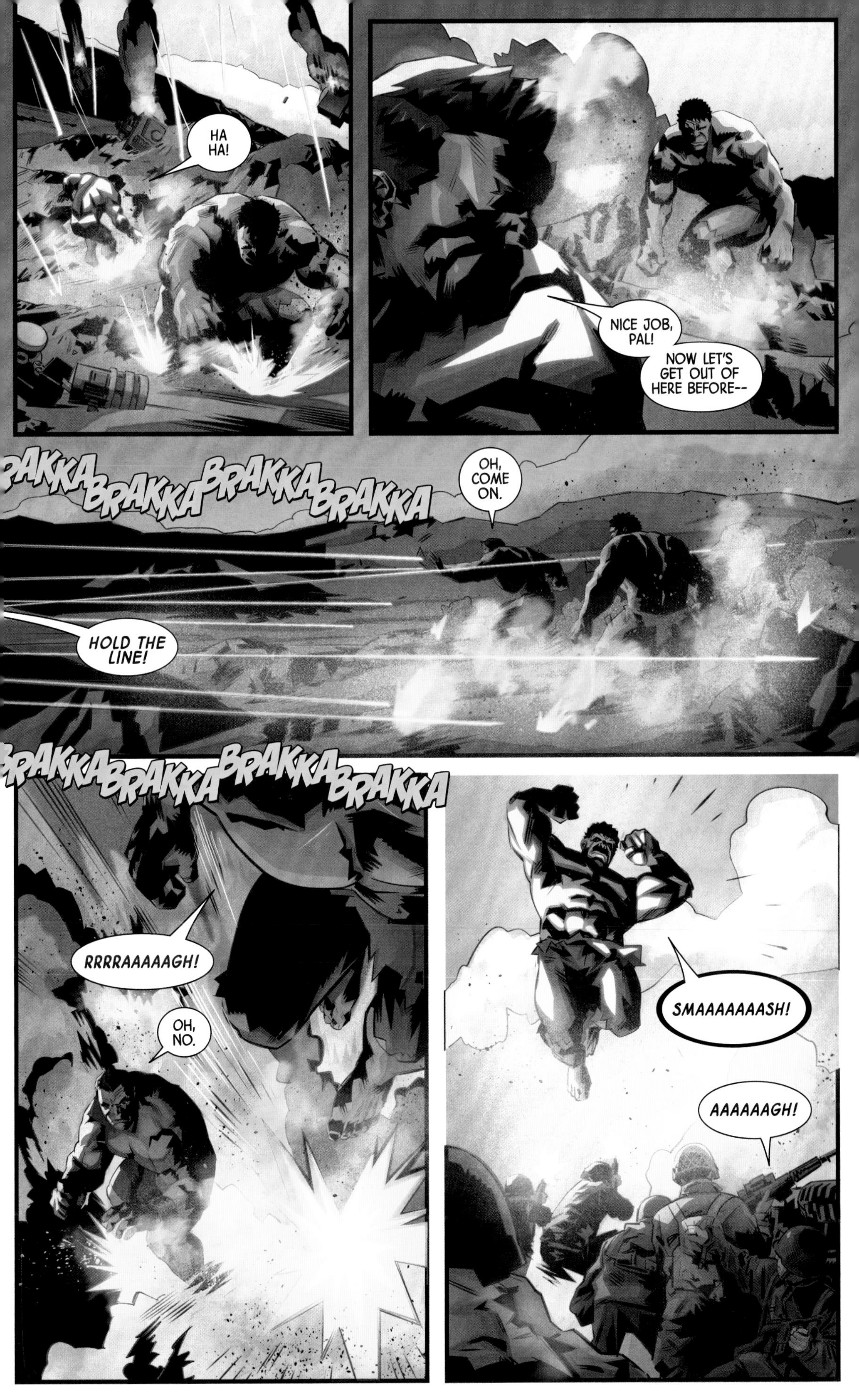
HA HA!
NICE JOB, PAL!
NOW LET'S GET OUT OF HERE BEFORE--
BRAKKA BRAKKA BRAKKA BRAKKA
OH, COME ON.
HOLD THE LINE!
BRAKKA BRAKKA BRAKKA BRAKKA
RRRRAAAAAGH!
OH, NO.
SMAAAAAAASH!
AAAAAAGH!

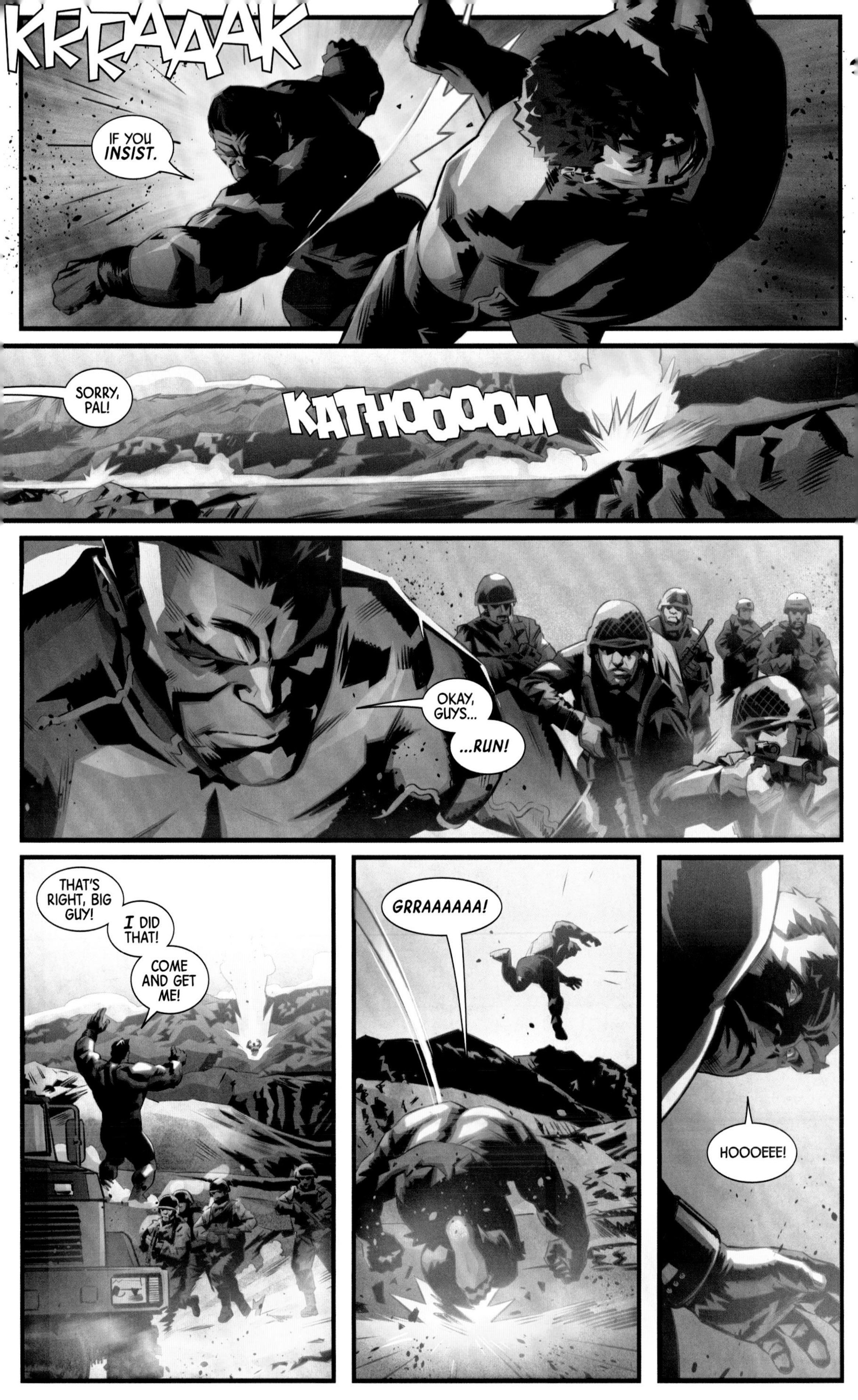
KRRAAAK
IF YOU INSIST.
SORRY, PAL!
KATHOOOOM
OKAY, GUYS...
...RUN!
THAT'S RIGHT, BIG GUY!
I DID THAT!
COME AND GET ME!
GRRAAAAAAA!
HOOOEEE!

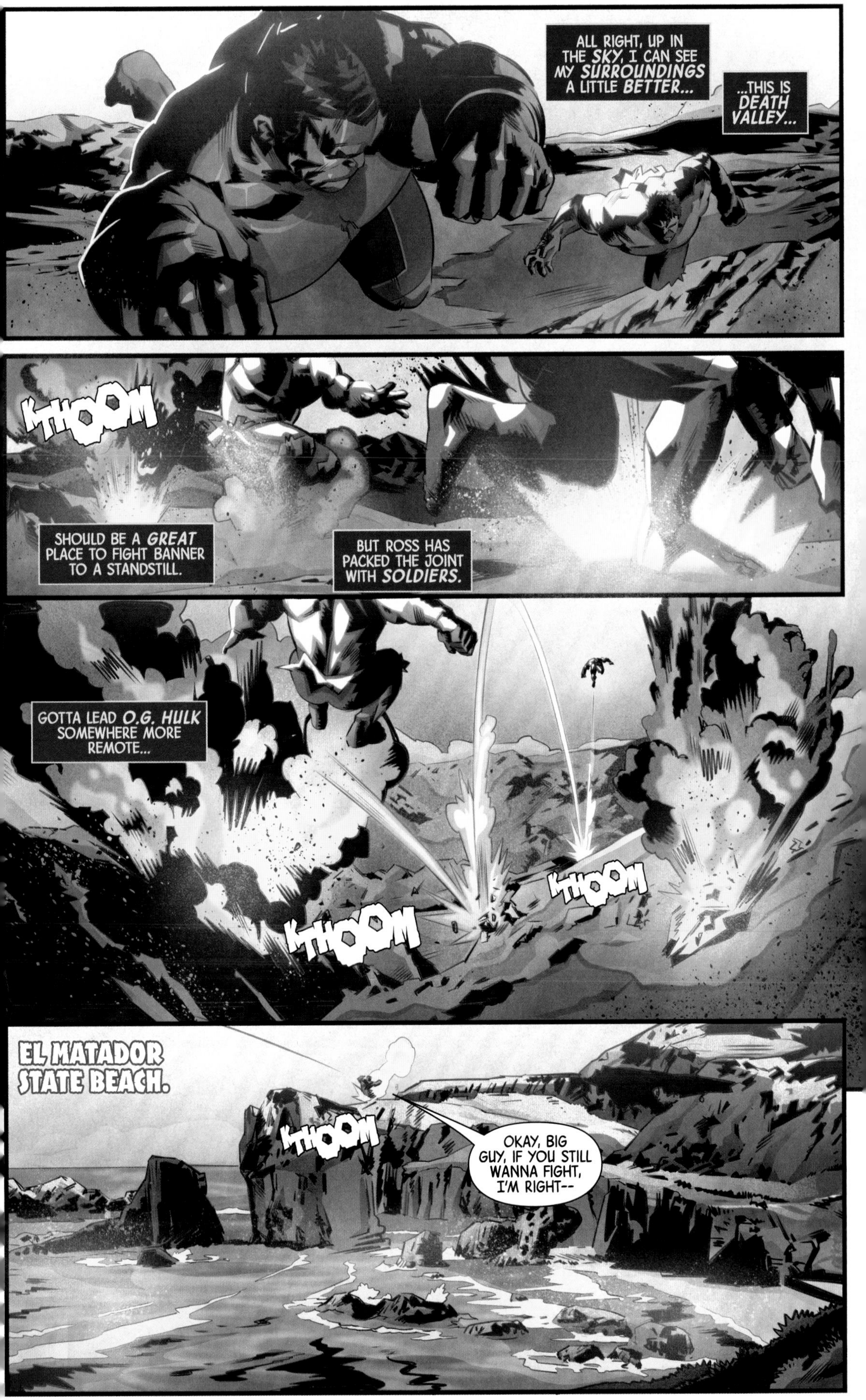
ALL RIGHT, UP IN THE SKY, I CAN SEE MY SURROUNDINGS A LITTLE BETTER...
...THIS IS DEATH VALLEY...
KTHOOM
SHOULD BE A GREAT PLACE TO FIGHT BANNER TO A STANDSTILL.
BUT ROSS HAS PACKED THE JOINT WITH SOLDIERS.
GOTTA LEAD O.G. HULK SOMEWHERE MORE REMOTE...
KTHOOM
KTHOOM
EL MATADOR STATE BEACH.
KTHOOM
OKAY, BIG GUY, IF YOU STILL WANNA FIGHT, I'M RIGHT--

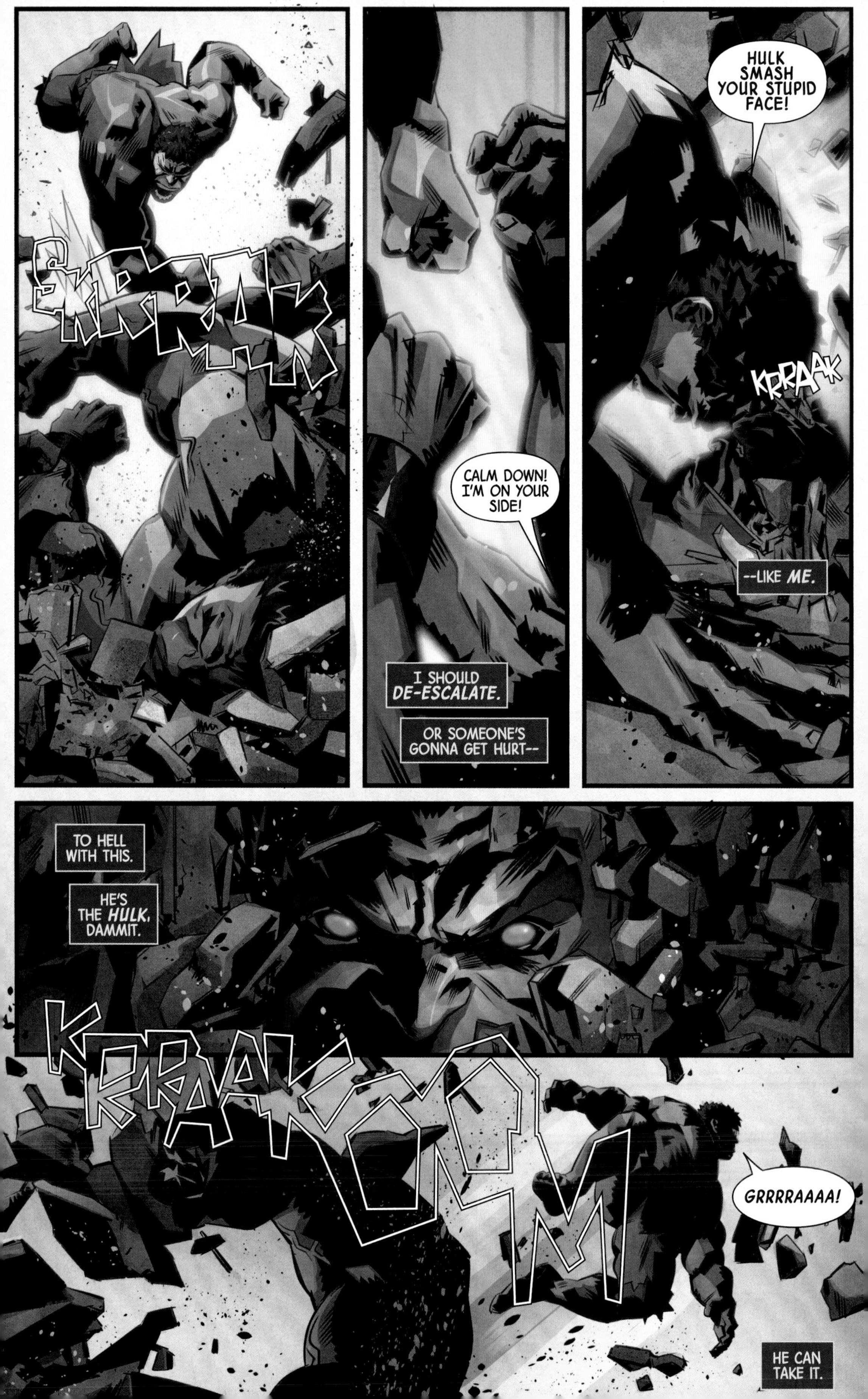
SKRAKK
CALM DOWN! I'M ON YOUR SIDE!
I SHOULD DE-ESCALATE.
OR SOMEONE'S GONNA GET HURT--
HULK SMASH YOUR STUPID FACE!
KRRAAK
--LIKE ME.
TO HELL WITH THIS.
HE'S THE HULK, DAMMIT.
KRRAAKOOM
GRRRRAAAA!
HE CAN TAKE IT.

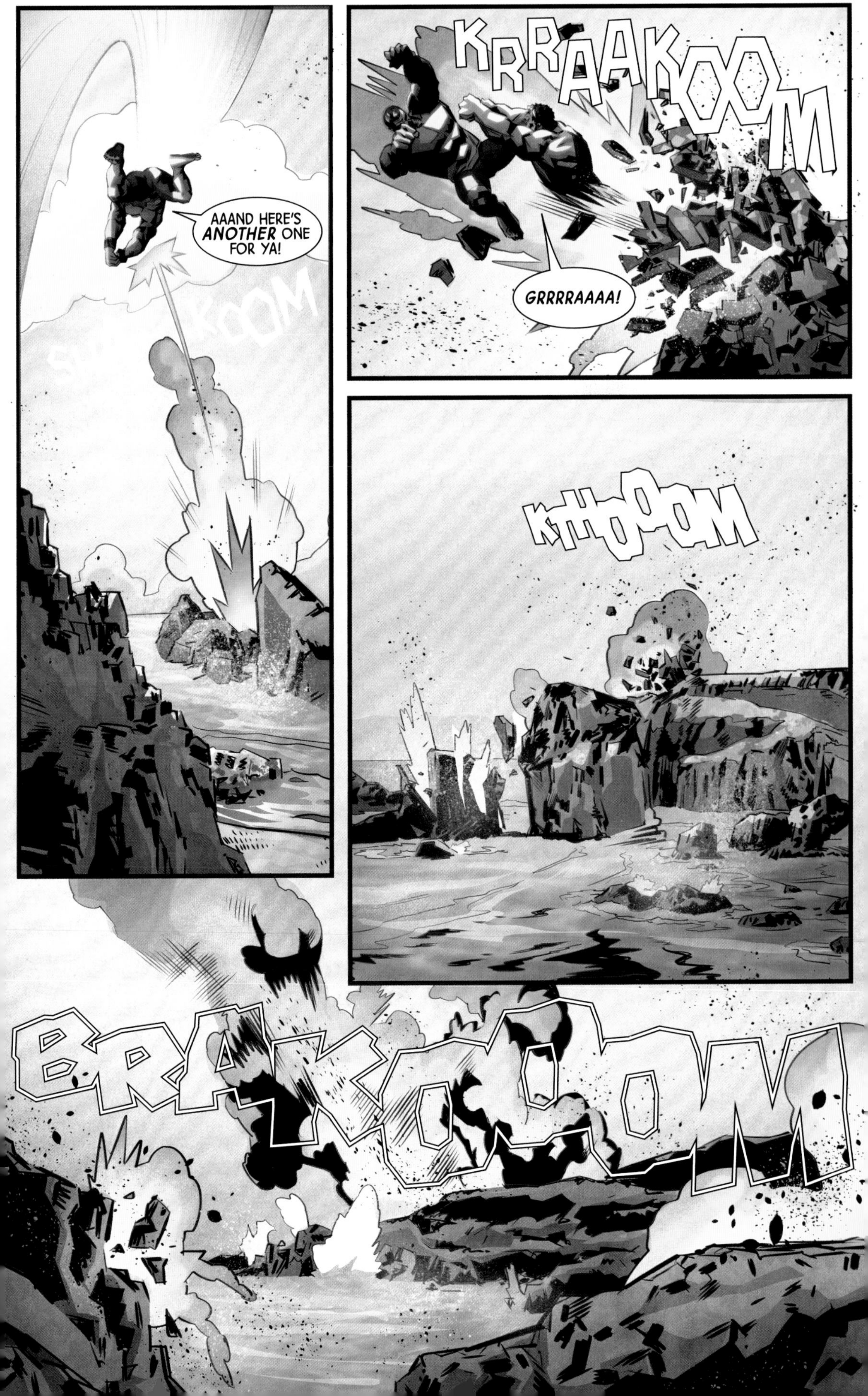
AAAND HERE'S *ANOTHER* ONE FOR YA!
KRRAAKOOOM
GRRRRAAAA!
KTHOOOM
BRAKOOOM

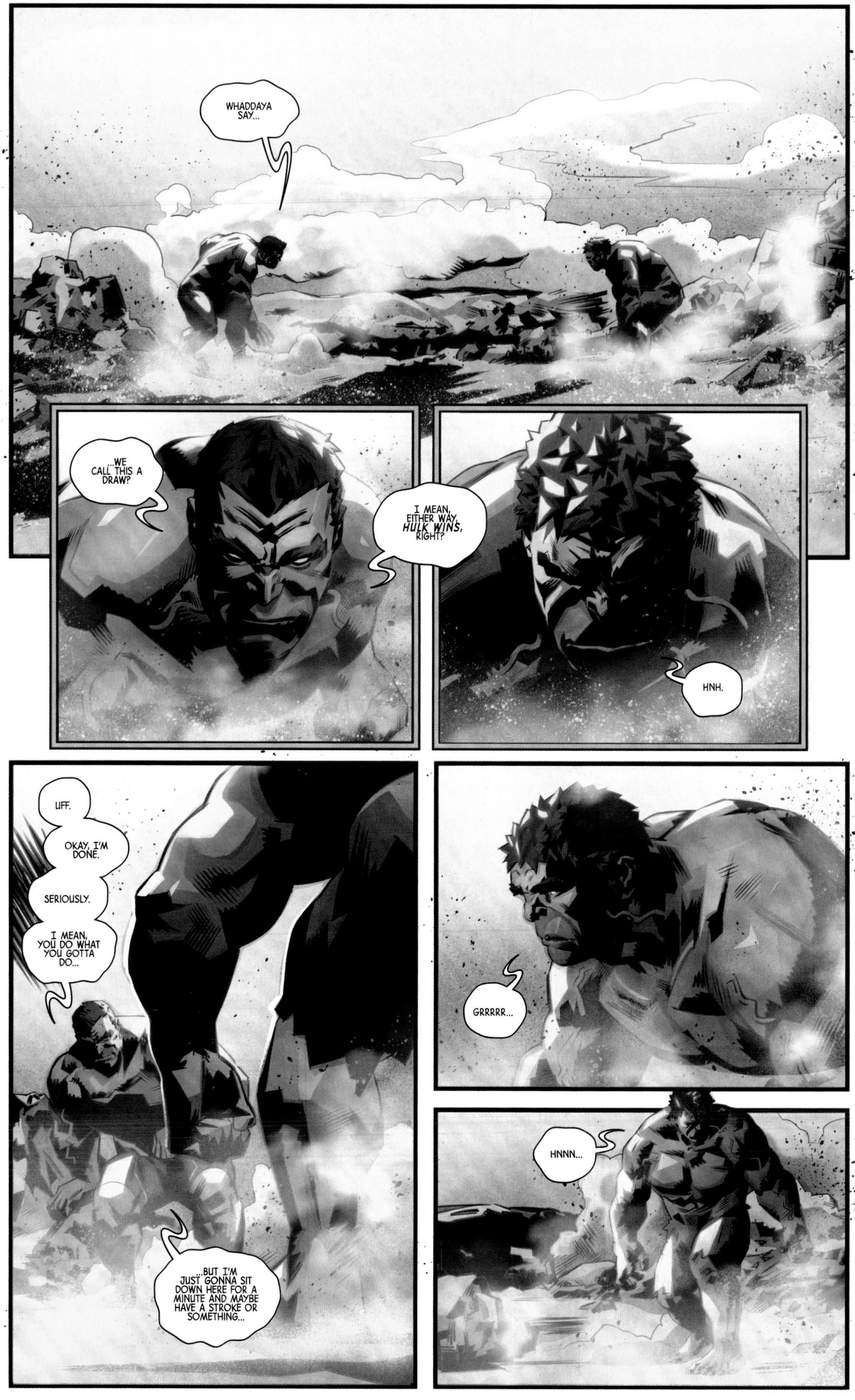
WHADDAYA SAY...
...WE CALL THIS A DRAW?
I MEAN, EITHER WAY, HULK WINS, RIGHT?
HNH.
UFF.
OKAY, I'M DONE.
SERIOUSLY.
I MEAN, YOU DO WHAT YOU GOTTA DO...
...BUT I'M JUST GONNA SIT DOWN HERE FOR A MINUTE AND MAYBE HAVE A STROKE OR SOMETHING...
GRRRRR...
HNNN...

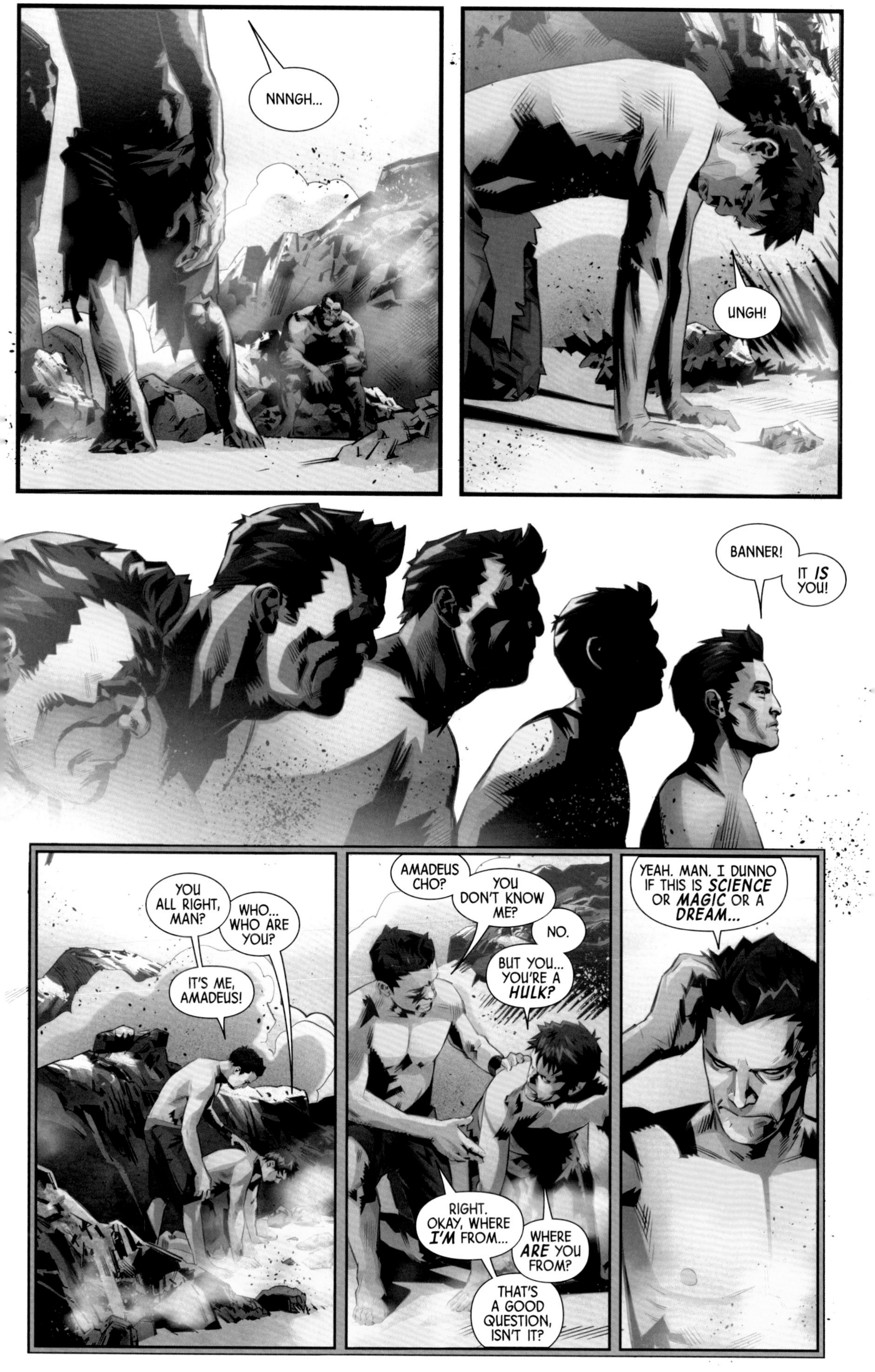
NNNGH...
UNGH!
BANNER!
IT IS YOU!
YOU ALL RIGHT, MAN?
WHO... WHO ARE YOU?
IT'S ME, AMADEUS!
AMADEUS CHO?
YOU DON'T KNOW ME?
NO.
BUT YOU... YOU'RE A HULK?
RIGHT. OKAY, WHERE I'M FROM...
WHERE ARE YOU FROM?
THAT'S A GOOD QUESTION, ISN'T IT?
YEAH. MAN. I DUNNO IF THIS IS SCIENCE OR MAGIC OR A DREAM...

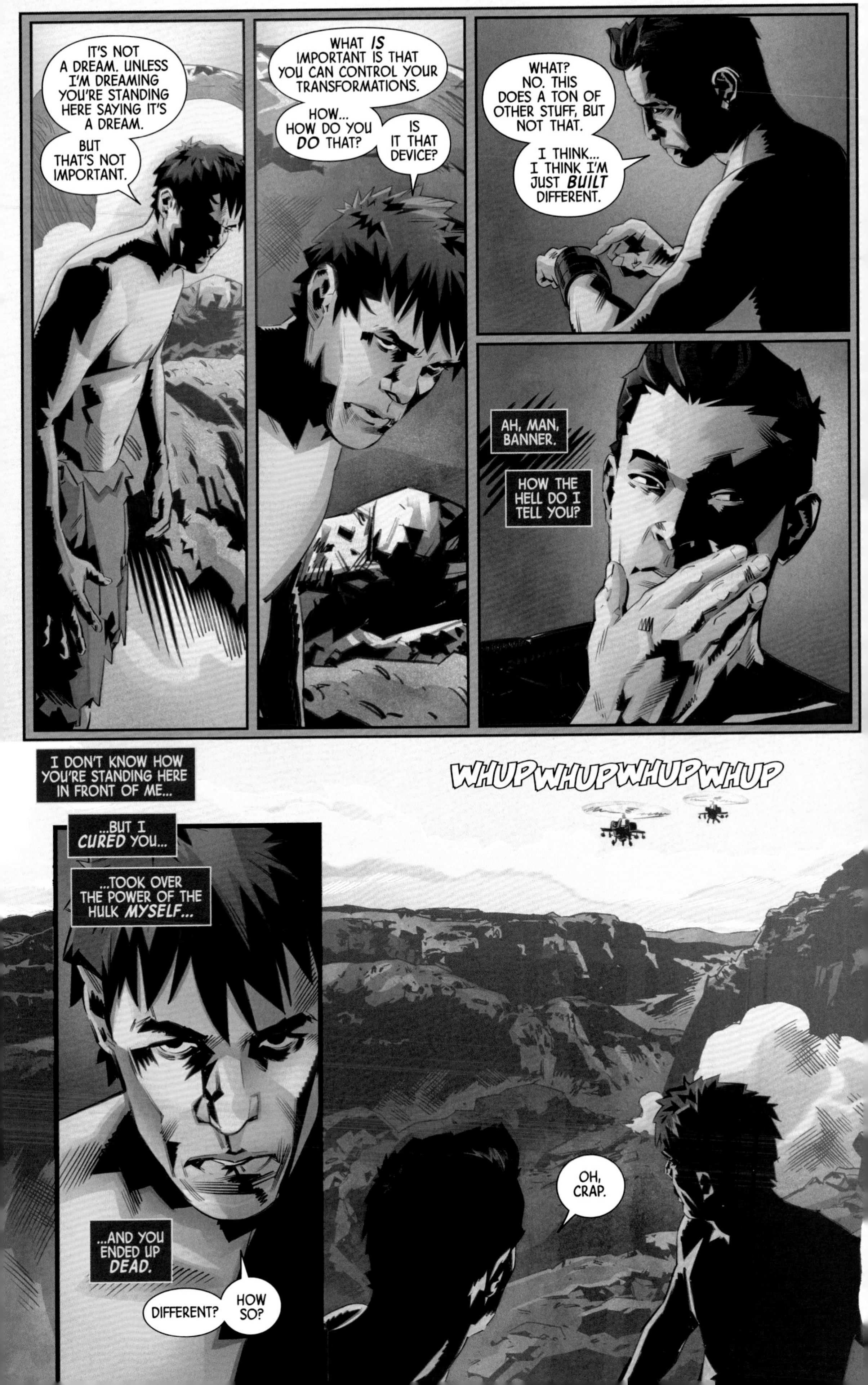
IT'S NOT A DREAM. UNLESS I'M DREAMING YOU'RE STANDING HERE SAYING IT'S A DREAM.
BUT THAT'S NOT IMPORTANT.
WHAT IS IMPORTANT IS THAT YOU CAN CONTROL YOUR TRANSFORMATIONS.
HOW... HOW DO YOU DO THAT?
IS IT THAT DEVICE?
WHAT? NO. THIS DOES A TON OF OTHER STUFF, BUT NOT THAT.
I THINK... I THINK I'M JUST BUILT DIFFERENT.
AH, MAN, BANNER.
HOW THE HELL DO I TELL YOU?
I DON'T KNOW HOW YOU'RE STANDING HERE IN FRONT OF ME...
...BUT I CURED YOU...
...TOOK OVER THE POWER OF THE HULK MYSELF...
...AND YOU ENDED UP DEAD.
DIFFERENT?
HOW SO?
WHUPWHUPWHUPWHUP
OH, CRAP.

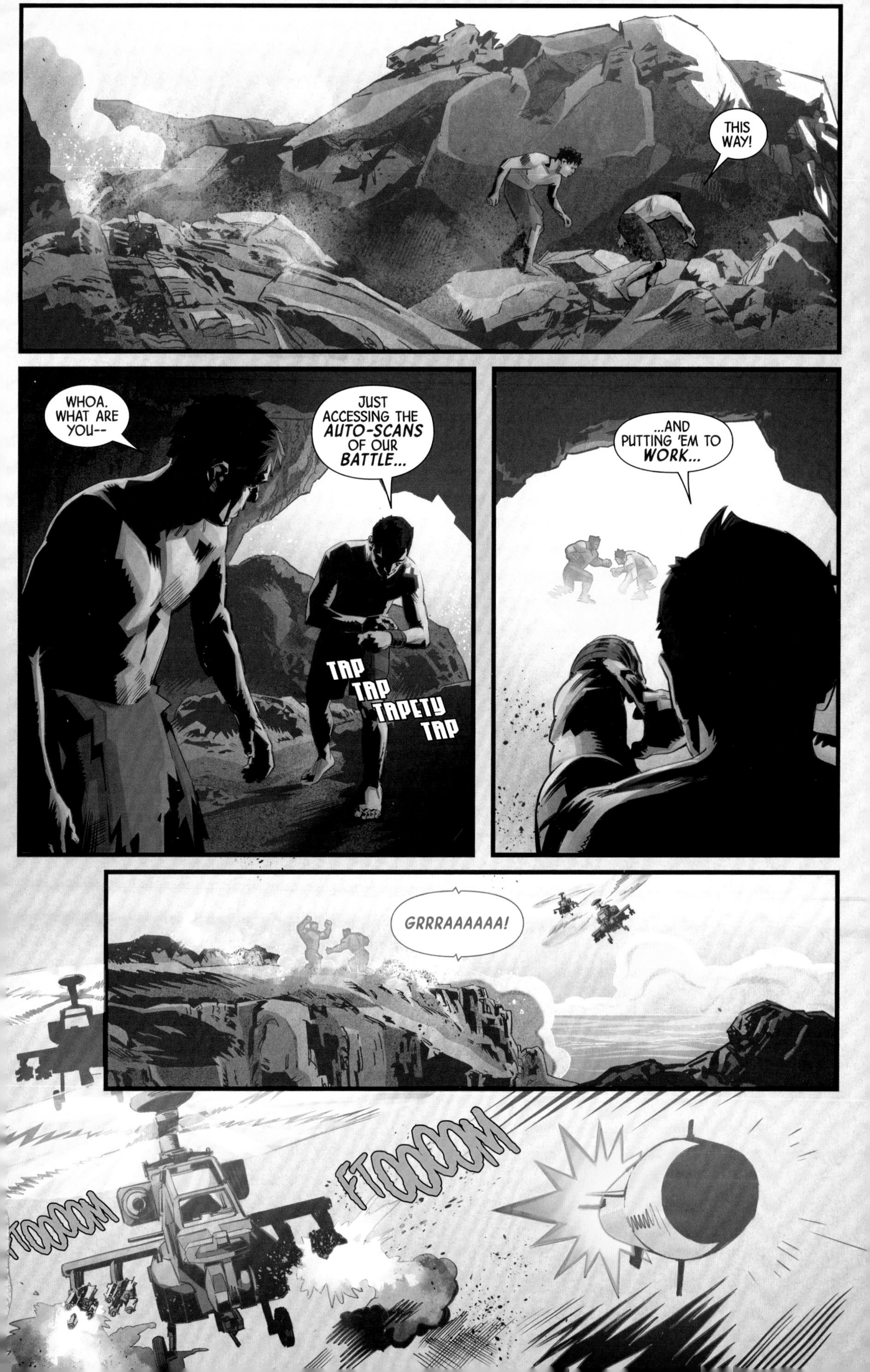
THIS WAY!
WHOA. WHAT ARE YOU--
JUST ACCESSING THE AUTO-SCANS OF OUR BATTLE...
TAP TAP TAPETY TAP
...AND PUTTING 'EM TO WORK...
GRRRAAAAAA!
FTOOOOM
FTOOOOM

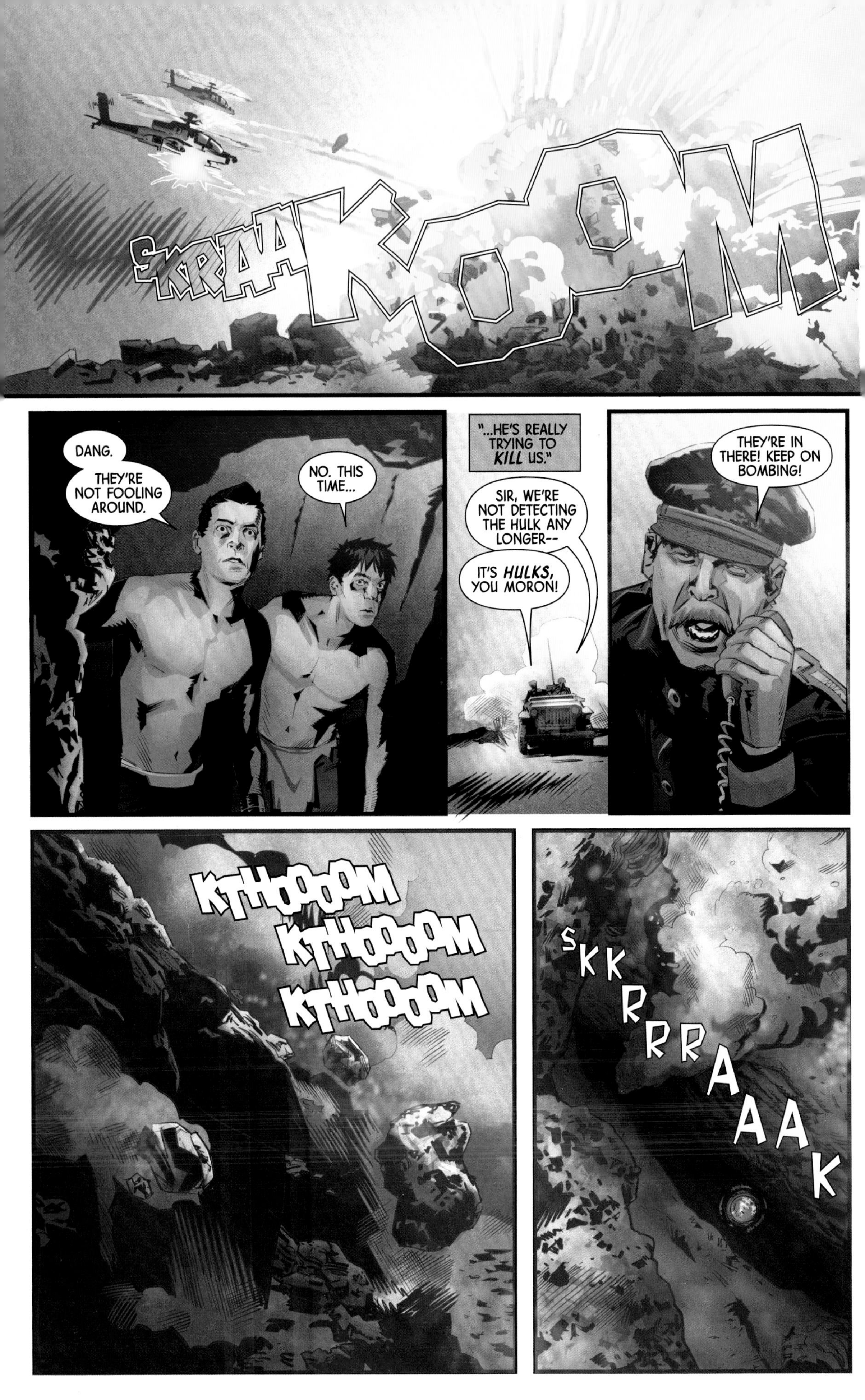
SKRAAKOOOM
DANG.
THEY'RE NOT FOOLING AROUND.
NO. THIS TIME...
"...HE'S REALLY TRYING TO KILL US."
SIR, WE'RE NOT DETECTING THE HULK ANY LONGER--
IT'S HULKS, YOU MORON!
THEY'RE IN THERE! KEEP ON BOMBING!
KTHOOOOM
KTHOOOOM
KTHOOOOM
SKKRRRAAAK

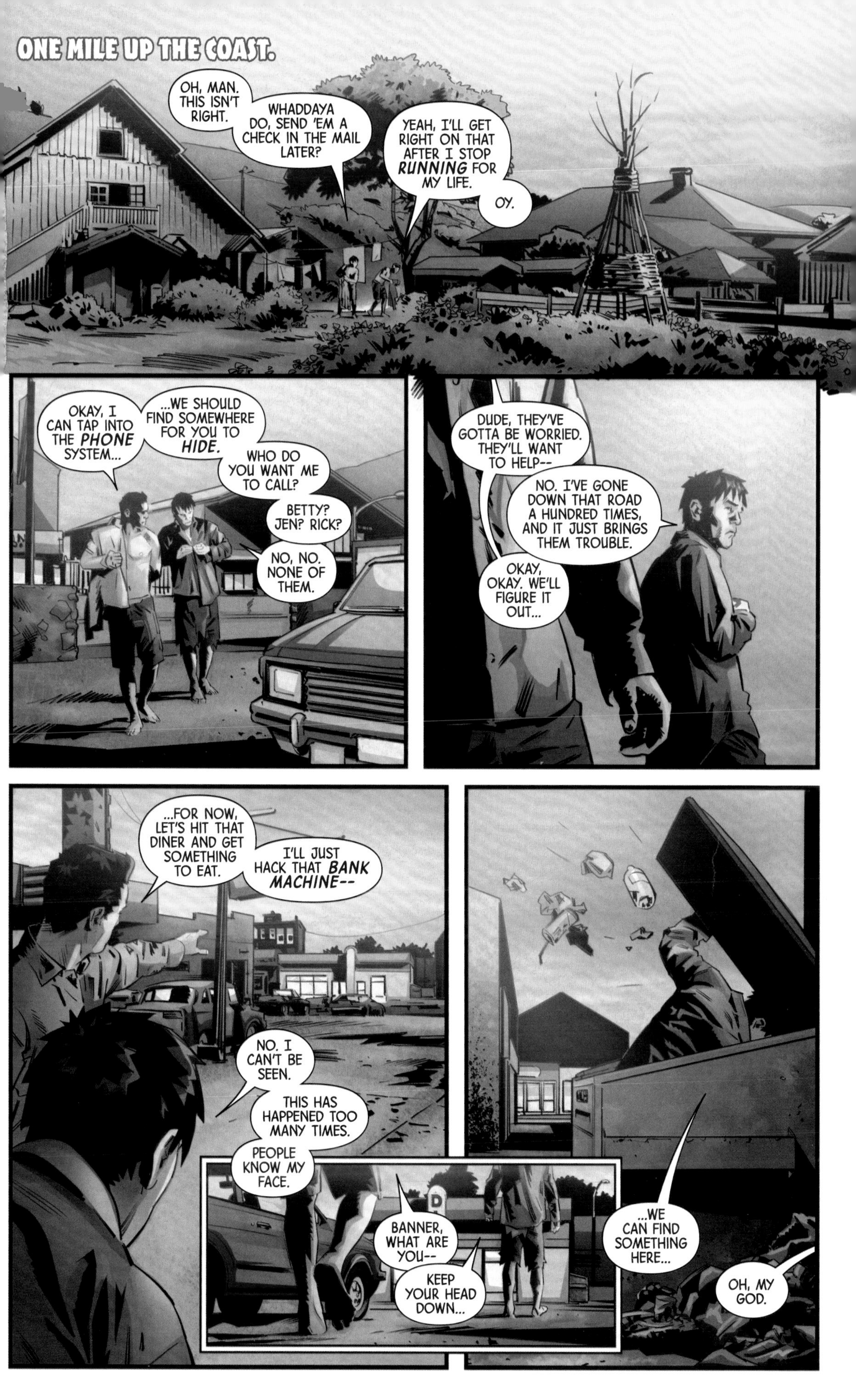
ONE MILE UP THE COAST.
OH, MAN. THIS ISN'T RIGHT.
WHADDAYA DO, SEND 'EM A CHECK IN THE MAIL LATER?
YEAH, I'LL GET RIGHT ON THAT AFTER I STOP RUNNING FOR MY LIFE.
OY.
OKAY, I CAN TAP INTO THE PHONE SYSTEM...
...WE SHOULD FIND SOMEWHERE FOR YOU TO HIDE.
WHO DO YOU WANT ME TO CALL?
BETTY? JEN? RICK?
NO, NO. NONE OF THEM.
DUDE, THEY'VE GOTTA BE WORRIED. THEY'LL WANT TO HELP--
NO. I'VE GONE DOWN THAT ROAD A HUNDRED TIMES, AND IT JUST BRINGS THEM TROUBLE.
OKAY, OKAY. WE'LL FIGURE IT OUT...
...FOR NOW, LET'S HIT THAT DINER AND GET SOMETHING TO EAT.
I'LL JUST HACK THAT BANK MACHINE--
NO. I CAN'T BE SEEN.
THIS HAS HAPPENED TOO MANY TIMES.
PEOPLE KNOW MY FACE.
BANNER, WHAT ARE YOU--
KEEP YOUR HEAD DOWN...
...WE CAN FIND SOMETHING HERE...
OH, MY GOD.

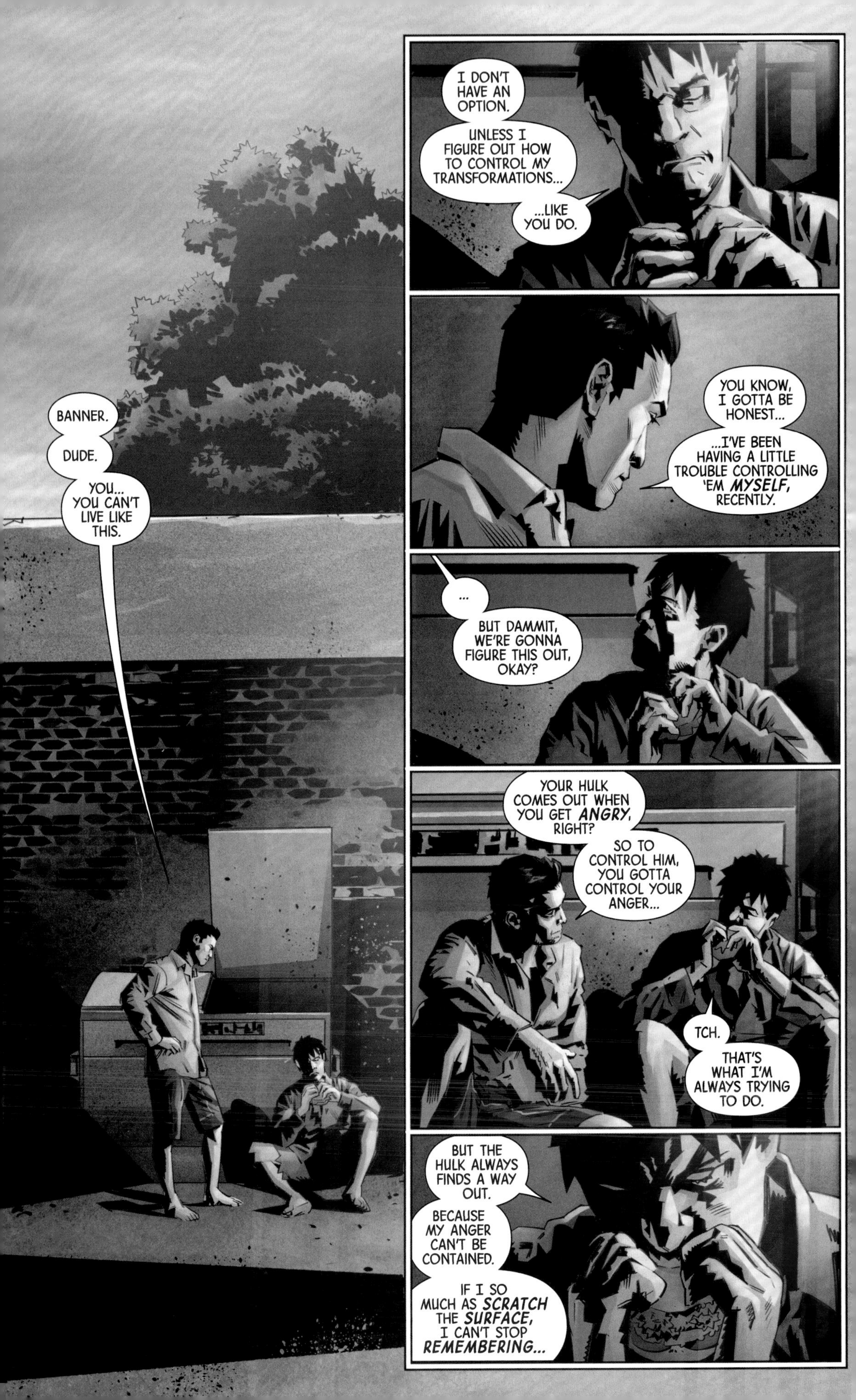

BANNER.
DUDE.
YOU... YOU CAN'T LIVE LIKE THIS.
I DON'T HAVE AN OPTION.
UNLESS I FIGURE OUT HOW TO CONTROL MY TRANSFORMATIONS...
...LIKE YOU DO.
YOU KNOW, I GOTTA BE HONEST...
...I'VE BEEN HAVING A LITTLE TROUBLE CONTROLLING 'EM MYSELF, RECENTLY.
...
BUT DAMMIT, WE'RE GONNA FIGURE THIS OUT, OKAY?
YOUR HULK COMES OUT WHEN YOU GET ANGRY, RIGHT?
SO TO CONTROL HIM, YOU GOTTA CONTROL YOUR ANGER...
TCH.
THAT'S WHAT I'M ALWAYS TRYING TO DO.
BUT THE HULK ALWAYS FINDS A WAY OUT.
BECAUSE MY ANGER CAN'T BE CONTAINED.
IF I SO MUCH AS SCRATCH THE SURFACE, I CAN'T STOP REMEMBERING...

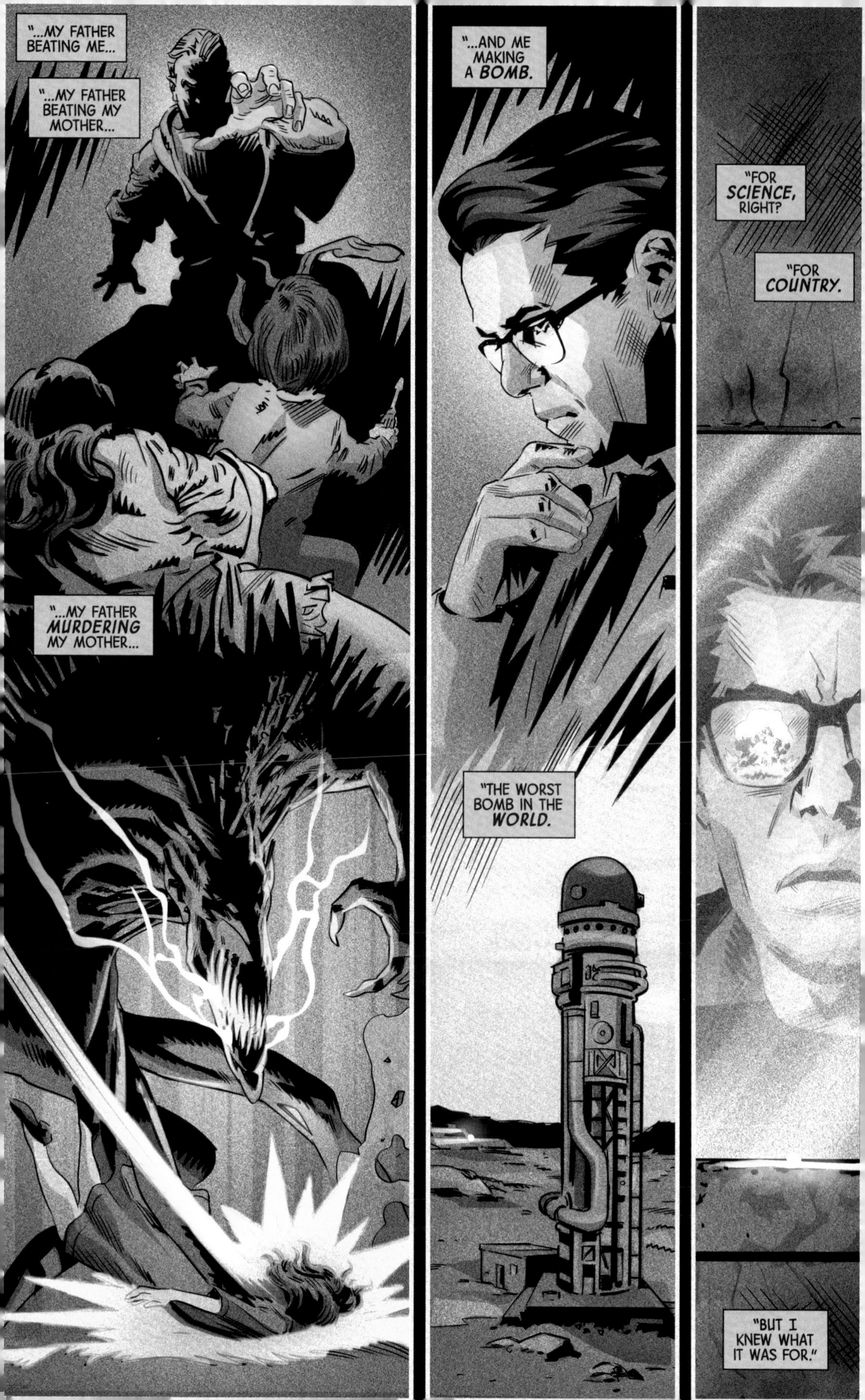
"...MY FATHER BEATING ME...
"...MY FATHER BEATING MY MOTHER...
"...MY FATHER *MURDERING* MY MOTHER...
"...AND ME MAKING A *BOMB.*
"THE WORST BOMB IN THE *WORLD.*
"FOR *SCIENCE,* RIGHT?
"FOR *COUNTRY.*
"BUT I KNEW WHAT IT WAS FOR."

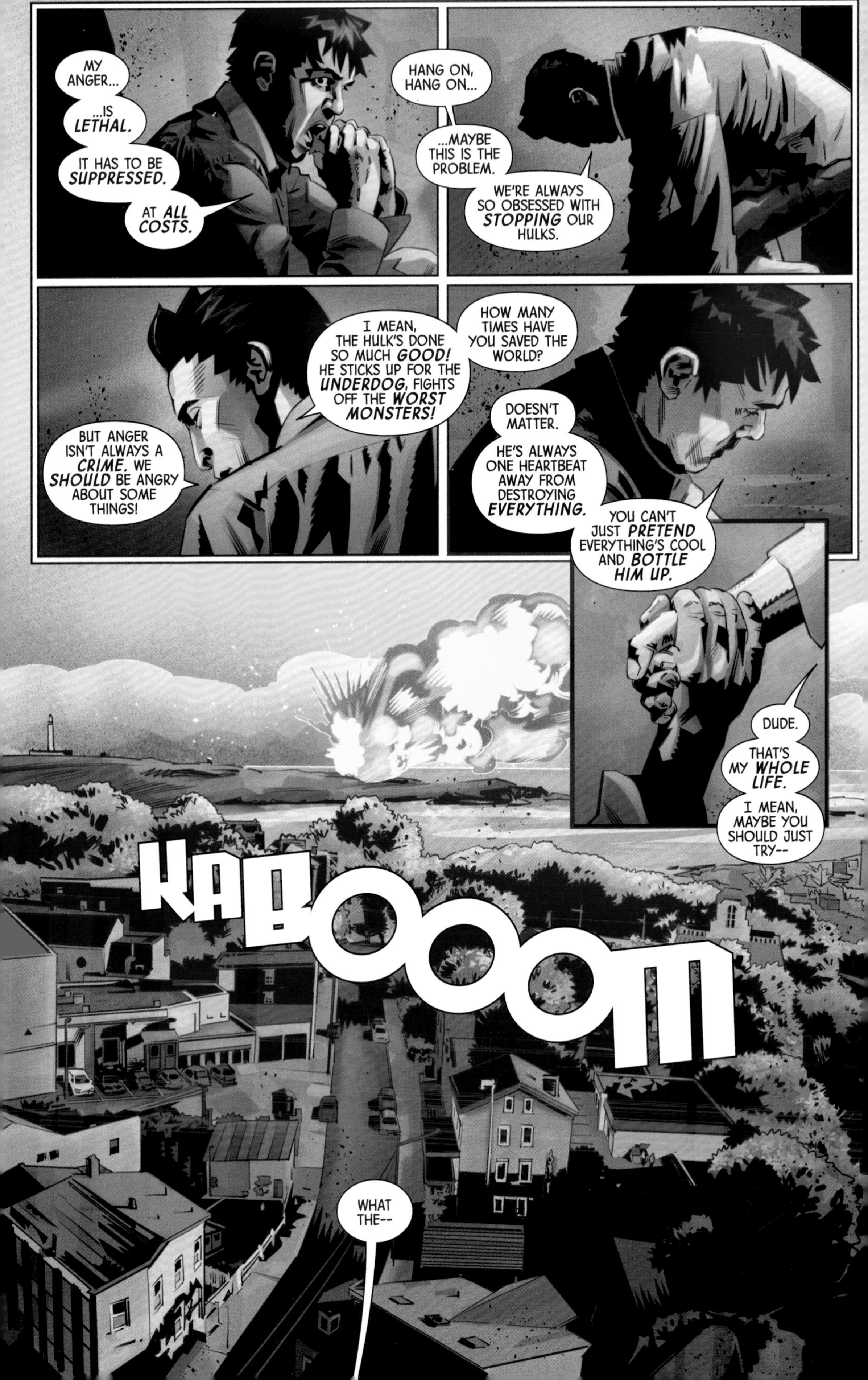
MY ANGER...
...IS LETHAL.
IT HAS TO BE SUPPRESSED.
AT ALL COSTS.
HANG ON, HANG ON...
...MAYBE THIS IS THE PROBLEM.
WE'RE ALWAYS SO OBSESSED WITH STOPPING OUR HULKS.
I MEAN, THE HULK'S DONE SO MUCH GOOD! HE STICKS UP FOR THE UNDERDOG, FIGHTS OFF THE WORST MONSTERS!
BUT ANGER ISN'T ALWAYS A CRIME. WE SHOULD BE ANGRY ABOUT SOME THINGS!
HOW MANY TIMES HAVE YOU SAVED THE WORLD?
DOESN'T MATTER.
HE'S ALWAYS ONE HEARTBEAT AWAY FROM DESTROYING EVERYTHING.
YOU CAN'T JUST PRETEND EVERYTHING'S COOL AND BOTTLE HIM UP.
DUDE.
THAT'S MY WHOLE LIFE.
I MEAN, MAYBE YOU SHOULD JUST TRY--
KABOOOM
WHAT THE--

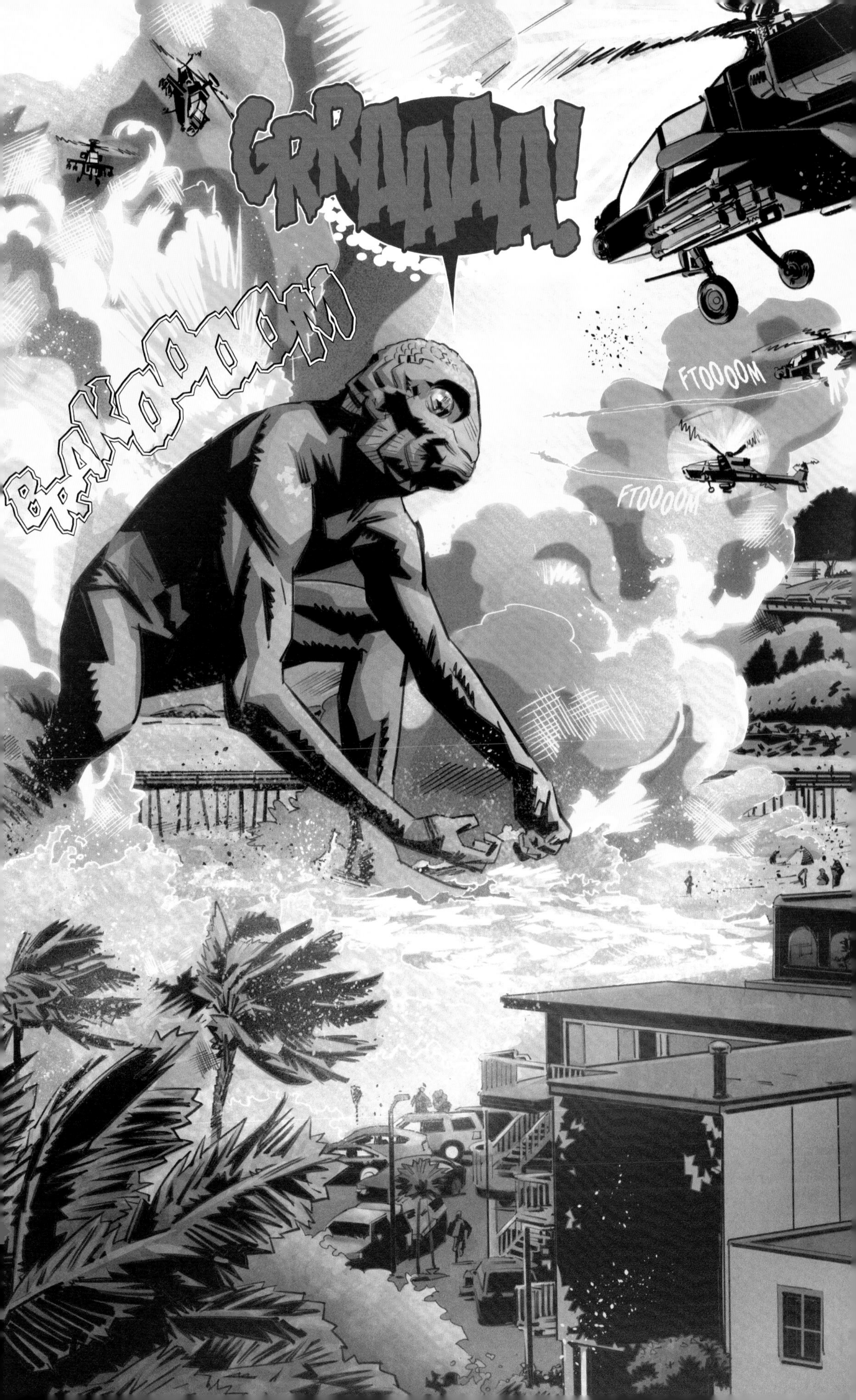
GRRAAAAA!
BRAKOOOOOM
FTOOOOM
FTOOOOM

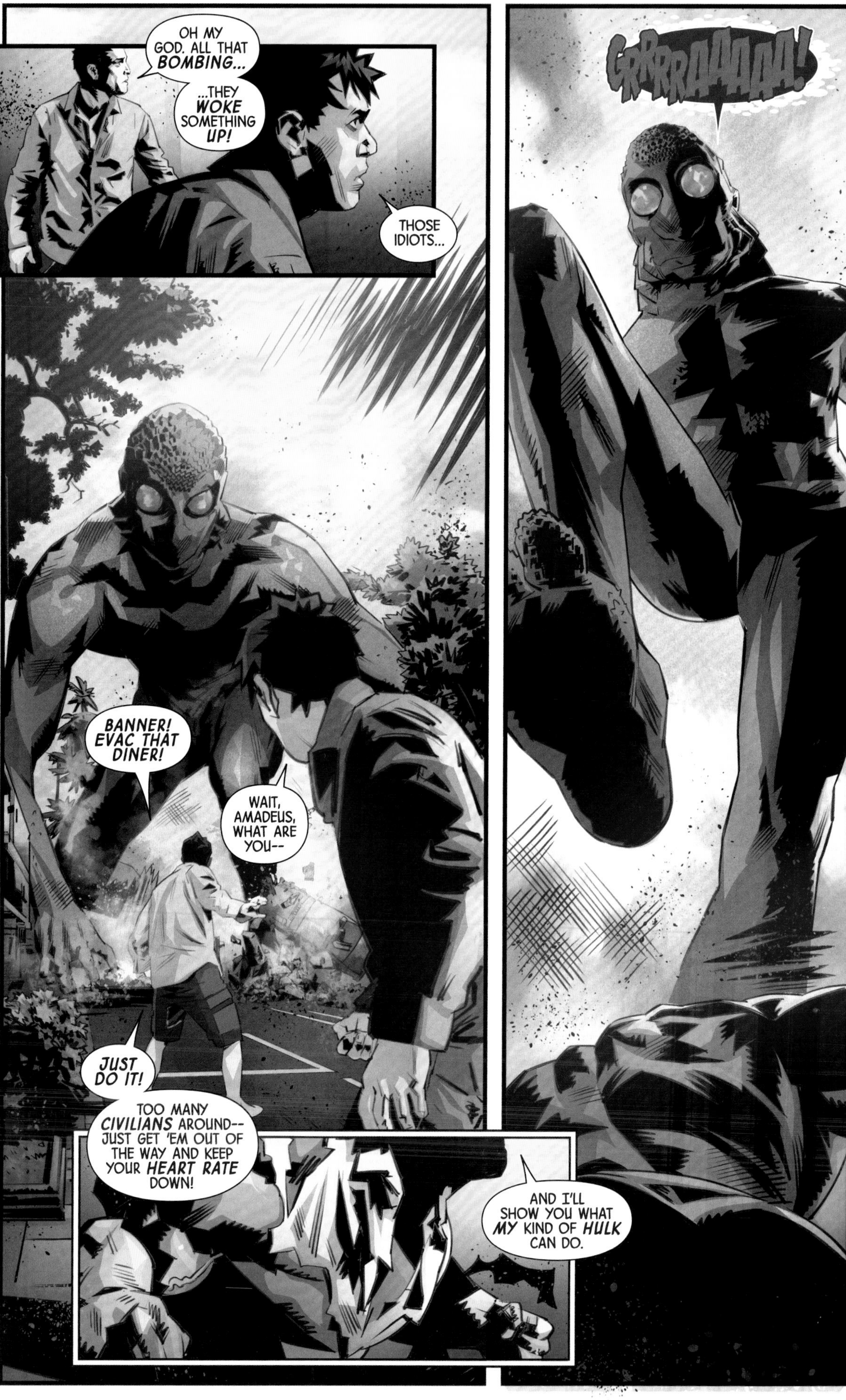
OH MY GOD. ALL THAT BOMBING...
...THEY WOKE SOMETHING UP!
THOSE IDIOTS...
BANNER! EVAC THAT DINER!
WAIT, AMADEUS, WHAT ARE YOU--
JUST DO IT!
TOO MANY CIVILIANS AROUND-- JUST GET 'EM OUT OF THE WAY AND KEEP YOUR HEART RATE DOWN!
AND I'LL SHOW YOU WHAT MY KIND OF HULK CAN DO.
GRRRAAAAA!

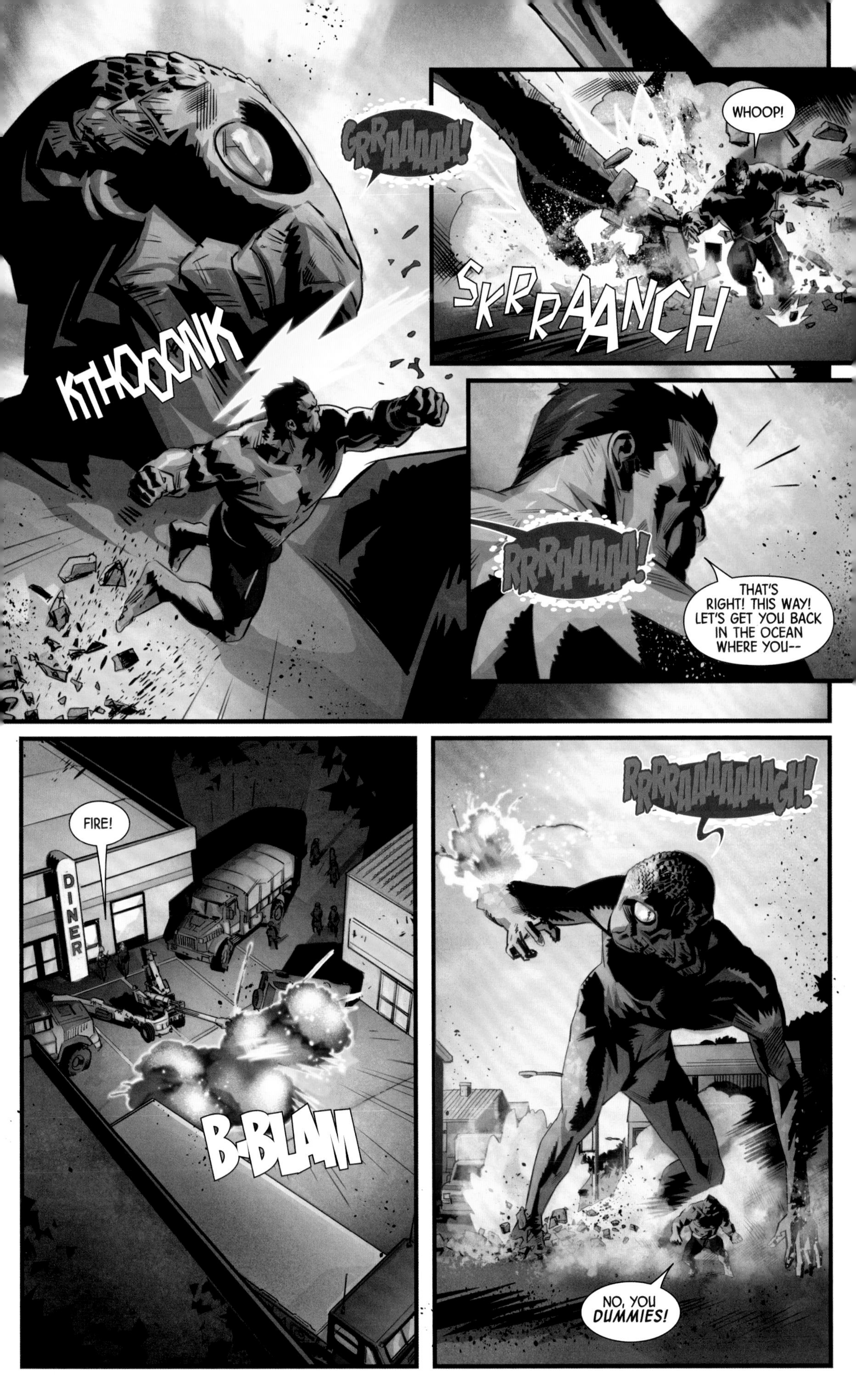
GRRAAAAA!
KTHOOONK
WHOOP!
SKRRAANCH
RRRAAAAA!
THAT'S RIGHT! THIS WAY! LET'S GET YOU BACK IN THE OCEAN WHERE YOU--
FIRE!
DINER
B-BLAM
RRRRAAAAAAAGH!
NO, YOU DUMMIES!

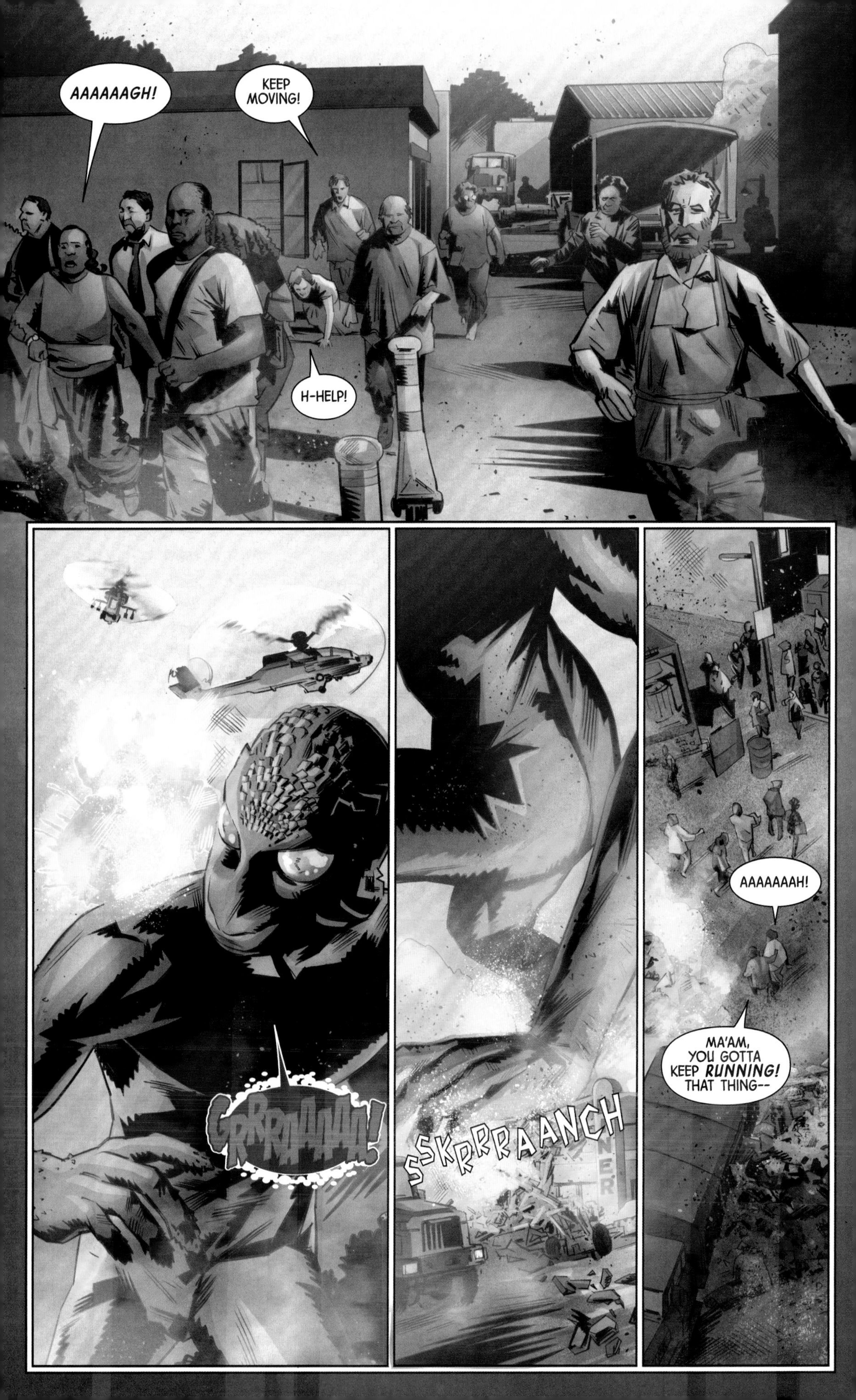
AAAAAAGH!
KEEP MOVING!
H-HELP!
GRRRAAAAA!
SSKRRRAANCH
AAAAAAAH!
MA'AM, YOU GOTTA KEEP RUNNING! THAT THING--

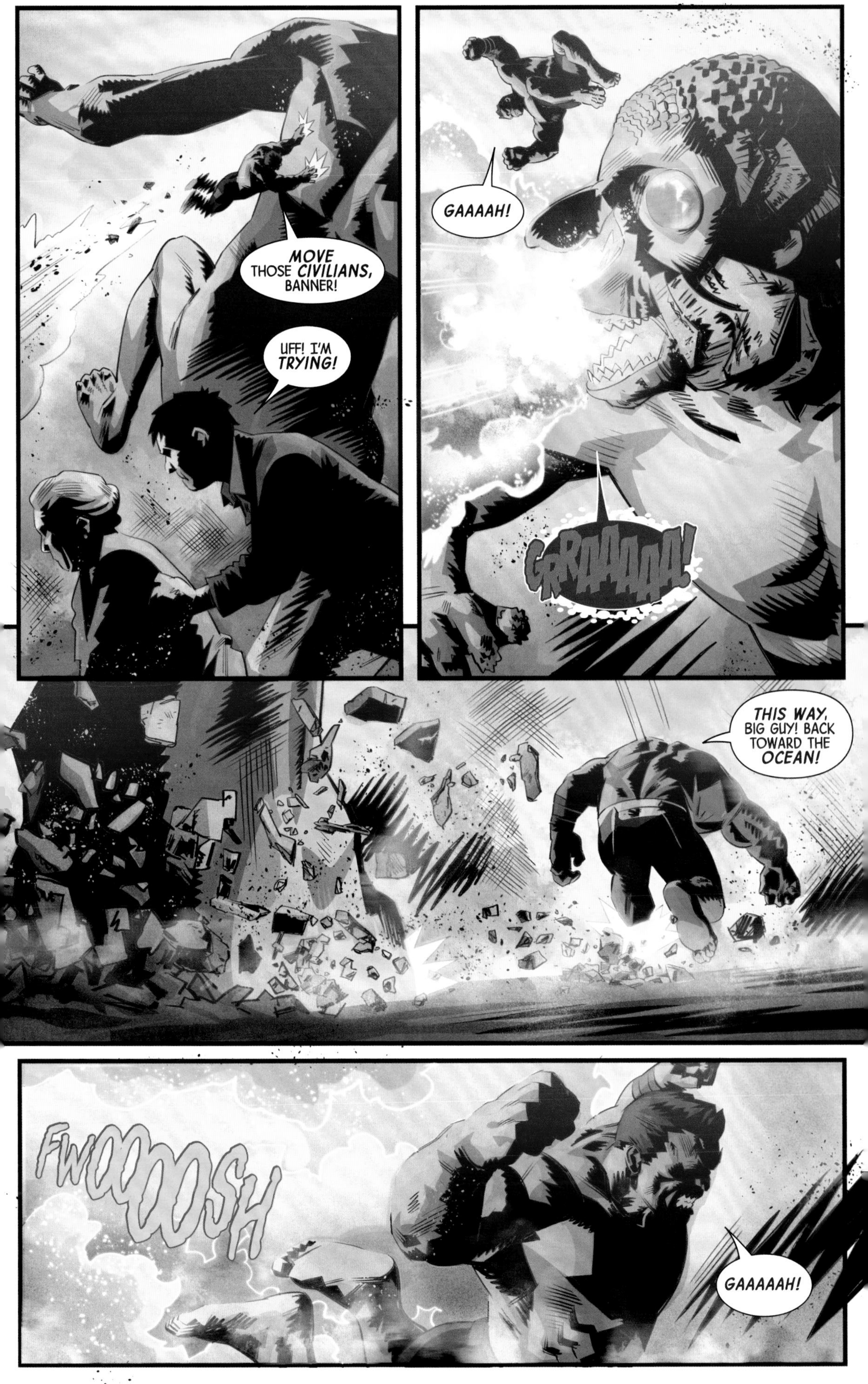
MOVE THOSE CIVILIANS, BANNER!
UFF! I'M TRYING!
GAAAAH!
GRAAAAAA!
THIS WAY, BIG GUY! BACK TOWARD THE OCEAN!
FWOOOOSH
GAAAAAH!

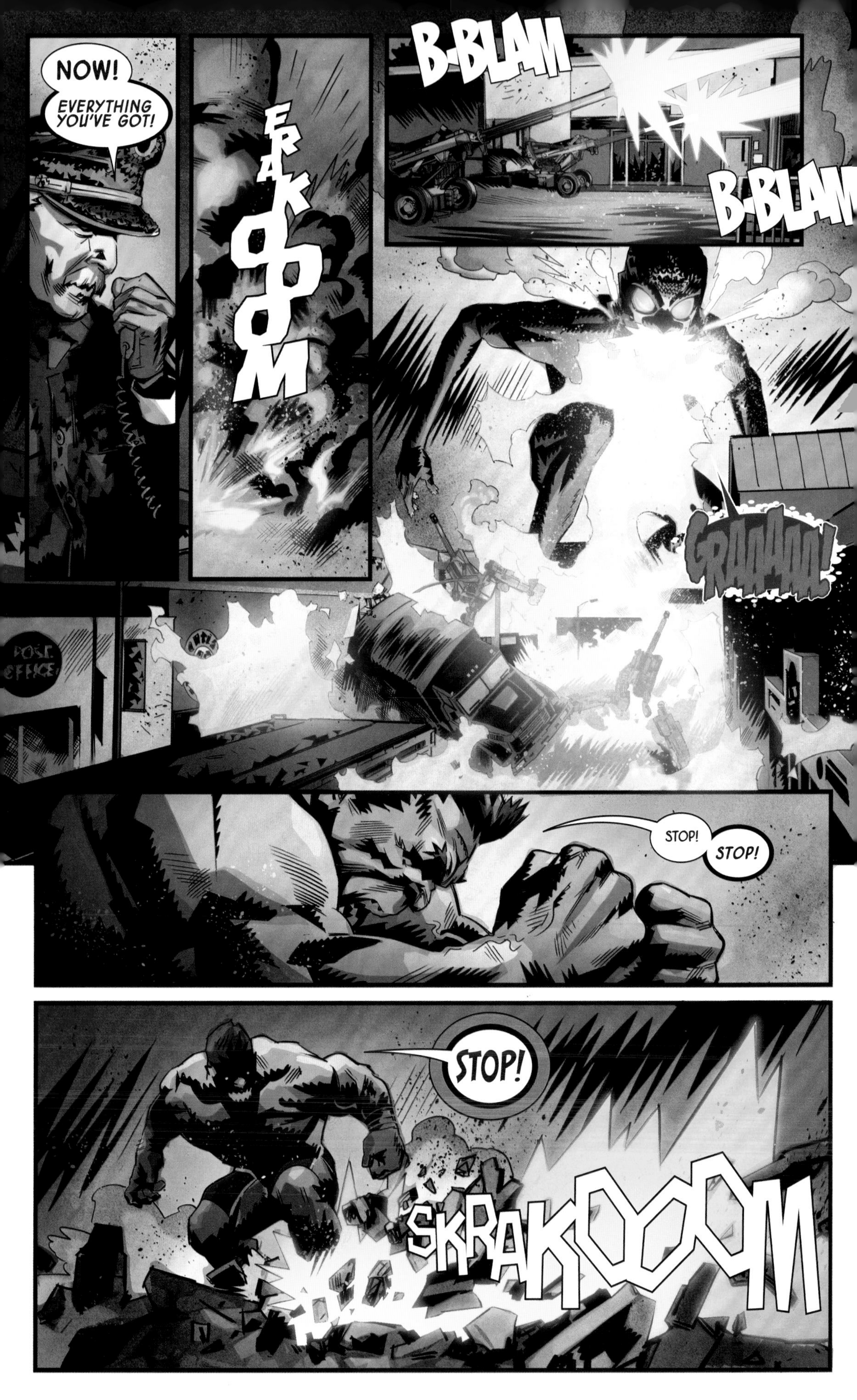
NOW!
EVERYTHING YOU'VE GOT!
ERAKOOOM
B-BLAM
B-BLAM
GRAAAAA!
POST OFFICE
STOP!
STOP!
STOP!
SKRAKOOOM

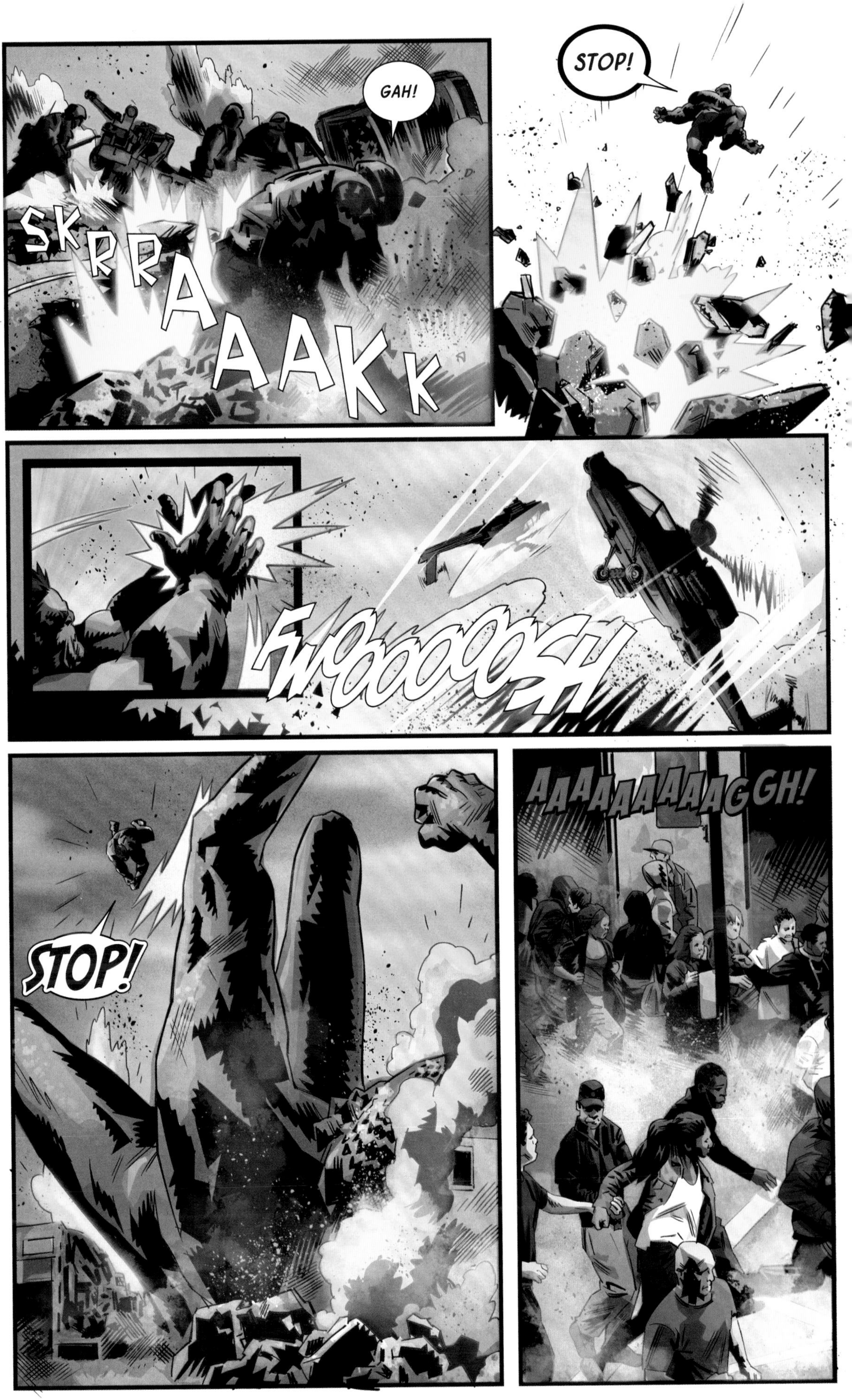
GAH!
SKRRAAAKK
STOP!
FWOOOOOSH
STOP!
AAAAAAAAAGGH!

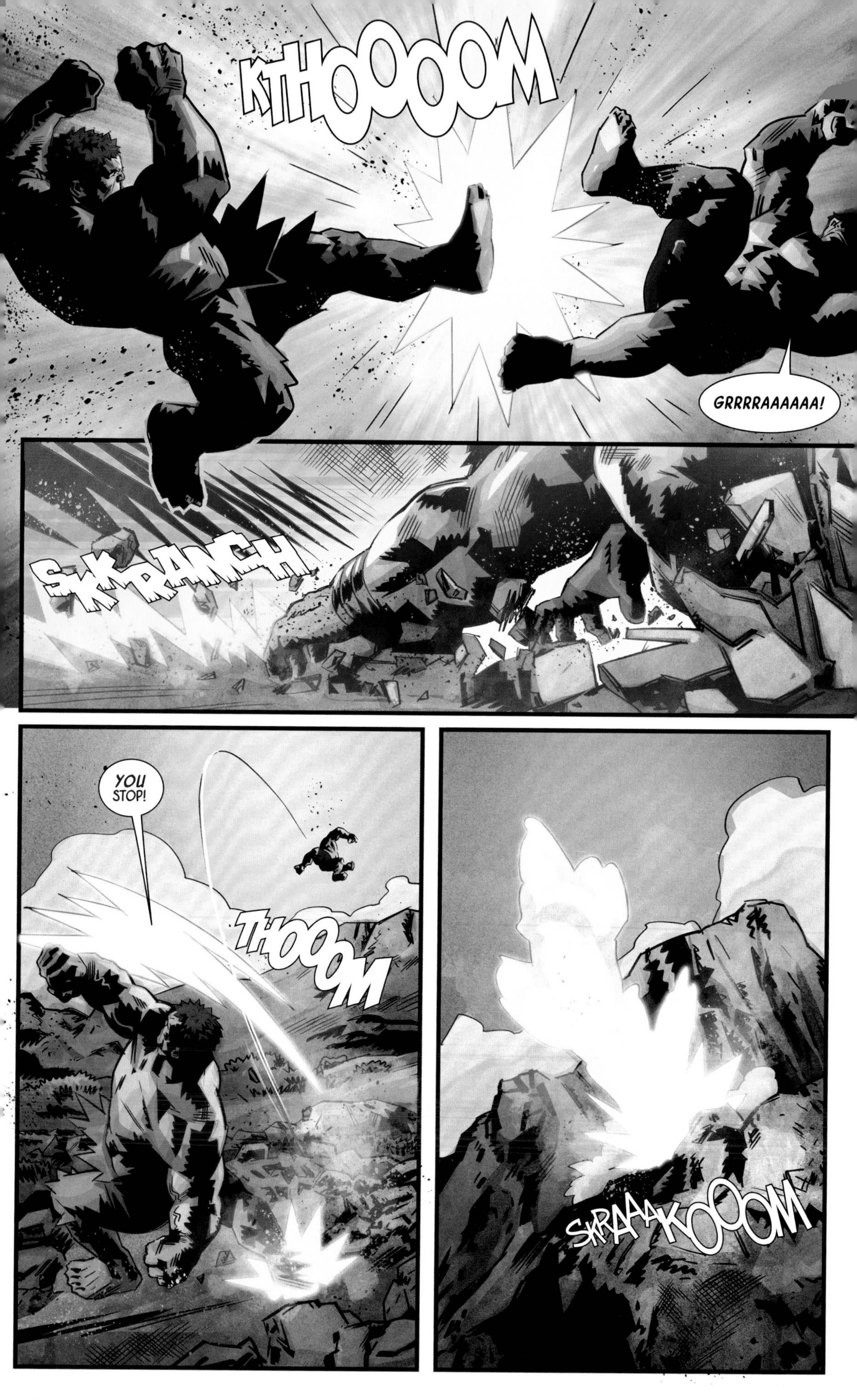
KTHOOOOOM
GRRRRAAAAAA!
SKRANCH
YOU STOP!
THOOOM
SKRAAAKOOOM

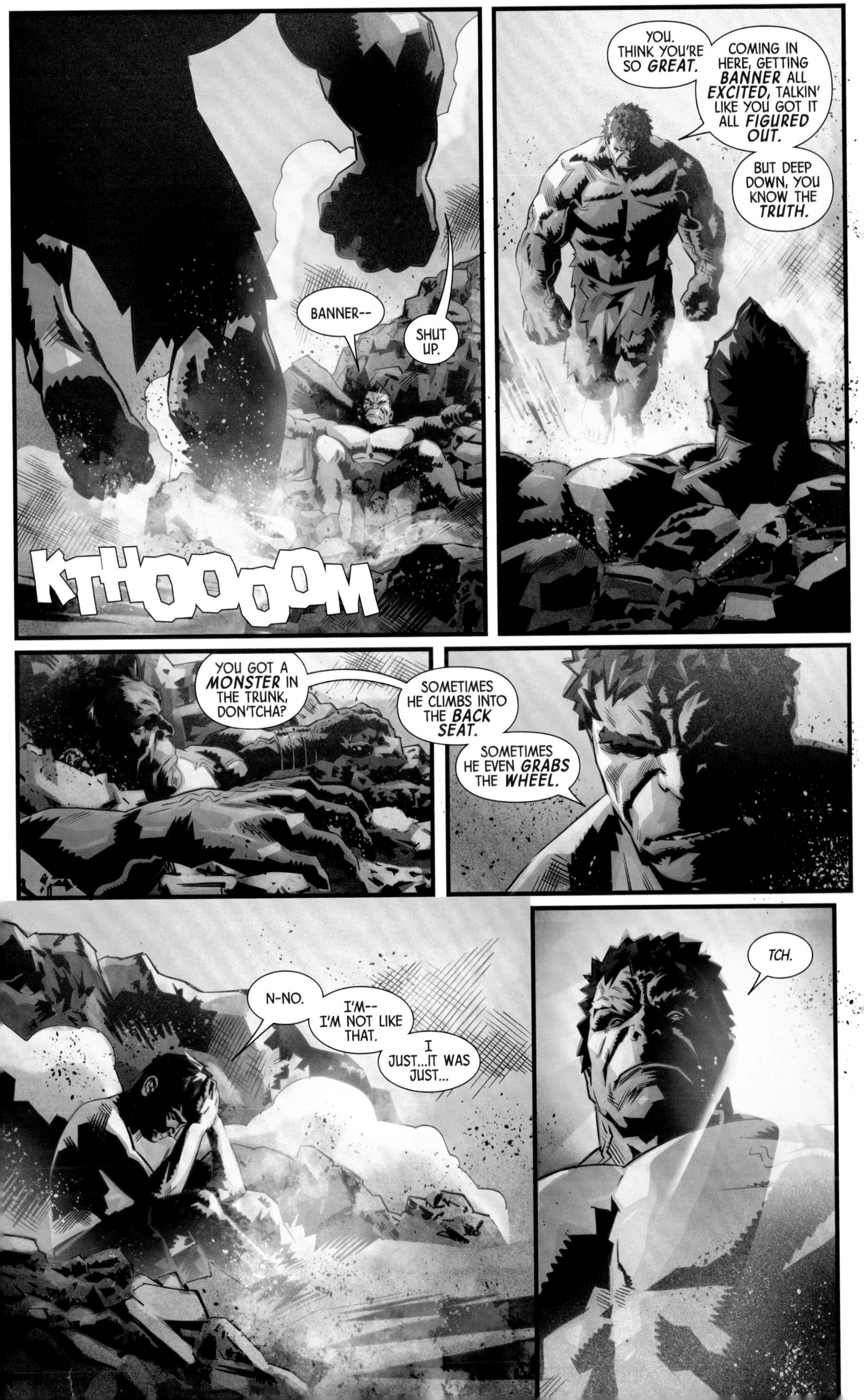
KTHOOOOOM
BANNER--
SHUT UP.
YOU. THINK YOU'RE SO GREAT.
COMING IN HERE, GETTING BANNER ALL EXCITED, TALKIN' LIKE YOU GOT IT ALL FIGURED OUT.
BUT DEEP DOWN, YOU KNOW THE TRUTH.
YOU GOT A MONSTER IN THE TRUNK, DON'TCHA?
SOMETIMES HE CLIMBS INTO THE BACK SEAT.
SOMETIMES HE EVEN GRABS THE WHEEL.
N-NO.
I'M-- I'M NOT LIKE THAT.
I JUST...IT WAS JUST...
TCH.

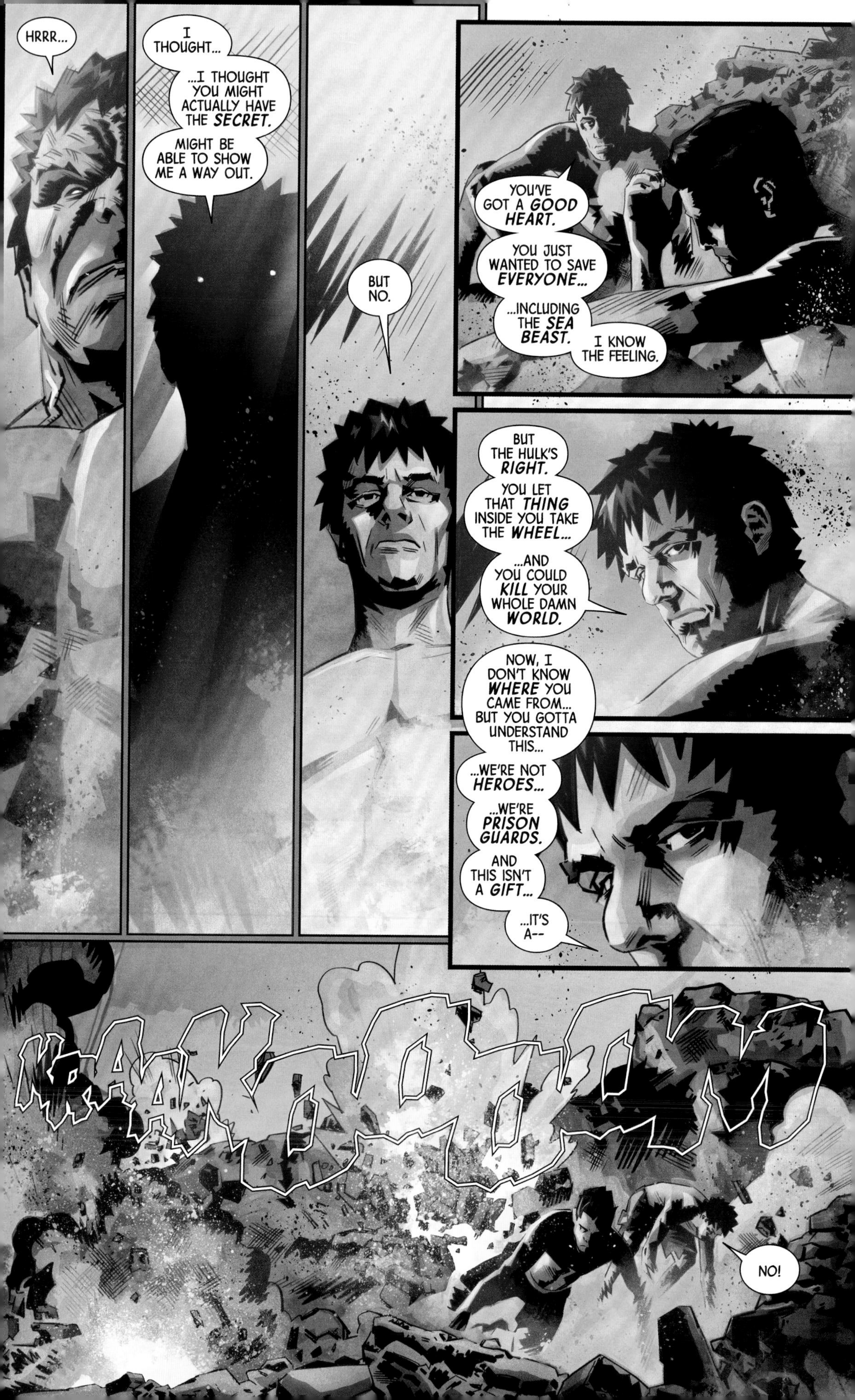
HRRR...
I THOUGHT...
...I THOUGHT YOU MIGHT ACTUALLY HAVE THE SECRET.
MIGHT BE ABLE TO SHOW ME A WAY OUT.
BUT NO.
YOU'VE GOT A GOOD HEART.
YOU JUST WANTED TO SAVE EVERYONE...
...INCLUDING THE SEA BEAST.
I KNOW THE FEELING.
BUT THE HULK'S RIGHT.
YOU LET THAT THING INSIDE YOU TAKE THE WHEEL...
...AND YOU COULD KILL YOUR WHOLE DAMN WORLD.
NOW, I DON'T KNOW WHERE YOU CAME FROM... BUT YOU GOTTA UNDERSTAND THIS...
...WE'RE NOT HEROES...
...WE'RE PRISON GUARDS.
AND THIS ISN'T A GIFT...
...IT'S A--
NO!

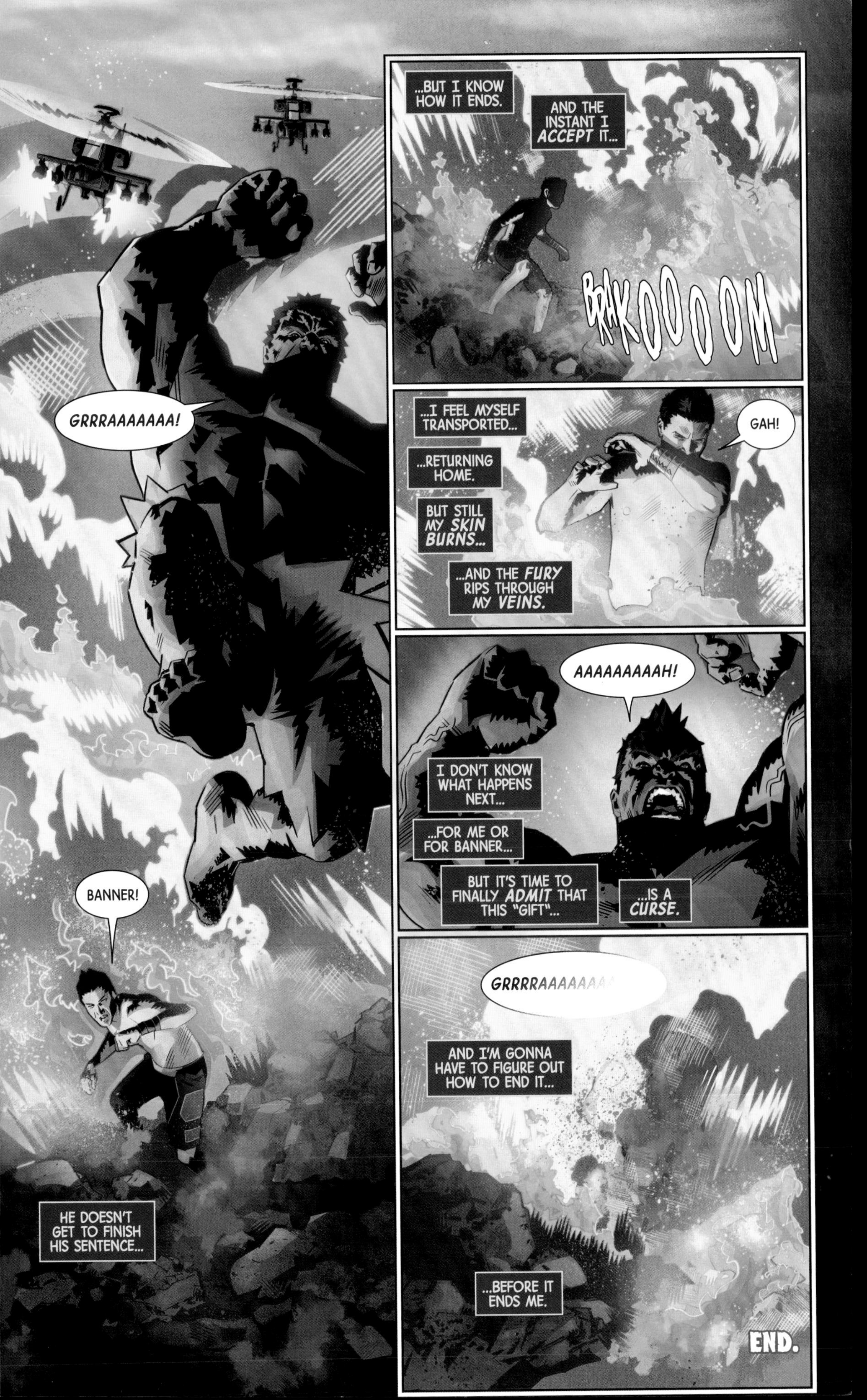
GRRRAAAAAAA!
BANNER!
HE DOESN'T GET TO FINISH HIS SENTENCE...
...BUT I KNOW HOW IT ENDS.
AND THE INSTANT I ACCEPT IT...
BRAKOOOOM
...I FEEL MYSELF TRANSPORTED...
...RETURNING HOME.
BUT STILL MY SKIN BURNS...
...AND THE FURY RIPS THROUGH MY VEINS.
GAH!
AAAAAAAAAH!
I DON'T KNOW WHAT HAPPENS NEXT...
...FOR ME OR FOR BANNER...
BUT IT'S TIME TO FINALLY ADMIT THAT THIS "GIFT"...
...IS A CURSE.
GRRRRAAAAAAA
AND I'M GONNA HAVE TO FIGURE OUT HOW TO END IT...
...BEFORE IT ENDS ME.
END.

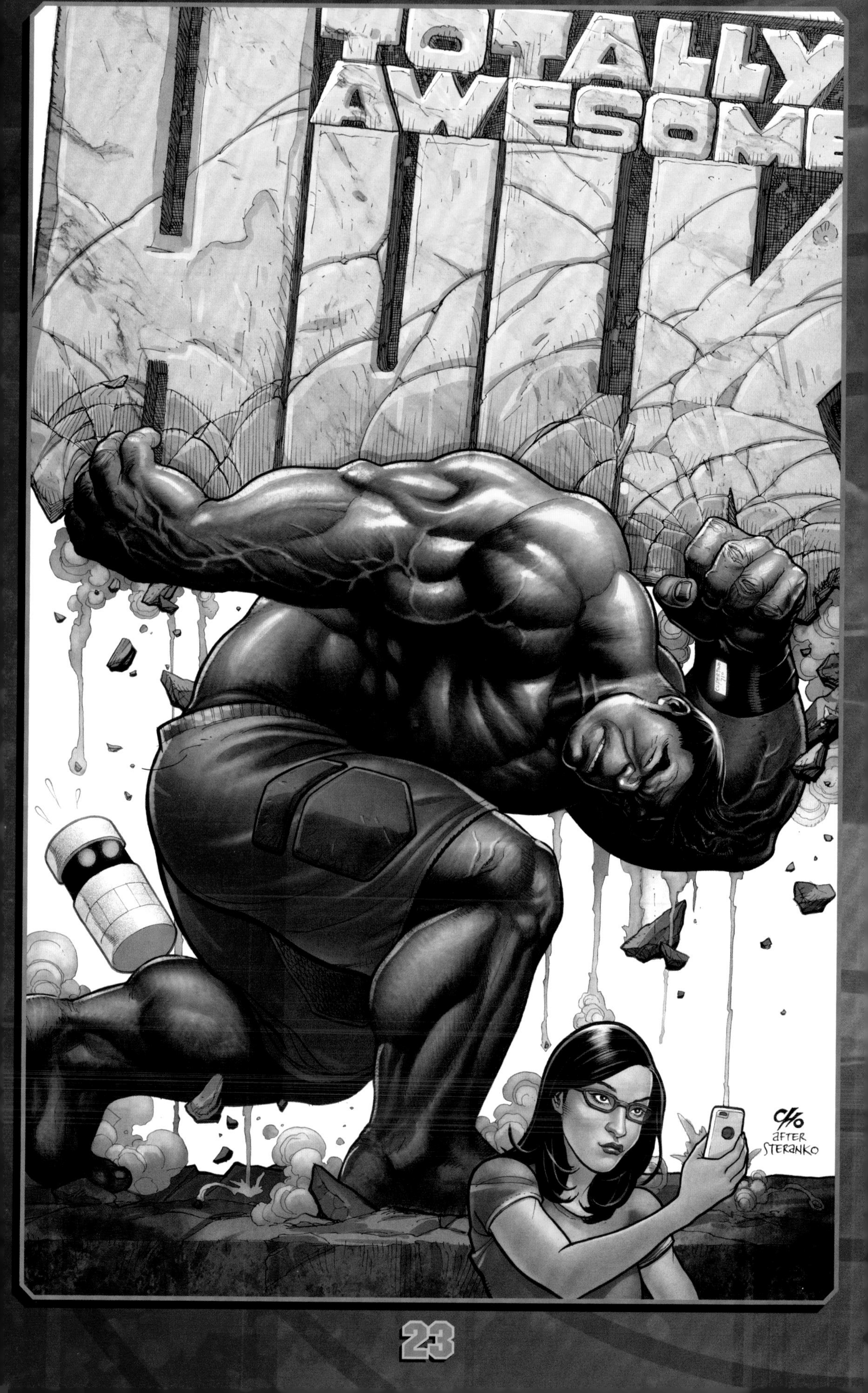
TOTALLY AWESOME
CHO after STERANKO

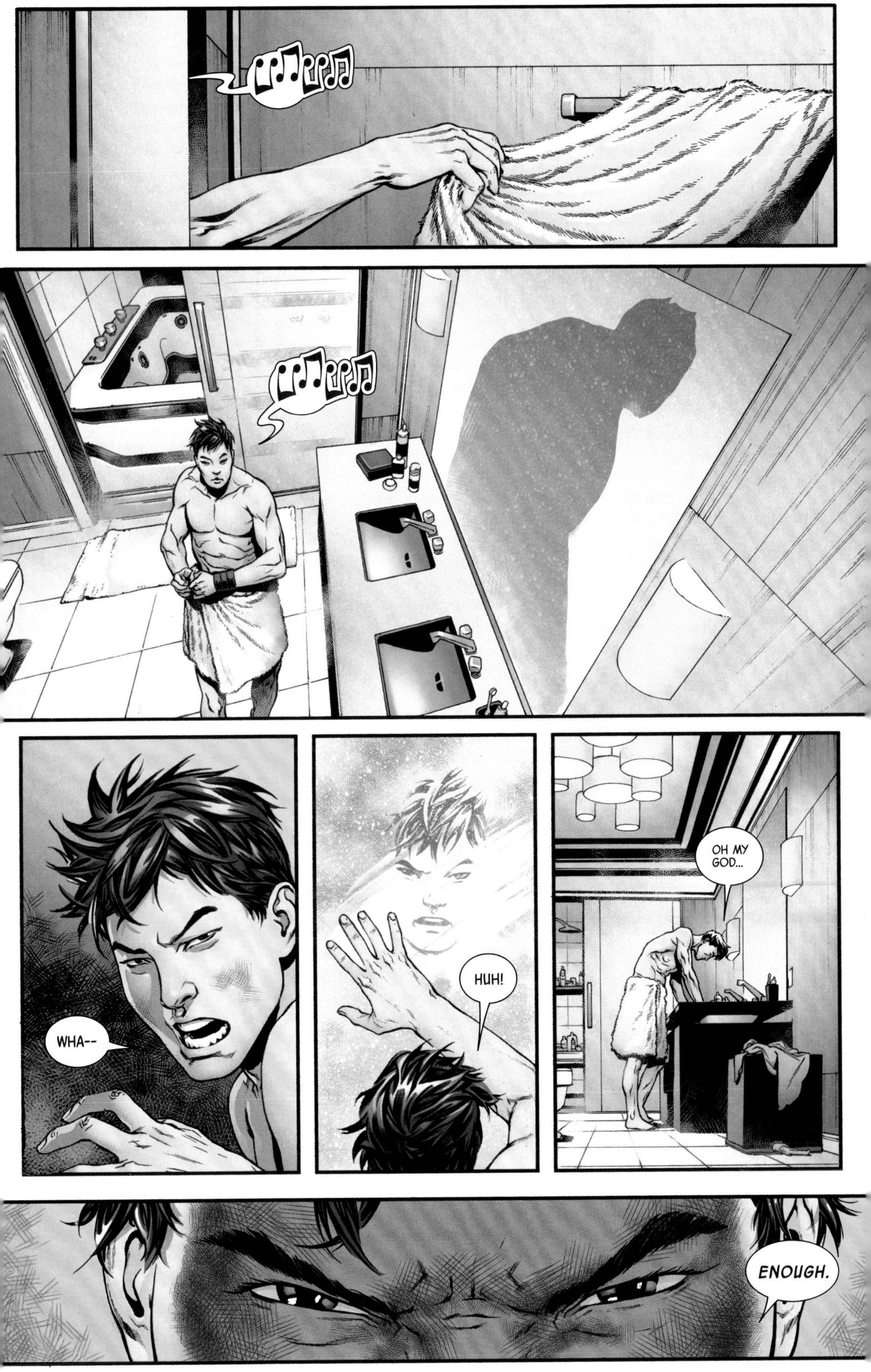
WHA--
HUH!
OH MY GOD...
ENOUGH.

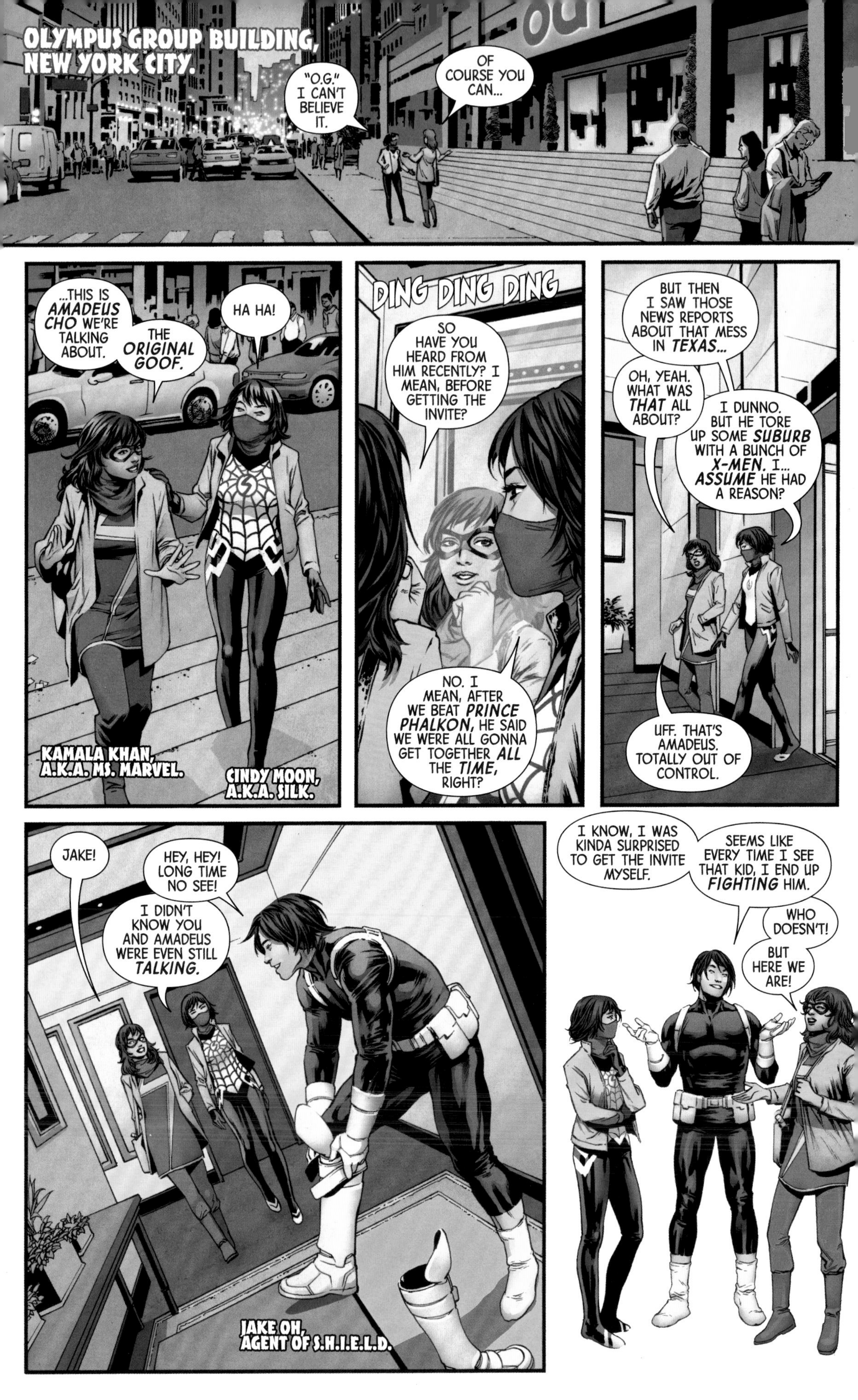
OLYMPUS GROUP BUILDING, NEW YORK CITY.
"O.G." I CAN'T BELIEVE IT.
OF COURSE YOU CAN...
...THIS IS AMADEUS CHO WE'RE TALKING ABOUT.
THE ORIGINAL GOOF.
HA HA!
KAMALA KHAN, A.K.A. MS. MARVEL.
CINDY MOON, A.K.A. SILK.
DING DING DING
SO HAVE YOU HEARD FROM HIM RECENTLY? I MEAN, BEFORE GETTING THE INVITE?
NO. I MEAN, AFTER WE BEAT PRINCE PHALKON, HE SAID WE WERE ALL GONNA GET TOGETHER ALL THE TIME, RIGHT?
BUT THEN I SAW THOSE NEWS REPORTS ABOUT THAT MESS IN TEXAS...
OH, YEAH. WHAT WAS THAT ALL ABOUT?
I DUNNO. BUT HE TORE UP SOME SUBURB WITH A BUNCH OF X-MEN. I... ASSUME HE HAD A REASON?
UFF. THAT'S AMADEUS. TOTALLY OUT OF CONTROL.
JAKE!
HEY, HEY! LONG TIME NO SEE!
I DIDN'T KNOW YOU AND AMADEUS WERE EVEN STILL TALKING.
JAKE OH, AGENT OF S.H.I.E.L.D.
I KNOW, I WAS KINDA SURPRISED TO GET THE INVITE MYSELF.
SEEMS LIKE EVERY TIME I SEE THAT KID, I END UP FIGHTING HIM.
WHO DOESN'T!
BUT HERE WE ARE!

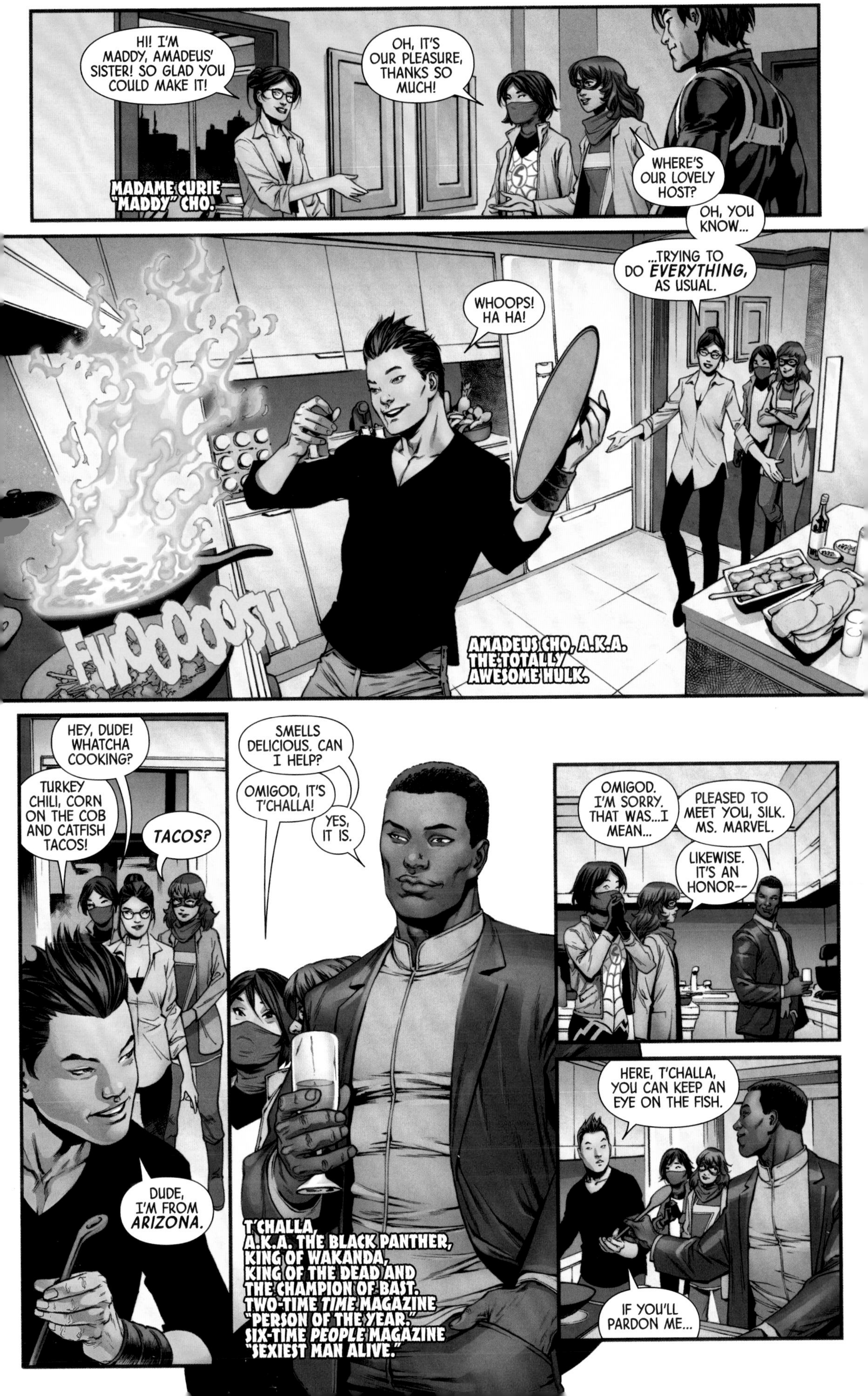
HI! I'M MADDY, AMADEUS' SISTER! SO GLAD YOU COULD MAKE IT!
OH, IT'S OUR PLEASURE, THANKS SO MUCH!
MADAME CURIE "MADDY" CHO.
WHERE'S OUR LOVELY HOST?
OH, YOU KNOW...
...TRYING TO DO EVERYTHING, AS USUAL.
WHOOPS! HA HA!
FWOOOOOSH
AMADEUS CHO, A.K.A. THE TOTALLY AWESOME HULK.
HEY, DUDE! WHATCHA COOKING?
TURKEY CHILI, CORN ON THE COB AND CATFISH TACOS!
TACOS?
DUDE, I'M FROM ARIZONA.
SMELLS DELICIOUS. CAN I HELP?
OMIGOD, IT'S T'CHALLA!
YES, IT IS.
T'CHALLA, A.K.A. THE BLACK PANTHER, KING OF WAKANDA, KING OF THE DEAD AND THE CHAMPION OF BAST. TWO-TIME TIME MAGAZINE "PERSON OF THE YEAR." SIX-TIME PEOPLE MAGAZINE "SEXIEST MAN ALIVE."
OMIGOD. I'M SORRY. THAT WAS...I MEAN...
PLEASED TO MEET YOU, SILK. MS. MARVEL.
LIKEWISE. IT'S AN HONOR--
HERE, T'CHALLA, YOU CAN KEEP AN EYE ON THE FISH.
IF YOU'LL PARDON ME...

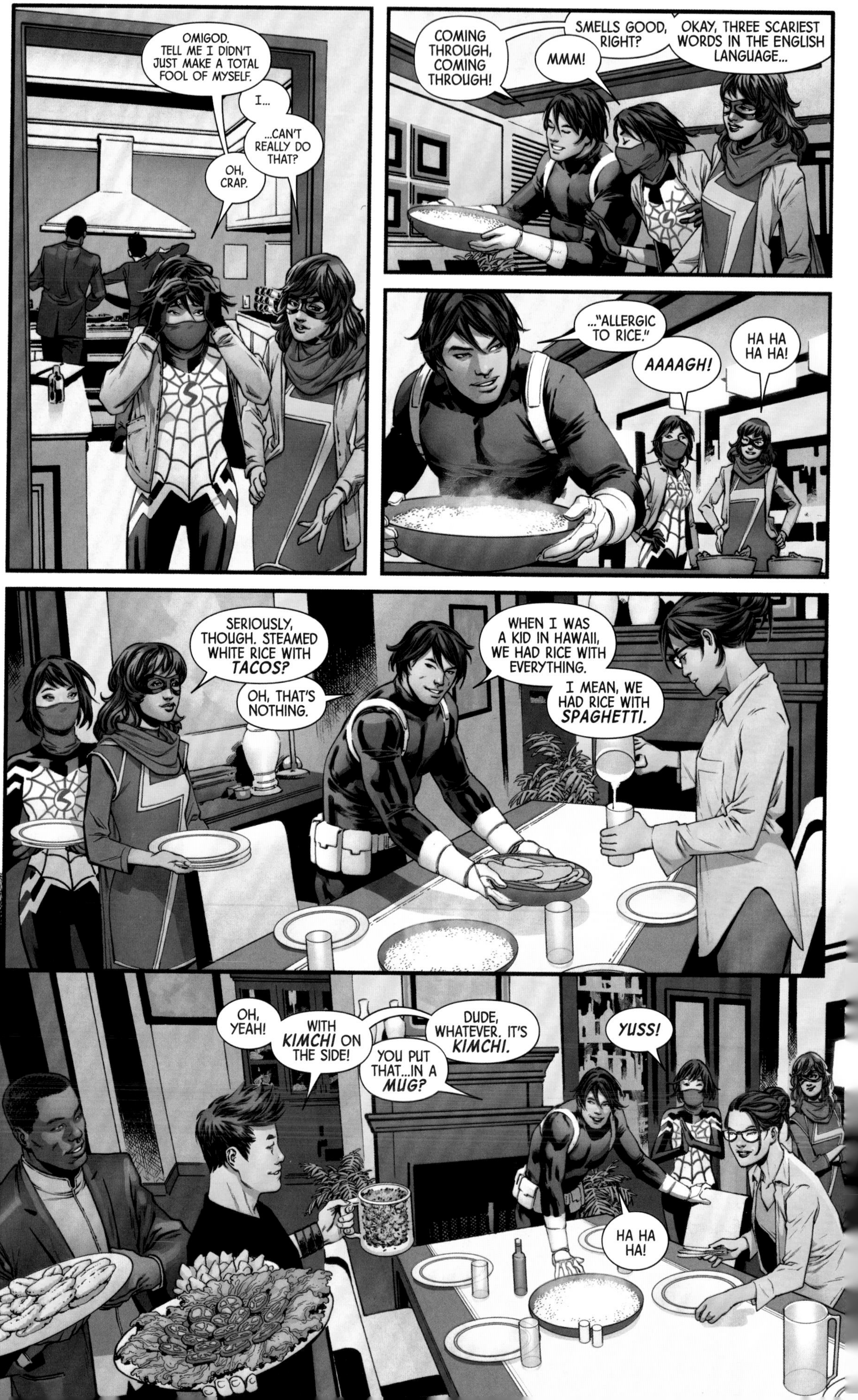
OMIGOD. TELL ME I DIDN'T JUST MAKE A TOTAL FOOL OF MYSELF.
I...
...CAN'T REALLY DO THAT?
OH, CRAP.
COMING THROUGH, COMING THROUGH!
SMELLS GOOD, RIGHT?
MMM!
OKAY, THREE SCARIEST WORDS IN THE ENGLISH LANGUAGE...
..."ALLERGIC TO RICE."
AAAAGH!
HA HA HA HA!
SERIOUSLY, THOUGH. STEAMED WHITE RICE WITH TACOS?
OH, THAT'S NOTHING.
WHEN I WAS A KID IN HAWAII, WE HAD RICE WITH EVERYTHING.
I MEAN, WE HAD RICE WITH SPAGHETTI.
OH, YEAH!
WITH KIMCHI ON THE SIDE!
YOU PUT THAT...IN A MUG?
DUDE, WHATEVER. IT'S KIMCHI.
YUSS!
HA HA HA!

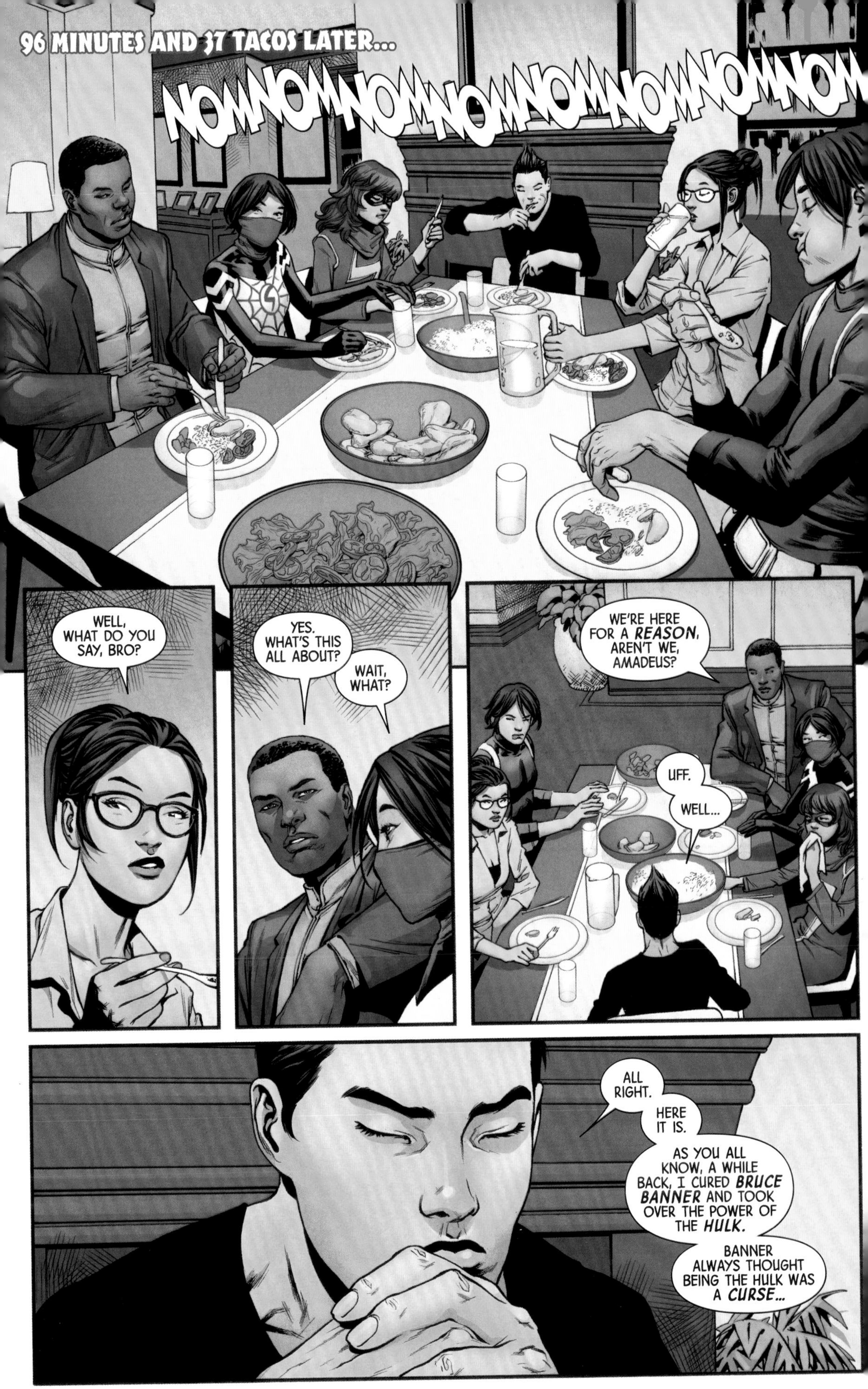
96 MINUTES AND 37 TACOS LATER...
NOMNOMNOMNOMNOMNOMNOMNOM
WELL, WHAT DO YOU SAY, BRO?
YES. WHAT'S THIS ALL ABOUT?
WAIT, WHAT?
WE'RE HERE FOR A REASON, AREN'T WE, AMADEUS?
UFF.
WELL...
ALL RIGHT.
HERE IT IS.
AS YOU ALL KNOW, A WHILE BACK, I CURED BRUCE BANNER AND TOOK OVER THE POWER OF THE HULK.
BANNER ALWAYS THOUGHT BEING THE HULK WAS A CURSE...

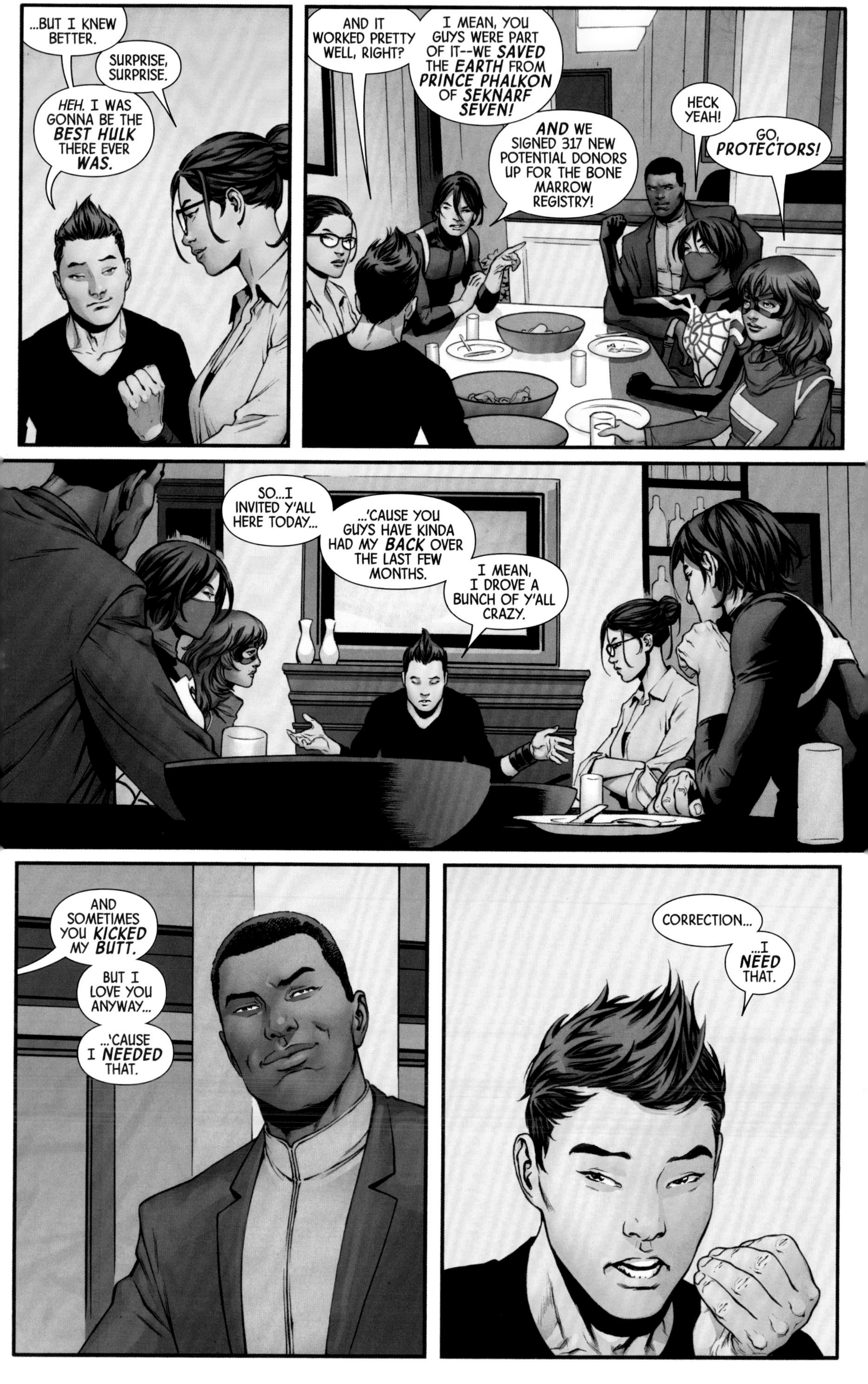
...BUT I KNEW BETTER.
SURPRISE, SURPRISE.
HEH. I WAS GONNA BE THE BEST HULK THERE EVER WAS.
AND IT WORKED PRETTY WELL, RIGHT?
I MEAN, YOU GUYS WERE PART OF IT--WE SAVED THE EARTH FROM PRINCE PHALKON OF SEKNARF SEVEN!
AND WE SIGNED 317 NEW POTENTIAL DONORS UP FOR THE BONE MARROW REGISTRY!
HECK YEAH!
GO, PROTECTORS!
SO...I INVITED Y'ALL HERE TODAY...
...'CAUSE YOU GUYS HAVE KINDA HAD MY BACK OVER THE LAST FEW MONTHS.
I MEAN, I DROVE A BUNCH OF Y'ALL CRAZY.
AND SOMETIMES YOU KICKED MY BUTT.
BUT I LOVE YOU ANYWAY...
...'CAUSE I NEEDED THAT.
CORRECTION...
...I NEED THAT.

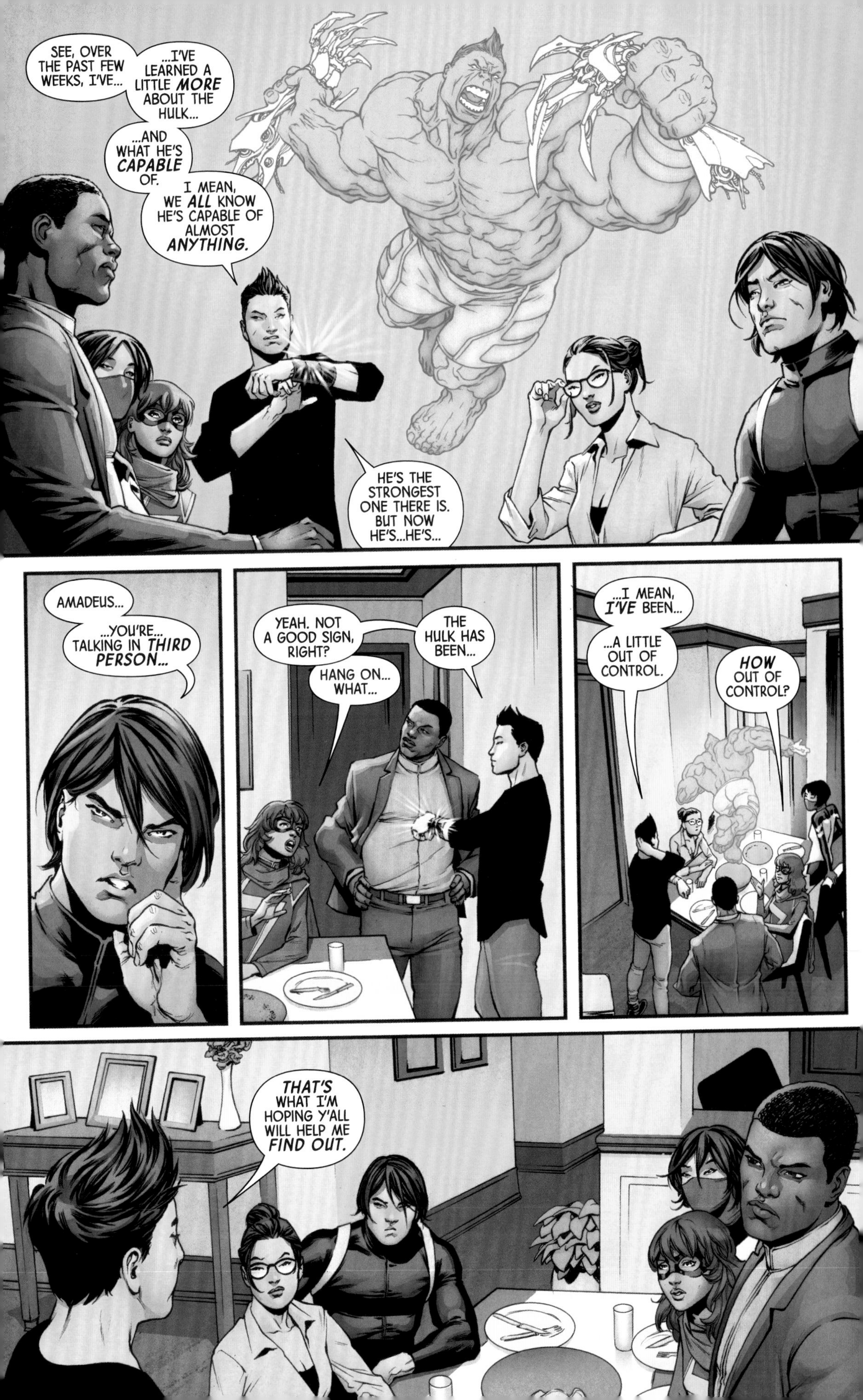
SEE, OVER THE PAST FEW WEEKS, I'VE...
...I'VE LEARNED A LITTLE MORE ABOUT THE HULK...
...AND WHAT HE'S CAPABLE OF.
I MEAN, WE ALL KNOW HE'S CAPABLE OF ALMOST ANYTHING.
HE'S THE STRONGEST ONE THERE IS. BUT NOW HE'S...HE'S...
AMADEUS...
...YOU'RE... TALKING IN THIRD PERSON...
YEAH. NOT A GOOD SIGN, RIGHT?
THE HULK HAS BEEN...
HANG ON... WHAT...
...I MEAN, I'VE BEEN...
...A LITTLE OUT OF CONTROL.
HOW OUT OF CONTROL?
THAT'S WHAT I'M HOPING Y'ALL WILL HELP ME FIND OUT.

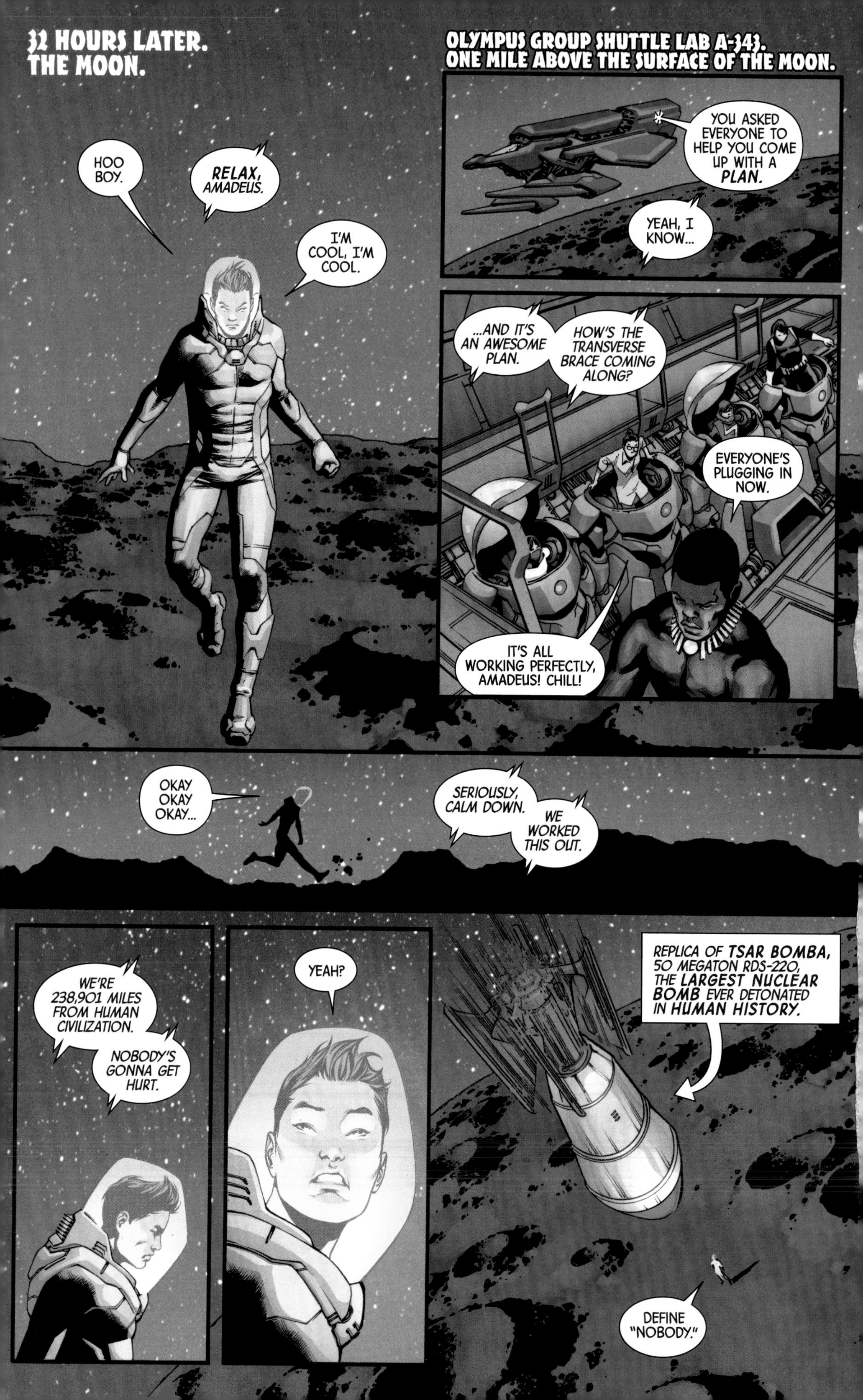
32 HOURS LATER.
THE MOON.
HOO BOY.
RELAX, AMADEUS.
I'M COOL, I'M COOL.
OLYMPUS GROUP SHUTTLE LAB A-343.
ONE MILE ABOVE THE SURFACE OF THE MOON.
YOU ASKED EVERYONE TO HELP YOU COME UP WITH A PLAN.
YEAH, I KNOW...
...AND IT'S AN AWESOME PLAN.
HOW'S THE TRANSVERSE BRACE COMING ALONG?
EVERYONE'S PLUGGING IN NOW.
IT'S ALL WORKING PERFECTLY, AMADEUS! CHILL!
OKAY OKAY OKAY...
SERIOUSLY, CALM DOWN.
WE WORKED THIS OUT.
WE'RE 238,901 MILES FROM HUMAN CIVILIZATION.
NOBODY'S GONNA GET HURT.
YEAH?
REPLICA OF TSAR BOMBA, 50 MEGATON RDS-220, THE LARGEST NUCLEAR BOMB EVER DETONATED IN HUMAN HISTORY.
DEFINE "NOBODY."

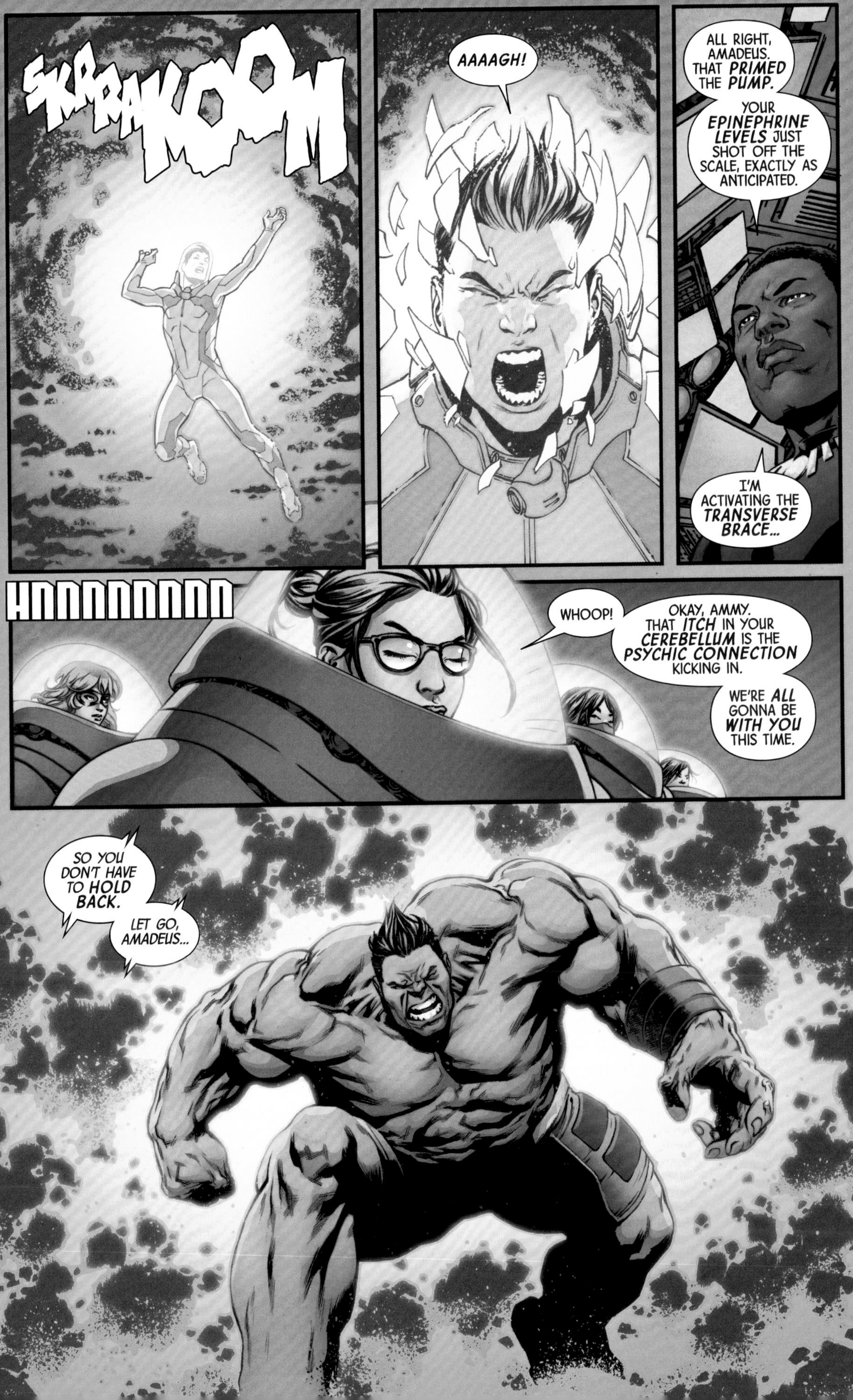
SKRRAKOOM
AAAAGH!
ALL RIGHT, AMADEUS. THAT PRIMED THE PUMP.
YOUR EPINEPHRINE LEVELS JUST SHOT OFF THE SCALE, EXACTLY AS ANTICIPATED.
I'M ACTIVATING THE TRANSVERSE BRACE...
HNNNNNNNN
WHOOP!
OKAY, AMMY. THAT ITCH IN YOUR CEREBELLUM IS THE PSYCHIC CONNECTION KICKING IN.
WE'RE ALL GONNA BE WITH YOU THIS TIME.
SO YOU DON'T HAVE TO HOLD BACK.
LET GO, AMADEUS...

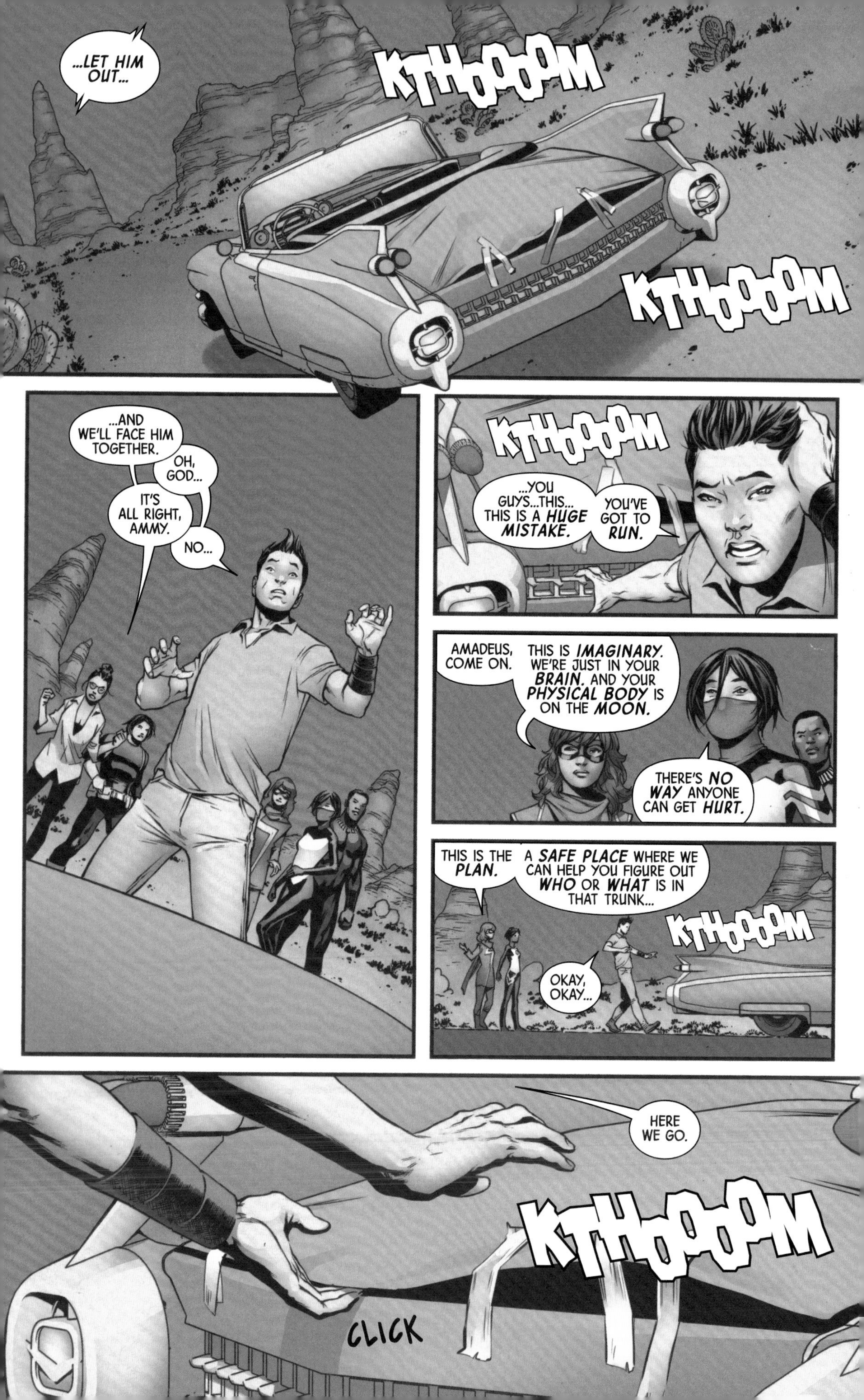

...LET HIM OUT...
KTHOOOOM
KTHOOOOM
...AND WE'LL FACE HIM TOGETHER.
OH, GOD...
IT'S ALL RIGHT, AMMY.
NO...
KTHOOOOM
...YOU GUYS...THIS... THIS IS A *HUGE* *MISTAKE.*
YOU'VE GOT TO *RUN.*
AMADEUS, COME ON.
THIS IS *IMAGINARY.* WE'RE JUST IN YOUR *BRAIN.* AND YOUR *PHYSICAL BODY* IS ON THE *MOON.*
THERE'S *NO* *WAY* ANYONE CAN GET *HURT.*
THIS IS THE *PLAN.*
A *SAFE PLACE* WHERE WE CAN HELP YOU FIGURE OUT *WHO* OR *WHAT* IS IN THAT TRUNK...
KTHOOOOM
OKAY, OKAY...
HERE WE GO.
KTHOOOOM
CLICK

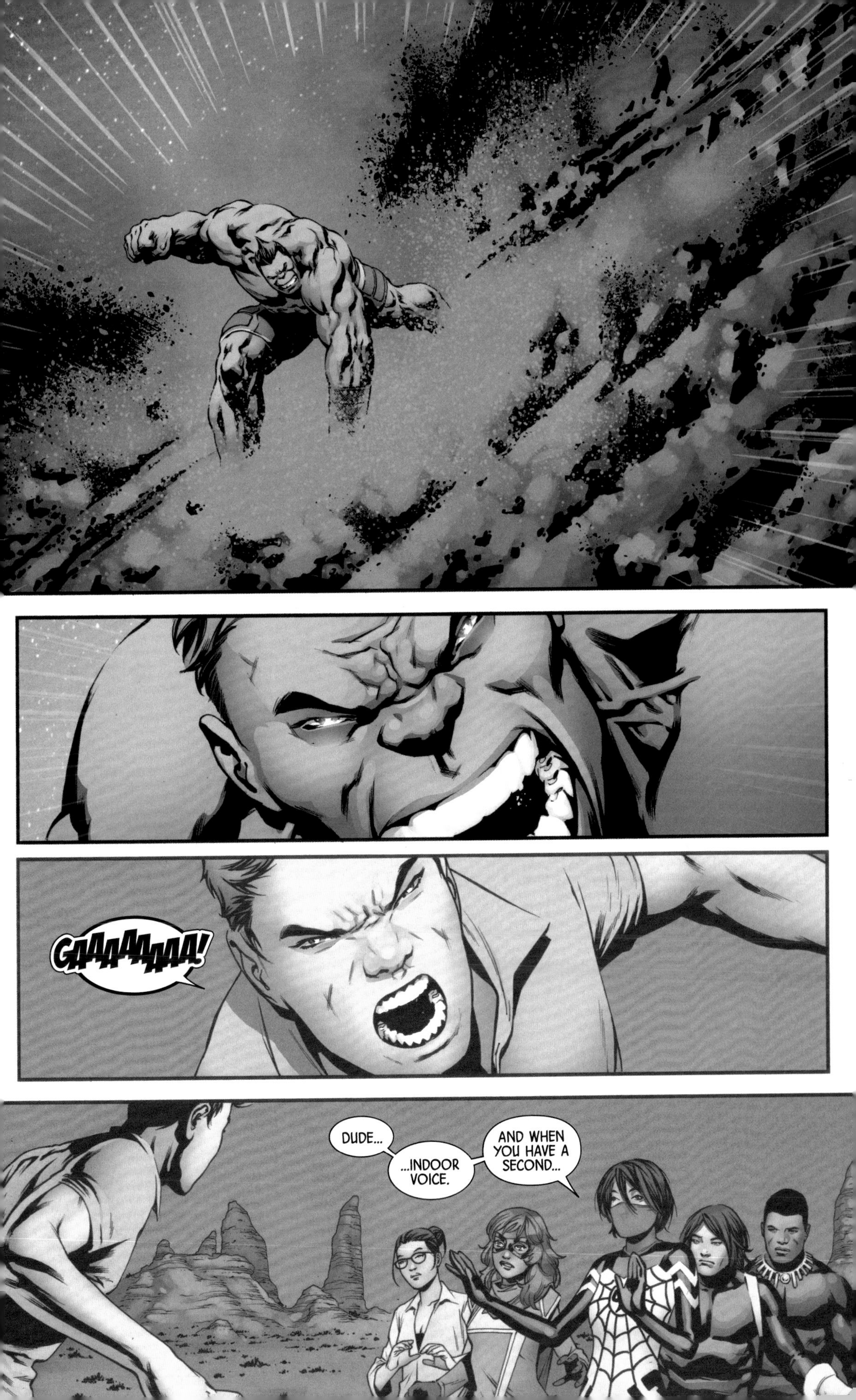
GAAAAAAAA!
DUDE...
...INDOOR VOICE.
AND WHEN YOU HAVE A SECOND...

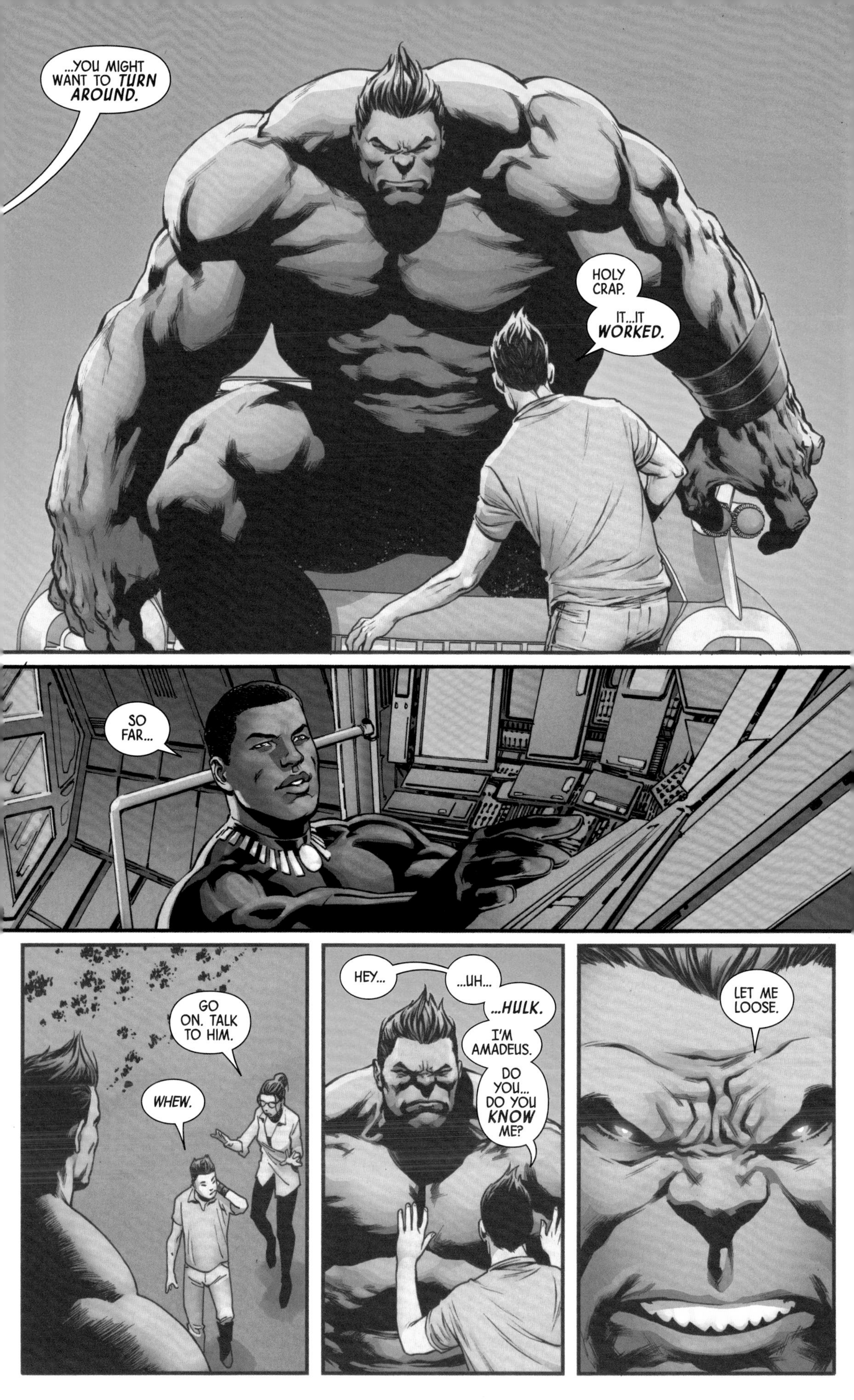

...YOU MIGHT WANT TO TURN AROUND.
HOLY CRAP.
IT...IT WORKED.
SO FAR...
GO ON. TALK TO HIM.
WHEW.
HEY...
...UH...
...HULK.
I'M AMADEUS.
DO YOU... DO YOU KNOW ME?
LET ME LOOSE.

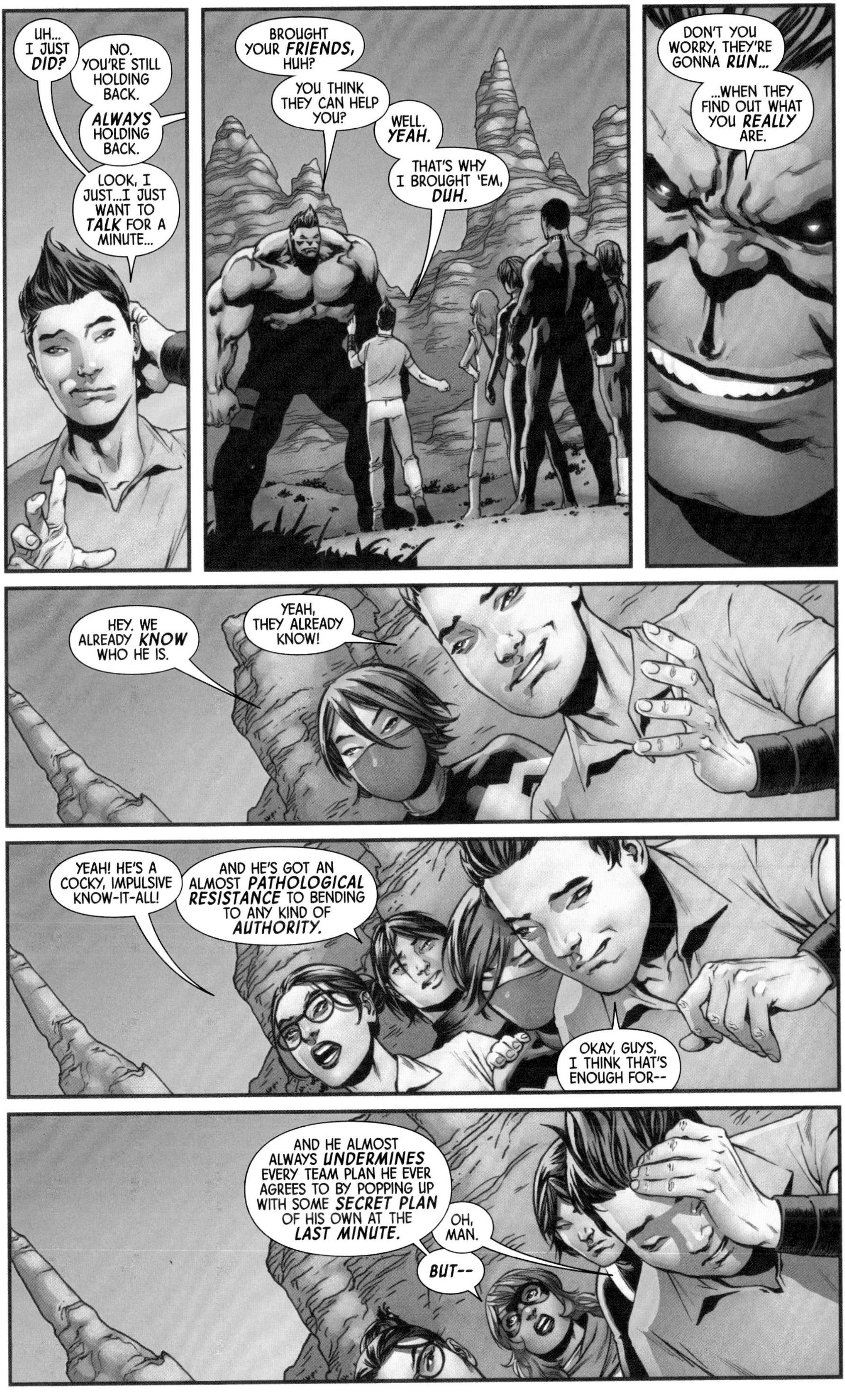
UH... I JUST DID?
NO. YOU'RE STILL HOLDING BACK.
ALWAYS HOLDING BACK.
LOOK, I JUST...I JUST WANT TO TALK FOR A MINUTE...
BROUGHT YOUR FRIENDS, HUH?
YOU THINK THEY CAN HELP YOU?
WELL. YEAH.
THAT'S WHY I BROUGHT 'EM, DUH.
DON'T YOU WORRY, THEY'RE GONNA RUN...
...WHEN THEY FIND OUT WHAT YOU REALLY ARE.
HEY. WE ALREADY KNOW WHO HE IS.
YEAH, THEY ALREADY KNOW!
YEAH! HE'S A COCKY, IMPULSIVE KNOW-IT-ALL!
AND HE'S GOT AN ALMOST PATHOLOGICAL RESISTANCE TO BENDING TO ANY KIND OF AUTHORITY.
OKAY, GUYS, I THINK THAT'S ENOUGH FOR--
AND HE ALMOST ALWAYS UNDERMINES EVERY TEAM PLAN HE EVER AGREES TO BY POPPING UP WITH SOME SECRET PLAN OF HIS OWN AT THE LAST MINUTE.
OH, MAN.
BUT--

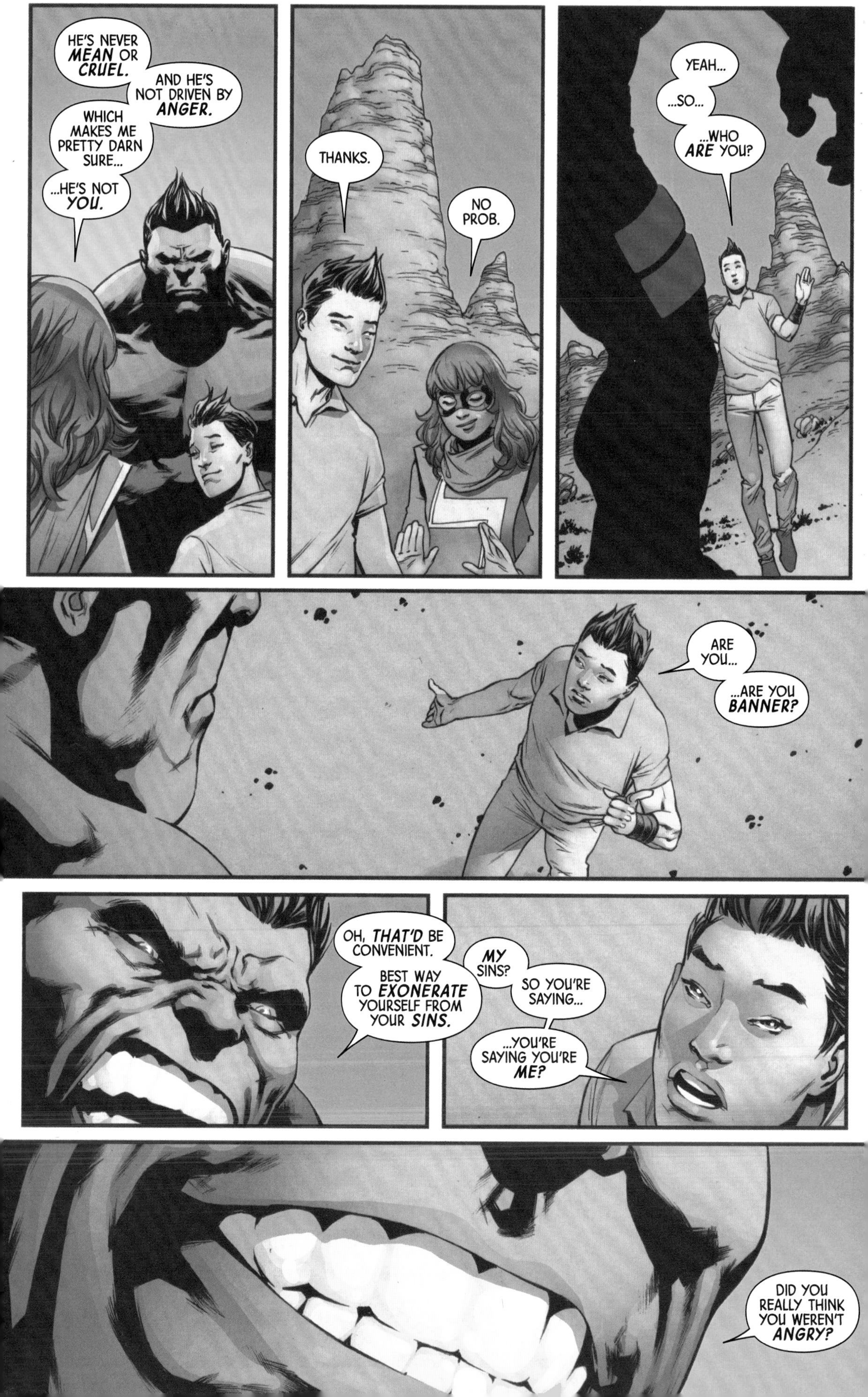
HE'S NEVER MEAN OR CRUEL.
AND HE'S NOT DRIVEN BY ANGER.
WHICH MAKES ME PRETTY DARN SURE...
...HE'S NOT YOU.
THANKS.
NO PROB.
YEAH...
...SO...
...WHO ARE YOU?
ARE YOU...
...ARE YOU BANNER?
OH, THAT'D BE CONVENIENT.
BEST WAY TO EXONERATE YOURSELF FROM YOUR SINS.
MY SINS?
SO YOU'RE SAYING...
...YOU'RE SAYING YOU'RE ME?
DID YOU REALLY THINK YOU WEREN'T ANGRY?

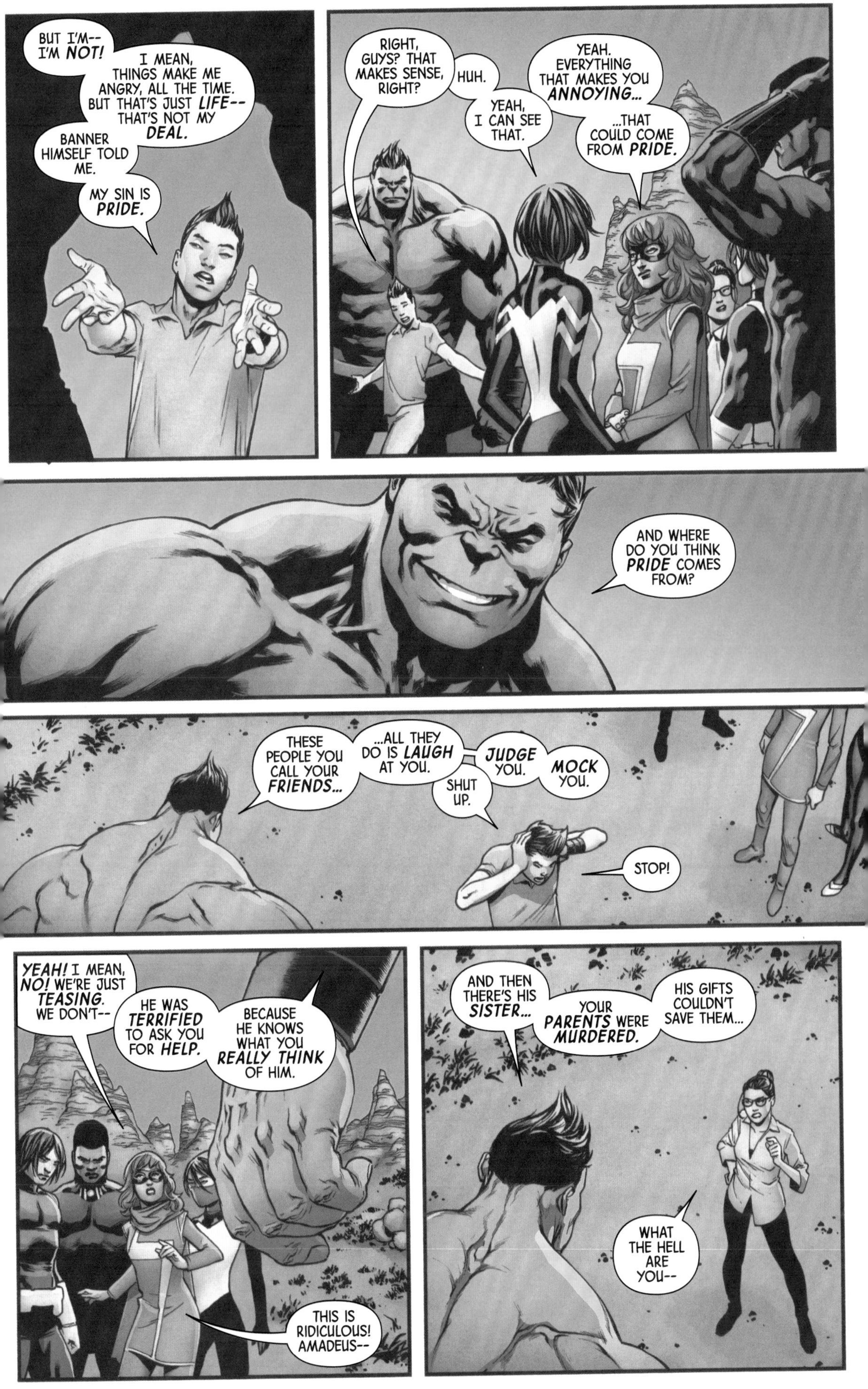

BUT I'M-- I'M NOT!
I MEAN, THINGS MAKE ME ANGRY, ALL THE TIME. BUT THAT'S JUST LIFE-- THAT'S NOT MY DEAL.
BANNER HIMSELF TOLD ME.
MY SIN IS PRIDE.
RIGHT, GUYS? THAT MAKES SENSE, RIGHT?
HUH.
YEAH, I CAN SEE THAT.
YEAH. EVERYTHING THAT MAKES YOU ANNOYING...
...THAT COULD COME FROM PRIDE.
AND WHERE DO YOU THINK PRIDE COMES FROM?
THESE PEOPLE YOU CALL YOUR FRIENDS...
...ALL THEY DO IS LAUGH AT YOU.
JUDGE YOU.
MOCK YOU.
SHUT UP.
STOP!
YEAH! I MEAN, NO! WE'RE JUST TEASING. WE DON'T--
HE WAS TERRIFIED TO ASK YOU FOR HELP.
BECAUSE HE KNOWS WHAT YOU REALLY THINK OF HIM.
THIS IS RIDICULOUS! AMADEUS--
AND THEN THERE'S HIS SISTER...
YOUR PARENTS WERE MURDERED.
HIS GIFTS COULDN'T SAVE THEM...
WHAT THE HELL ARE YOU--

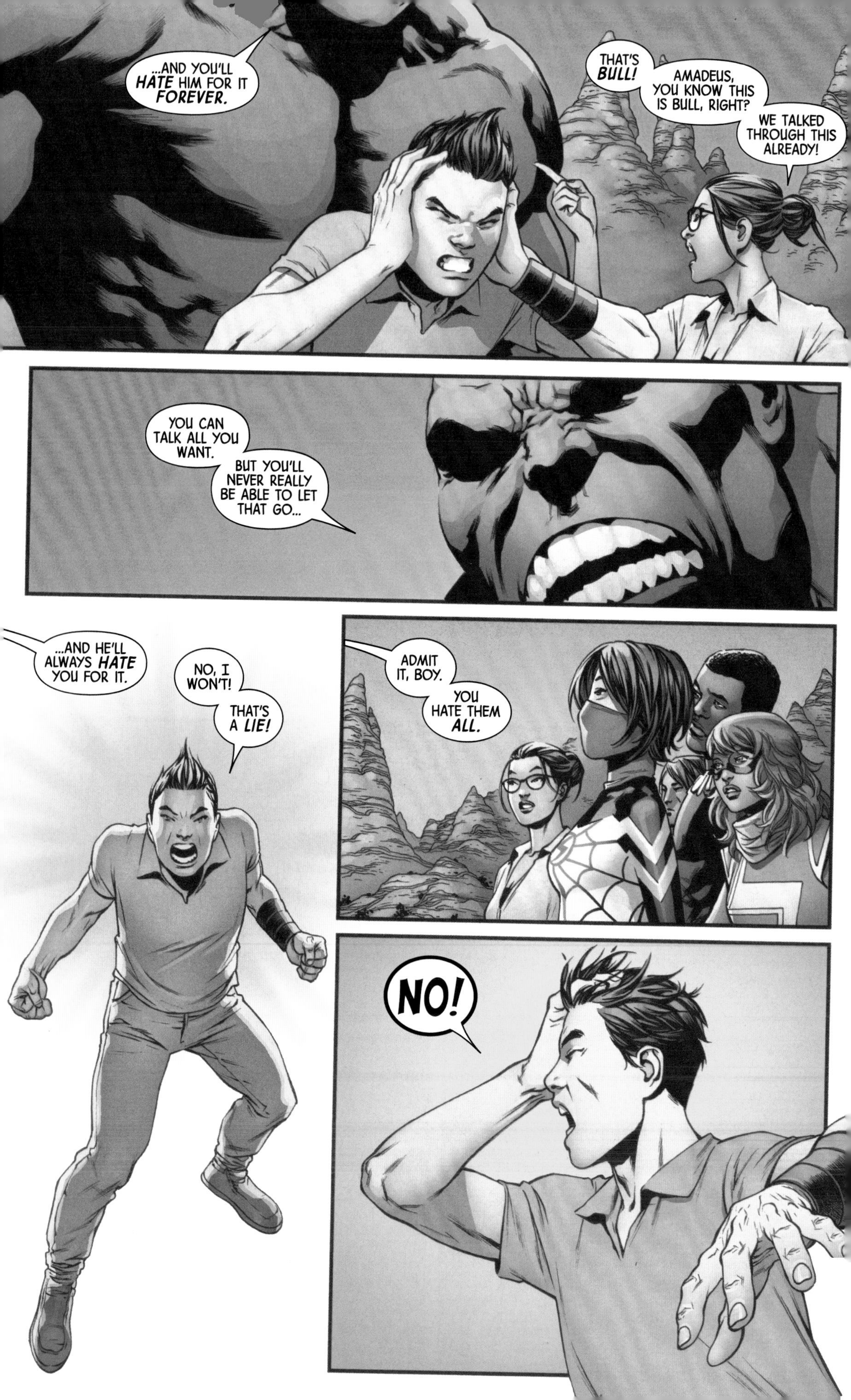
...AND YOU'LL HATE HIM FOR IT FOREVER.
THAT'S BULL!
AMADEUS, YOU KNOW THIS IS BULL, RIGHT?
WE TALKED THROUGH THIS ALREADY!
YOU CAN TALK ALL YOU WANT.
BUT YOU'LL NEVER REALLY BE ABLE TO LET THAT GO...
...AND HE'LL ALWAYS HATE YOU FOR IT.
NO, I WON'T!
THAT'S A LIE!
ADMIT IT, BOY.
YOU HATE THEM ALL.
NO!

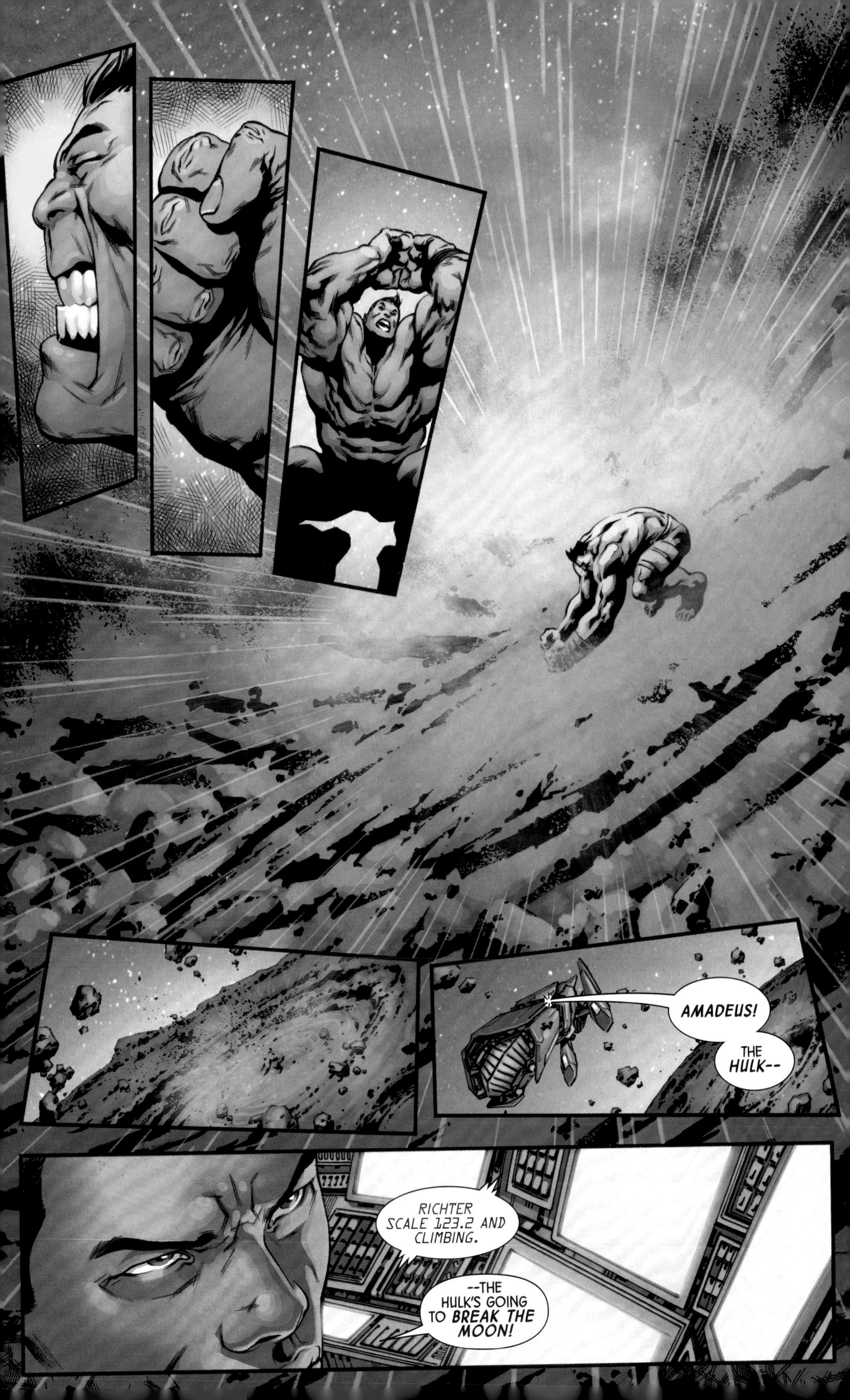
AMADEUS!
THE HULK--
RICHTER SCALE 123.2 AND CLIMBING.
--THE HULK'S GOING TO BREAK THE MOON!

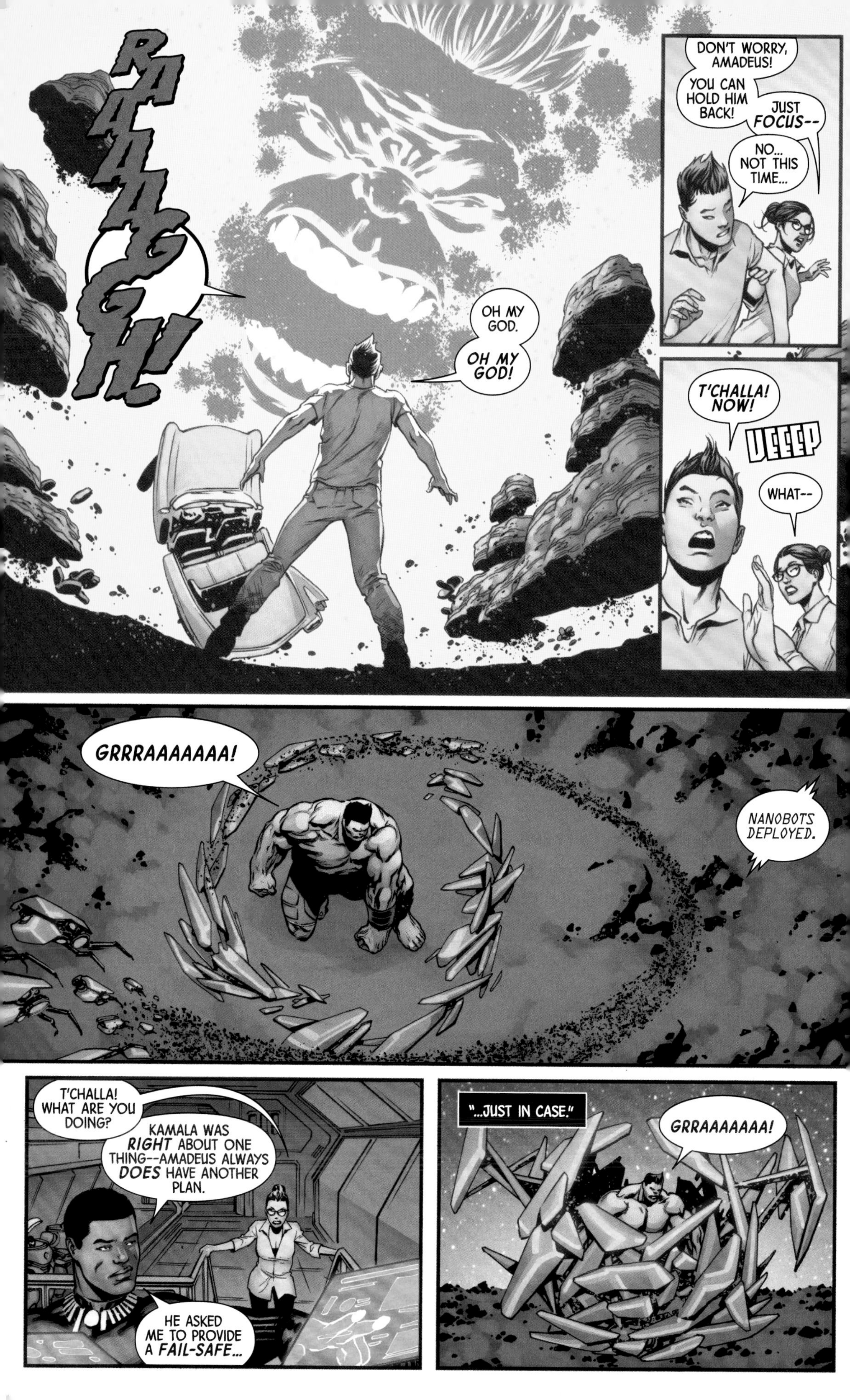
RAAAAGH!
OH MY GOD.
OH MY GOD!
DON'T WORRY, AMADEUS!
YOU CAN HOLD HIM BACK!
JUST FOCUS--
NO... NOT THIS TIME...
T'CHALLA! NOW!
VEEEP
WHAT--
GRRRAAAAAAA!
NANOBOTS DEPLOYED.
T'CHALLA! WHAT ARE YOU DOING?
KAMALA WAS RIGHT ABOUT ONE THING--AMADEUS ALWAYS DOES HAVE ANOTHER PLAN.
HE ASKED ME TO PROVIDE A FAIL-SAFE...
"...JUST IN CASE."
GRRAAAAAAA!

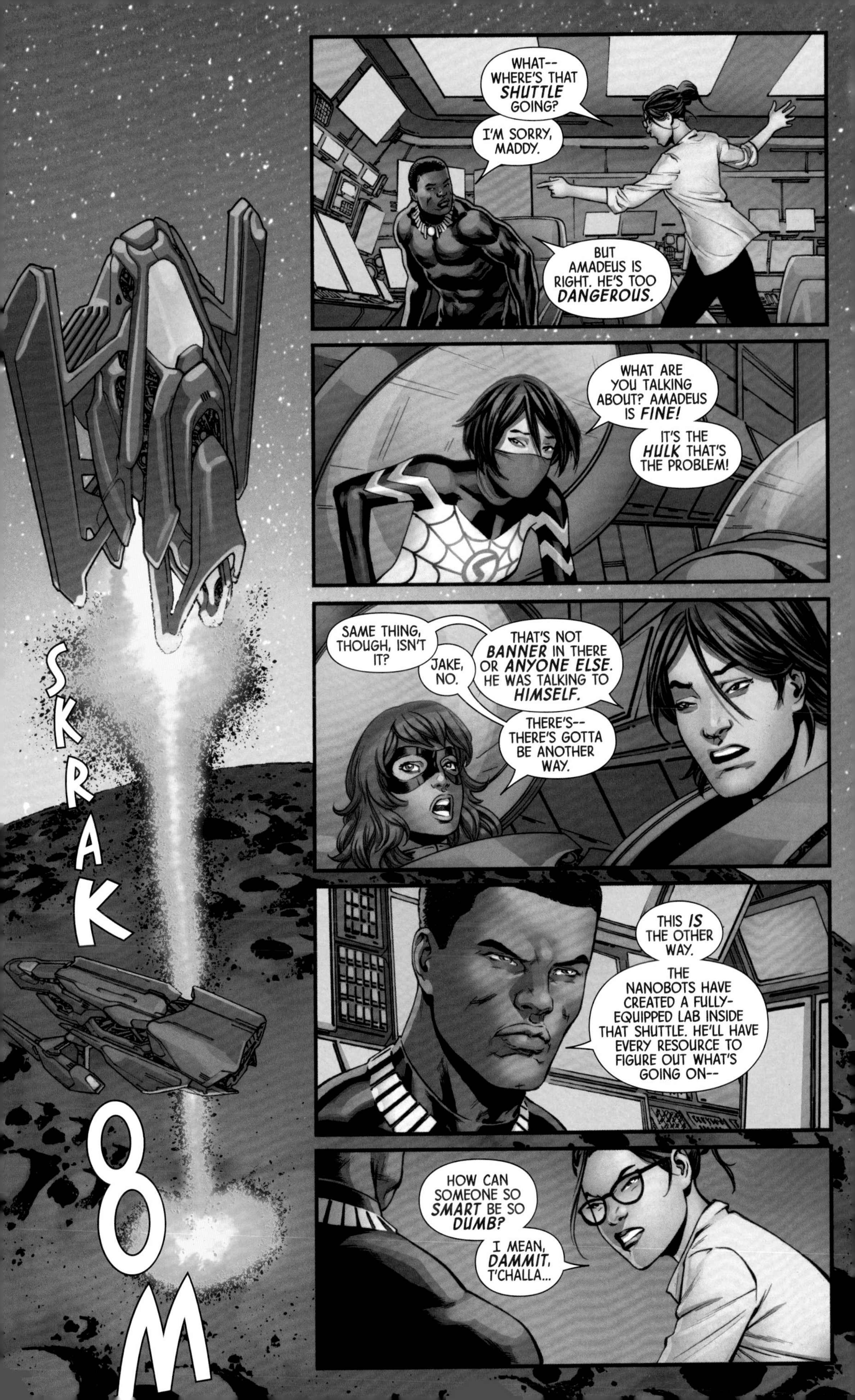
WHAT-- WHERE'S THAT SHUTTLE GOING?
I'M SORRY, MADDY.
BUT AMADEUS IS RIGHT. HE'S TOO DANGEROUS.
WHAT ARE YOU TALKING ABOUT? AMADEUS IS FINE!
IT'S THE HULK THAT'S THE PROBLEM!
SAME THING, THOUGH, ISN'T IT?
JAKE, NO.
THAT'S NOT BANNER IN THERE OR ANYONE ELSE. HE WAS TALKING TO HIMSELF.
THERE'S-- THERE'S GOTTA BE ANOTHER WAY.
SKRAK
THIS IS THE OTHER WAY.
THE NANOBOTS HAVE CREATED A FULLY-EQUIPPED LAB INSIDE THAT SHUTTLE. HE'LL HAVE EVERY RESOURCE TO FIGURE OUT WHAT'S GOING ON--
BOOM
HOW CAN SOMEONE SO SMART BE SO DUMB?
I MEAN, DAMMIT, T'CHALLA...

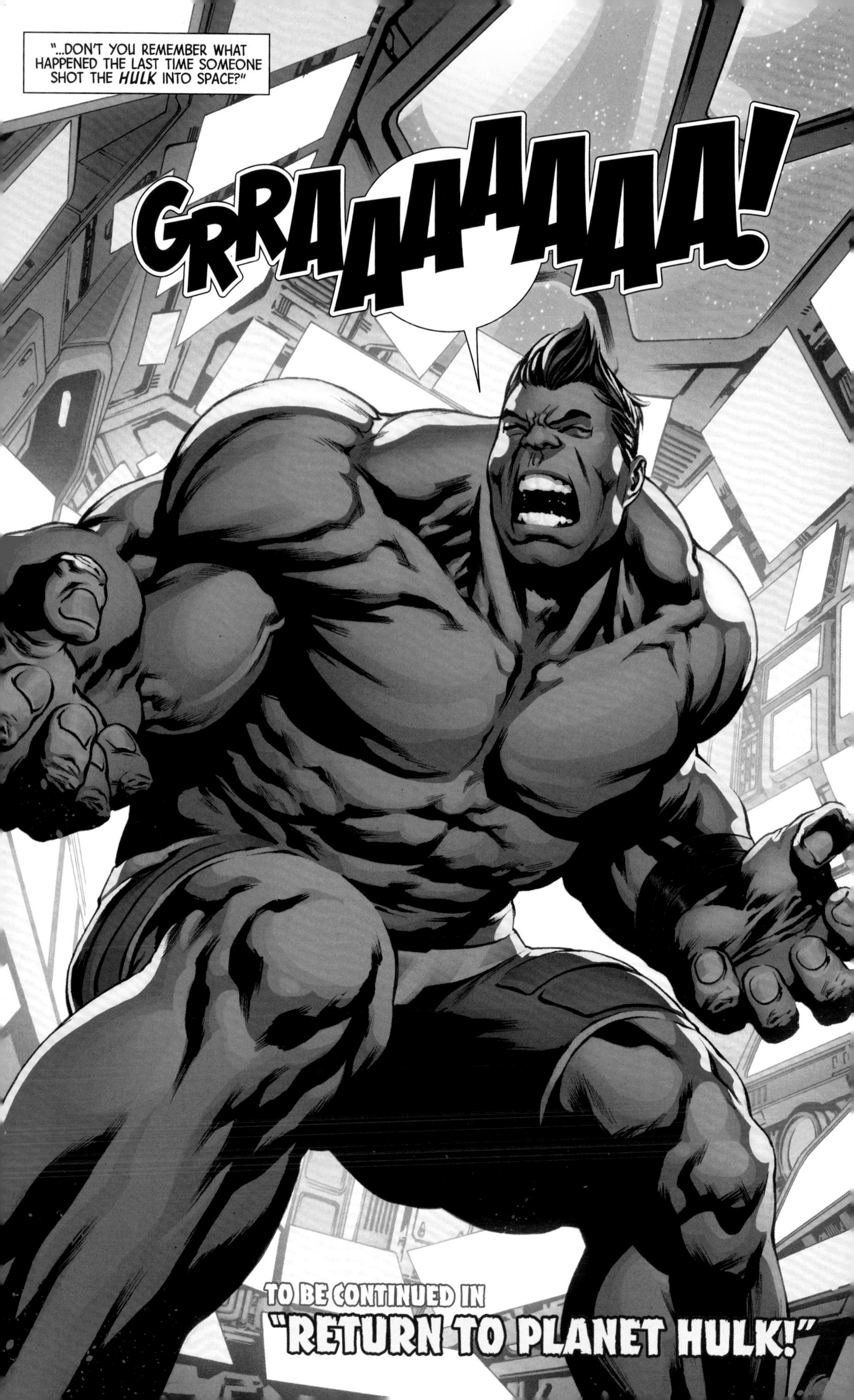
"...DON'T YOU REMEMBER WHAT HAPPENED THE LAST TIME SOMEONE SHOT THE HULK INTO SPACE?"
GRRAAAAAAA!
TO BE CONTINUED IN
"RETURN TO PLANET HULK!"

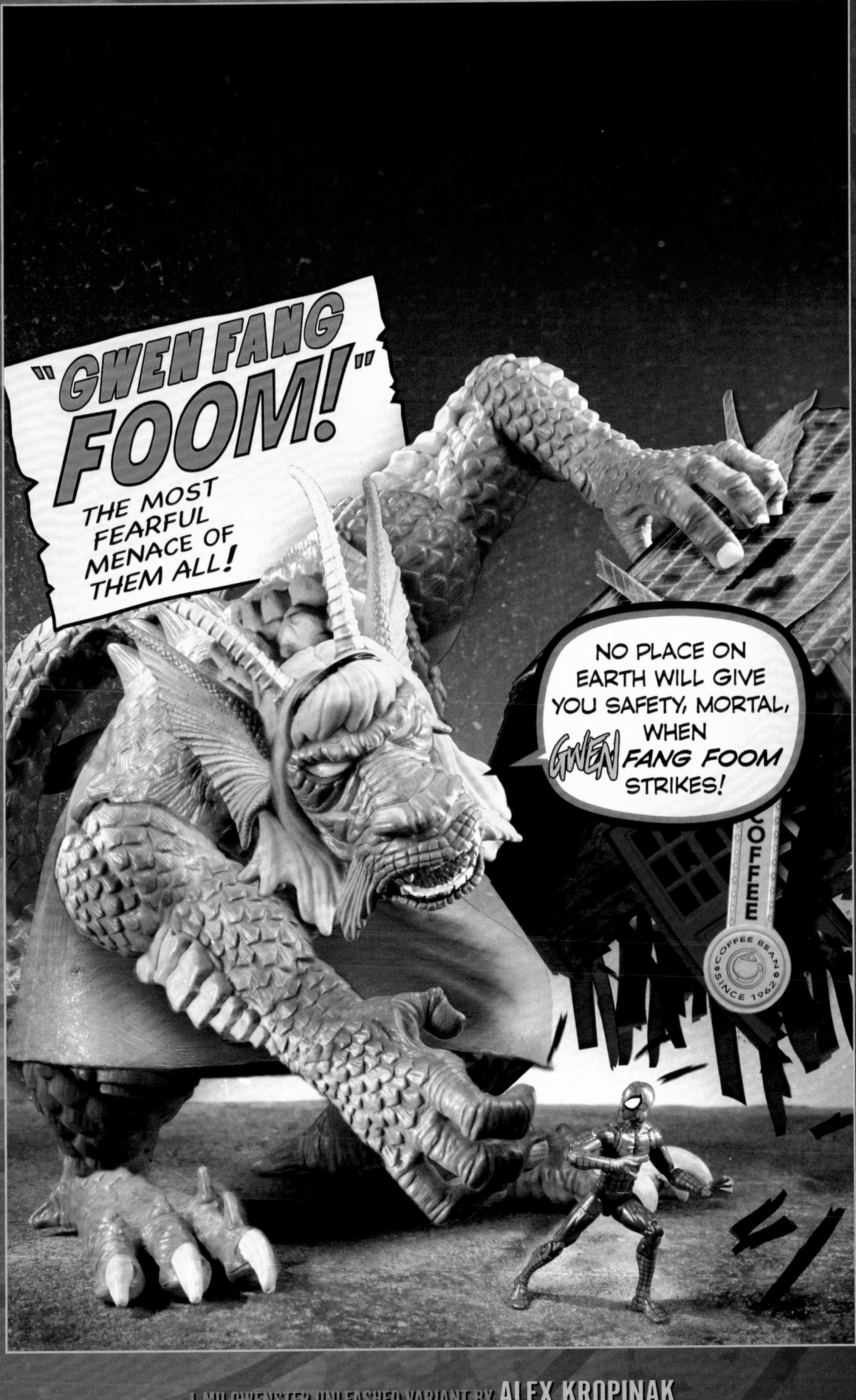
"GWEN FANG FOOM!"
THE MOST FEARFUL MENACE OF THEM ALL!
NO PLACE ON EARTH WILL GIVE YOU SAFETY, MORTAL, WHEN GWEN FANG FOOM STRIKES!
COFFEE
COFFEE BEAN SINCE 1962

1.MU GWENSTER UNLEASHED VARIANT BY ALEX KROPINAK

GENERATIONS VARIANT BY **GREG HORN**

GENERATIONS VARIANT BY **MATTEO BUFFAGNI**

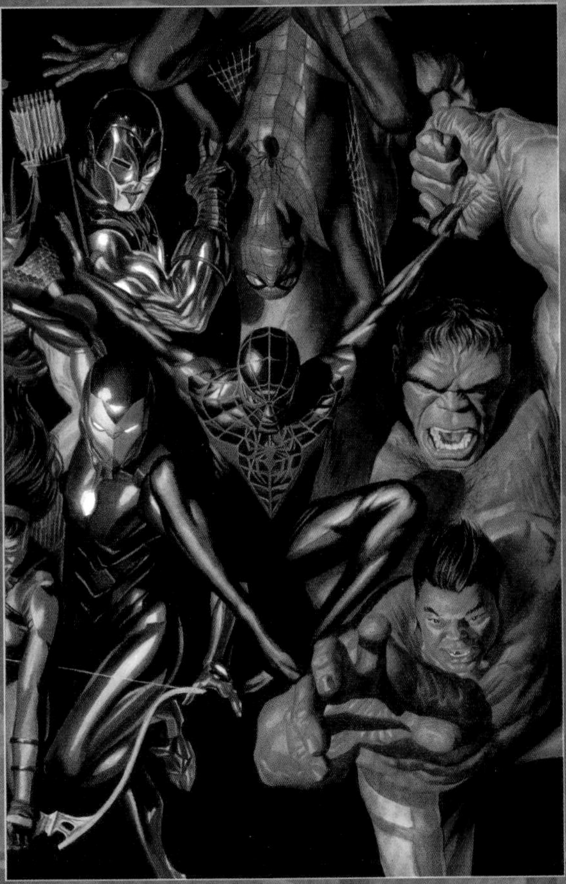

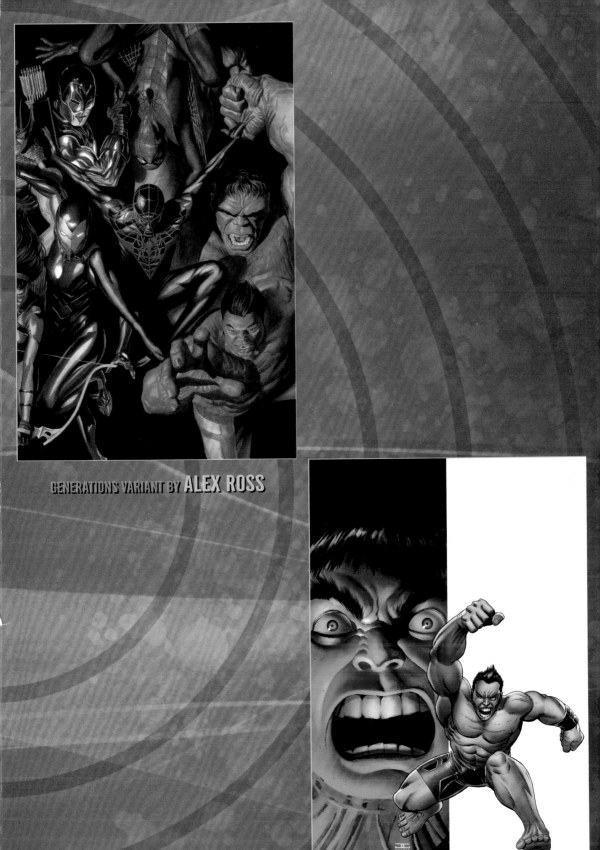

GENERATIONS VARIANT BY ALEX ROSS

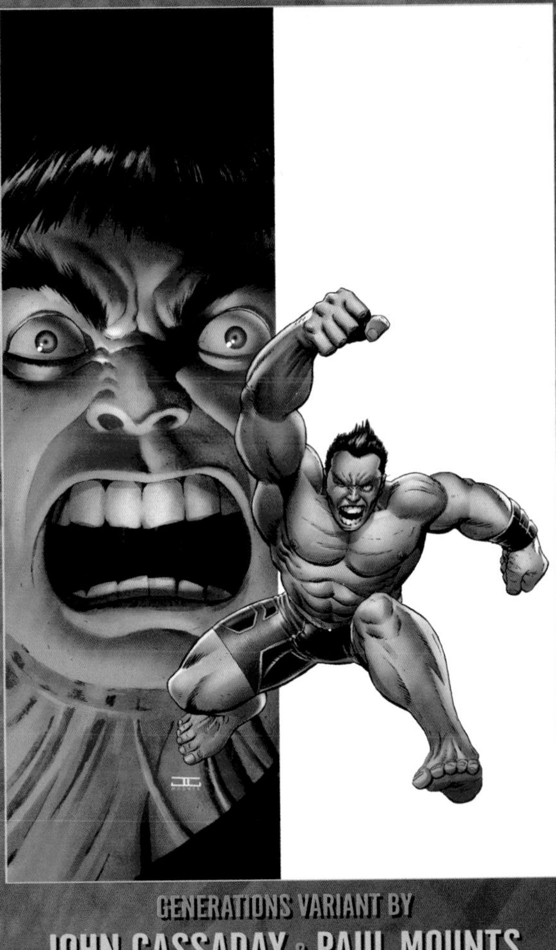

GENERATIONS VARIANT BY
JOHN CASSADAY & PAUL MOUNTS

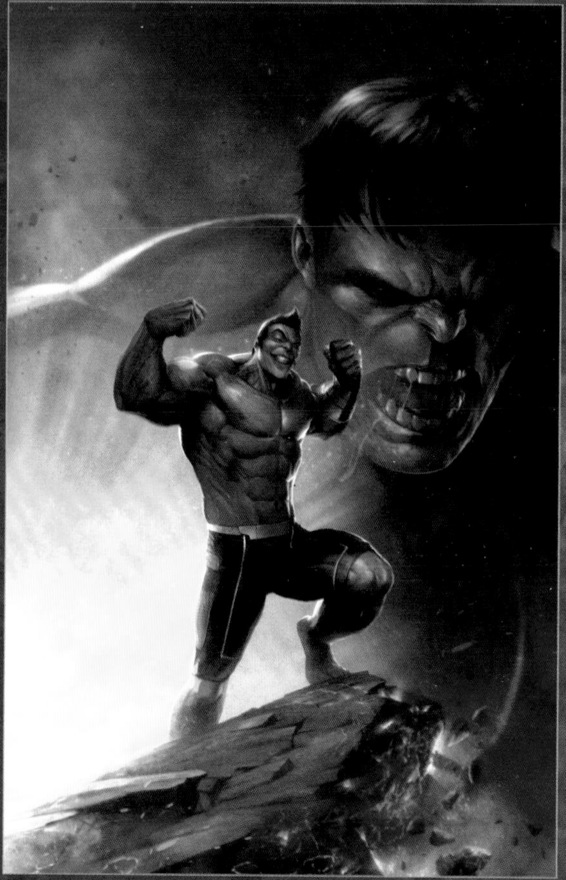

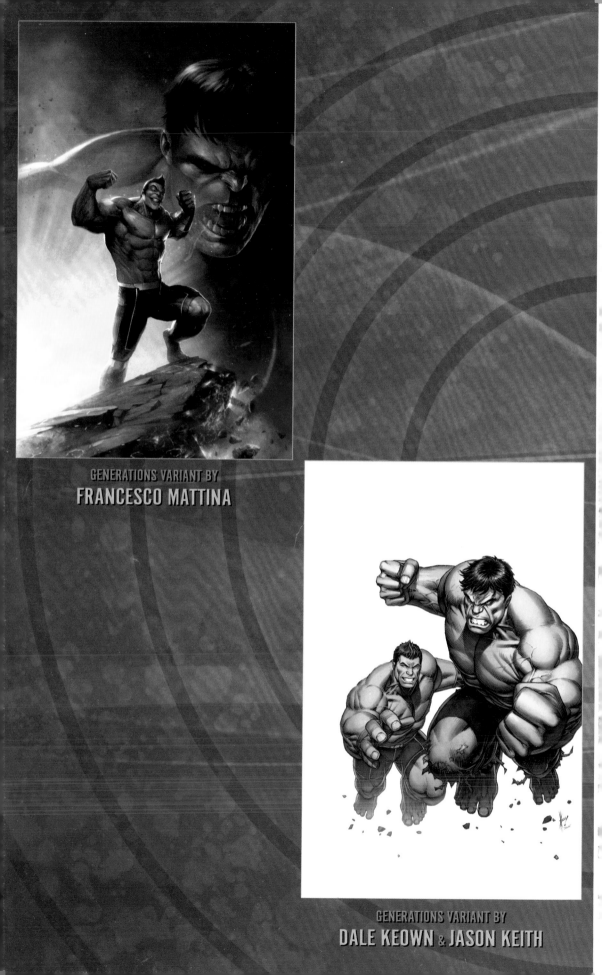

GENERATIONS VARIANT BY
FRANCESCO MATTINA

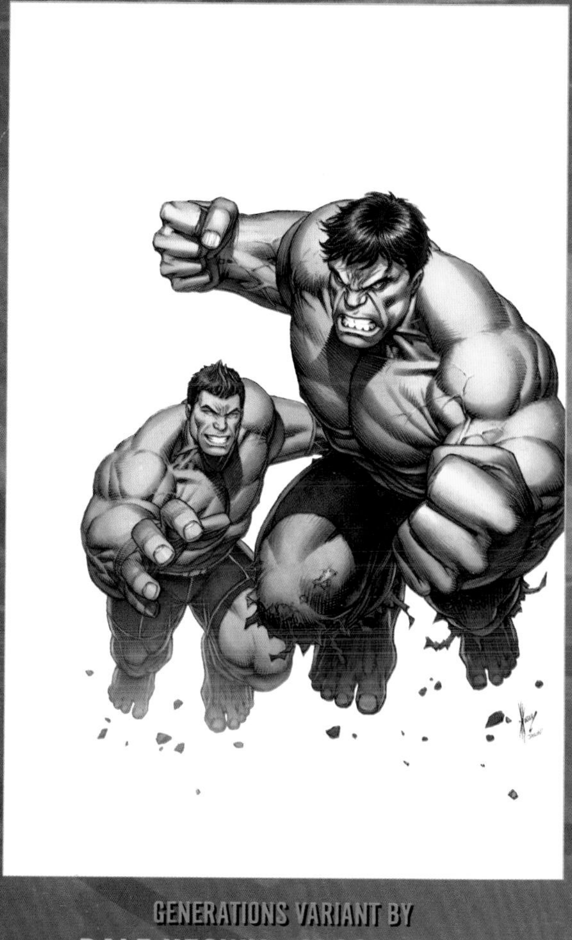

GENERATIONS VARIANT BY
DALE KEOWN & JASON KEITH